E. Margaret Evans, Ph.D.
Center for Human Growth & Dev.
University of Michigan
300 N. Ingalls Building, 10th Floor
Ann Arbor, MI 48109-0406

Statistical
Power
Analysis

A Simple and General Model
for Traditional and Modern Hypothesis Tests

THIRD EDITION

Statistical Power Analysis

A Simple and General Model for Traditional and Modern Hypothesis Tests

THIRD EDITION

Kevin R. Murphy
Pennsylvania State University

Brett Myors
Griffith University

Allen Wolach
Illinois Institute of Technology

Routledge
Taylor & Francis Group
New York London

Routledge
Taylor & Francis Group
270 Madison Avenue
New York, NY 10016

Routledge
Taylor & Francis Group
2 Park Square
Milton Park, Abingdon
Oxon OX14 4RN

Printed in the United States of America on acid-free paper
10 9 8 7 6 5 4 3 2 1

International Standard Book Number-13: 978-1-84169-774-1 (Softcover) 978-1-84169-775-8 (Hardcover)

Library of Congress Cataloging-in-Publication Data

Murphy, Kevin R., 1952-
    Statistical power analysis : a simple and general model for traditional and modern hypothesis tests / Kevin R. Murphy, Brett Myron, Allen Wolach. -- 3rd ed.
        p. cm.
    ISBN 978-1-84169-774-1 (pbk.) -- ISBN 978-0-415-96555-2 (hardback)
    1. Statistical hypothesis testing. 2. Statistical power analysis. I. Myron, Brett. II. Wolach, Allen H. III. Title.

QA277.M87 2008
519.5'6--dc22   2008037988

Visit the Taylor & Francis Web site at
http://www.taylorandfrancis.com

and the Psychology Press Web site at
http://www.psypress.com

Contents

Preface

One of the most common statistical procedures in the behavioral and social sciences is to test the hypothesis that treatments or interventions have no effect, or that the correlation between two variables is equal to zero, etc.— i.e., tests of the null hypothesis. Researchers have long been concerned with the possibility that they will reject the null hypothesis when it is in fact correct (i.e., make a Type I error), and an extensive body of research and data-analytic methods exists to help understand and control these errors. Less attention has been devoted to the possibility that researchers will fail to reject the null hypothesis, when in fact treatments, interventions, etc., have some real effect (i.e., make a Type II error). Statistical tests that fail to detect the real effects of treatments or interventions might substantially impede the progress of scientific research.

The statistical power of a test is the probability that it will lead you to reject the null hypothesis when that hypothesis is in fact wrong. Because most statistical tests are conducted in contexts where treatments have at least some effect (although it might be minuscule), power often translates into the probability that your test will you lead to a correct conclusion about the null hypothesis. Viewed in this light, it is obvious why researchers have become interested in the topic of statistical power and in methods of assessing and increasing the power of their tests.

This book presents a simple and general model for statistical power analysis that is based on the widely used F statistic. A wide variety of statistics used in the social and behavioral sciences can be thought of as special applications of the "general linear model" (e.g., t-tests, analysis of variance and covariance, correlation, multiple regression), and the F statistic can be used in testing hypotheses about virtually any of these specialized applications. The model for power analysis laid out here is quite simple, and it illustrates how these analyses work and how they can be applied to problems of study design, to evaluating others' research, and even to problems such as choosing the appropriate criterion for defining "statistically significant" outcomes.

In response to criticisms of traditional null hypothesis testing, several researchers have developed methods for testing what we refer to as "minimum-effect" hypotheses—i.e., the hypothesis that the effect of treatments, interventions, etc., exceeds some specific minimal level. Ours is the first book to discuss in detail the application of power analysis to both traditional null hypothesis tests and minimum-effect tests. We show how the same basic model applies to both types of testing and illustrate applications of power analysis to both traditional null hypothesis tests (i.e., tests of the hypothesis that treatments have no effect) and to minimum-effect tests (i.e., tests of the hypothesis that the effects of treatments exceeds some minimal level).

Most of the analyses presented in this book can be carried out using a single table, the One-Stop F Table presented in Appendix B. Appendix C presents a comparable table that expresses statistical results in terms of the percentage of variance (PV) explained rather than the F statistic. These two tables make it easy to move back and forth between assessments of statistical significance and assessments of the strength of various effects in a study. The One-Stop F Table can be used to answer many questions that relate to the power of statistical tests. A computer program, the One-Stop F Calculator, is on the book's website www.psypress.com/statistical-power-analysis. The One-Stop F Calculator can be used as a substitute for the One-Stop F Table. This computer program allows users more flexibility in defining the hypothesis to be tested, the desired power level, and the alpha level than is typical for power analysis software. The One-Stop F Calculator also makes it unnecessary to interpolate between values in a table.

This book is intended for a wide audience, including advanced students and researchers in the social and behavioral sciences, education, health sciences, and business. Presentations are kept simple and nontechnical whenever possible. Although most of the examples in this book come from the social and behavioral sciences, general principles explained in this book should be useful to researchers in diverse disciplines.

Changes in the New Edition

This third edition includes expanded coverage of power analysis for multifactor analysis of variance (ANOVA), including split-plot and randomized block factorial designs. Although conceptual issues for power analysis are similar in factorial ANOVA and other methods of analysis, special features of ANOVA require explicit attention. The present edition of the book also shows how to calculate power for simple main effects tests and *t* tests that are performed after an analysis of variance is performed, and it provides a more detailed examination of *t* tests than was included in our first and second editions.

Perhaps the most important addition to this third edition is a set of examples, illustrations, and discussions included in Chapters 1 through 8 in boxed sections. This material is set off for easy reference, and it provides examples of power analysis in action and discussions of unique issues that arise as a result of applying power analyses in different designs.

Other highlights of the third edition include the following:

- A completely redesigned, user-friendly software program that allows users to carry out all of the analysis described in this book and to conduct a wide range of tests; this new program allows users to conduct significance tests, power analyses, and assessments of N and alpha needed for traditional and minimum-effects tests
- New chapters (Chapters 7 and 8) demonstrating the application of POWER in complex ANOVA designs, including randomized block, split-plot, and repeated measures designs
- A separate chapter (chapter 3) describing the rationale and operation of minimum effects tests
- Worked examples in all chapters
- Expanded coverage of the concepts behind power analysis (Chapters 1 and 4) and the application of these concepts in correlational studies (Chapter 5)

Using the One-Stop *F* Calculator

A book-specific website www.psypress.com/statistical-power-analysis includes the One-Stop F Calculator, which is a program designed to run on most Windows-compatible computers. Following the philosophy that drives our book, the program is simple to install and use. Visit this website, and you will receive instructions for quickly installing the program. The program asks you to make some simple decisions about the analysis you have in mind, and it provides information about statistical power, effect sizes, *F* values, and/or significance tests. Chapter 2 illustrates the use of this program.

Acknowledgments

We are grateful for the comments and suggestions of several reviewers, including Stephen Brand, University of Rhode Island; Jaihyun Park, Baruch College–CUNY; Eric Turkheimer, University of Virginia; and Connie Zimmerman, Illinois State University.

1

The Power of Statistical Tests

▼ ▼ ▼ ▼ ▼

In the social and behavioral sciences, statistics serve two general purposes. First, they can be used to describe what happened in a particular study (descriptive statistics). Second, they can be used to help draw conclusions about what those results mean in some broader context (inferential statistics). The main question in inferential statistics is whether a result, finding, or observation from a study reflects some meaningful phenomenon in the population from which that study was drawn. For example, if 100 college sophomores are surveyed and it is determined that a majority of them prefer pizza to hot dogs, does this mean that people in general (or college students in general) also prefer pizza? If a medical treatment yields improvements in 6 out of 10 patients, does this mean that it is an effective treatment that should be approved for general use? The goal of inferential statistics is to determine what sorts of inferences and generalizations can be made on the basis of data of this type and to assess the strength of evidence and the degree of confidence one can have in these inferences.

The process of drawing inferences about populations from samples is a risky one, and a great deal has been written about the causes and cures for errors in statistical inference. Statistical power analysis (Cohen, 1988; Kraemer & Thiemann, 1987; Lipsey, 1990) falls under this general heading. Studies with too little statistical power can lead to erroneous conclusions about the meaning of the results of a particular study. In the example cited above, the fact that a medical treatment worked for 6 out of 10 patients is probably insufficient evidence that it is truly safe and effective; and if you have nothing more than this study to rely on, you might conclude that the treatment had not been proven effective. Does this mean that you should abandon the treatment or that it is unlikely to work in a broader population? The conclusion that the treatment has not been shown to be effective may say as much about the low level of statistical power in your study as about the value of the treatment.

In this chapter, we will describe the rationale for and applications of statistical power analysis. In most of our examples, we describe or apply power analysis in studies that assess the effect of some treatment or intervention (e.g., psychotherapy, reading instruction, performance incentives) by comparing outcomes for those who have received the treatment to outcomes of those who have not (nontreatment or control group). However, power analysis is applicable to a very wide range of statistical tests, and the same simple and general model can be applied to virtually all of the statistical analyses you are likely to encounter in the social and behavioral sciences.

The Structure of Statistical Tests

To understand statistical power, you must first understand the ideas that underlie statistical hypothesis testing. Suppose 100 children are randomly divided into two groups. Fifty children receive a new method of reading instruction, and their performance on reading tests is on average 6 points higher (on a 100-point test) than the other 50 children who received standard methods of instruction. Does this mean that the new method is truly better? A 6-point difference *might* mean that the new method is really better, but it is also possible that there is no real difference between the two methods, and that this observed difference is the result of the sort of random fluctuation you might expect when you use the results from a single sample to draw inferences about the effects of these two methods of instruction in the population.

One of the most basic ideas in statistical analysis is that results obtained in a sample do not necessarily reflect the state of affairs in the population from which that sample was drawn. For example, the fact that scores averaged 6 points higher in this particular group of children does not necessarily mean that scores will be 6 points higher in the population, or that the same 6-point difference would be found in another study examining a new group of students. Because samples do not (in general) perfectly represent the populations from which they were drawn, you should expect some instability in the results obtained from each sample. This instability is usually referred to as "sampling error." The presence of sampling error is what makes drawing inferences about populations from samples difficult. One of the key goals of statistical theory is to estimate the amount of sampling error that is likely to be present in different statistical procedures and tests and thereby gaining some idea about the amount of risk involved in using a particular procedure.

Statistical significance tests can be thought of as decision aids. That is, these tests can help you reach conclusions about whether the findings of your particular study are likely to represent real population effects or whether they fall within the range of outcomes that might be produced by random sampling error. For example, there are two possible interpretations of the findings in this study of reading instruction:

1. The difference between average scores from the two programs is so small that it might reasonably represent nothing more than sampling error.

versus

2. The difference between average scores from the two programs is so large that it cannot be reasonably explained in terms of sampling error.

The most common statistical procedure in the social and behavioral sciences is to pit a null hypothesis (H_0) against an alternative (H_1). In this example, the null and alternative hypotheses might take the forms:

H_0—Reading instruction has no effect. It doesn't matter how you teach children to read, because in the population there is no difference in the average scores of children receiving either method of instruction.

versus

H_1—Reading instruction has an effect. It does matter how you teach children to read, because in the population there *is* a difference in the average scores of children receiving different methods of instruction.

Although null hypotheses usually refer to "no difference" or "no effect," it is important to understand that there is nothing magic about the hypothesis that the difference between two groups is zero. It might be perfectly reasonable to evaluate the following set of possibilities:

H_0—In the population, the difference in the average scores of those receiving these two methods of reading instruction is 6 points.

versus

H_1—In the population, the difference in the average scores of those receiving these two methods of reading instruction is *not* 6 points.

Another possible set of hypotheses is:

H_0—In the population, the new method of reading instruction is *not* better than the old method; the new method might even be worse.

versus

H_1—In the population, the new method of reading instruction *is* better than the old method.

This set of hypotheses leads to what is often called a "one-tailed" statistical test, in which the researcher not only asserts that there is a real difference between these two methods, but also describes the direction or the nature of this difference (i.e., that the new method is not just different from the old one, it is also better). We discuss one-tailed tests in several sections of this book, but in most cases we will focus on the more widely used two-tailed tests that compare the null hypothesis that nothing happened with the alternative hypothesis that something happened. Unless we specifically note otherwise, the traditional null hypothesis tests discussed in this book will be assumed to be two-tailed. However, the minimum effect tests we introduce in Chapter 2 and discuss extensively throughout the book have all of the advantages and few of the drawbacks of traditional one-tailed tests of the null hypothesis.

Null Hypotheses Versus Nil Hypotheses

The most common structure for tests of statistical significance is to pit the null hypothesis that treatments have no effect, or that there is no difference between groups, or that there is no correlation between two variables against the alternative hypotheses that there is *some* treatment effect. In fact, this structure is so common that most people assume that the "null hypothesis" is essentially a statement that there is no difference between groups, no treatment effect, no correlation between variables, etc. This is not true. The null hypothesis is simply the hypothesis you actually test, and if you reject the null, you are left with the alternative. That is, if you reject the hypothesis that the effect of an intervention of treatment is *X*, you are left to conclude that the alternative hypothesis that the effect of treatments is *not-X* must be true. If you test and reject the hypothesis that treatments have no effect, you are left with the conclusion that they must have some effect. If you test and reject the hypothesis that a particular diet will lead to a 20% weight loss, you are left with the conclusion that the diet will *not* lead to a 20%

weight loss (it might have no effect; it might have a smaller effect; it might even have a larger effect).

Following Cohen's (1994) suggestion, we think it is useful to distinguish between the null hypothesis in general and its very special and very common form, the "nil hypothesis" (i.e., the hypothesis that treatments, interventions, etc., have no effect whatsoever). The nil hypothesis is common because it is very easy to test and because it leaves you with a fairly simple and concrete alternative. If you reject the nil hypothesis that nothing happened, the alternative hypothesis you should accept is that something happened. However, as we show in this chapter and in the chapters that follow, there are often important advantages to testing null hypotheses that are broader than the traditional nil hypothesis.

Most treatments of power analysis focus on the statistical power of tests of the nil hypothesis (i.e., tests of the hypothesis that treatments or interventions have no effect whatsoever). However, there are a number of advantages to posing and testing substantive hypotheses about the size of treatment effects (Murphy & Myors, 1999). For example, it is easy to test the hypothesis that the effects of treatments are negligibly small (e.g., they account for 1% or less of the variance in outcomes, or that the standardized mean difference is .10 or less). If you test and reject this hypothesis, you are left with the alternative hypothesis that the effect of treatments is *not* negligibly small, but rather large enough to deserve at least some attention. The methods of power analysis described in this book are easily extended to such minimum-effect tests and are not limited to traditional tests of the null hypothesis that treatments have no effect.

What determines the outcomes of statistical tests? There are four outcomes that are possible when you use the results obtained in a particular sample to draw inferences about a population; these outcomes are shown in Figure 1.1.

As Figure 1.1 shows, there are two ways to make errors when testing hypotheses. First, it is possible that the treatment (e.g., a new method of instruction) has no real effect in the population, but the results in your sample might lead you to believe that it does have some effect. If the results of this study lead you to incorrectly conclude that the new method of instruction does work better than the current method, when in fact there were no differences, you would be making a *Type I* error (sometimes called an *alpha* error). Type I errors might lead you to waste time and resources by pursuing what are essentially dead ends, and researchers have traditionally gone to great lengths to avoid Type I errors.

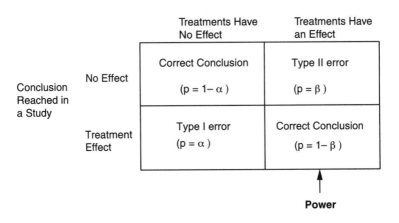

Figure 1.1   Outcomes of statistical tests.

There is an extensive literature dealing with methods of estimating and minimizing the occurrence of Type I errors (e.g., Zwick & Marascuilo, 1984). The probability of making a Type I error is in part a function of the standard or decision criterion used in testing your hypothesis (often referred to as alpha, or α). A very lenient standard (e.g., if there is *any* difference between the two samples, you will conclude that there is also a difference in the population) might lead to more frequent Type I errors, whereas a more stringent standard might lead to fewer Type I errors.[1]

A second type of error (referred to as *Type II* error, or *beta* error) is also common in statistical hypothesis testing (Cohen, 1994; Sedlmeier & Gigerenzer, 1989). A Type II error occurs when you conclude in favor of H_0, when in fact H_1 is true. For example, if you conclude that there are no real differences in the outcomes of these two methods of instruction, when in fact one really is better than the other in the population, you have made a Type II error.

Statistical power analysis is concerned with Type II errors (i.e., if the probability of making a Type II error is β, power = $1 - \beta$). Another way of saying this is to note that power is the (conditional) probability that you will

---

[1] It is important to note that Type I errors can only occur when the null hypothesis is actually true. If the null hypothesis is that there is no true treatment effect (a nil hypothesis), this will rarely be the case. As a result, Type I errors are probably quite rare in tests of the traditional null hypothesis, and efforts to control these errors at the expense of making more Type II errors might be ill advised (Murphy, 1990).

avoid a Type II error. Studies with high levels of statistical power will rarely fail to detect the effects of treatments. If we assume that most treatments have at least *some* effect, the statistical power of a study often translates into the probability that the study will lead to the correct conclusion (i.e., that it will detect the effects of treatments).

Understanding Conditional Probability

Figure 1.1 illustrates four different possible outcomes of a statistical test. You might notice that the probabilities of these four events do not sum to 1.0. That is because the probabilities illustrated in Figure 1.1 are *conditional* probabilities.

Look at the right-hand column of Figure 1.1 (the column labeled "Treatments have an effect"). If treatments do have some effect in the population, your statistical test can lead to two possible outcomes. You might correctly conclude that there is a difference between these two treatments (the probability that this will occur is 1 − β), or you might mistakenly conclude that there is no real difference between treatments (the probability that this will occur is β). We refer to these as conditional probabilities because these two events are conditioned by, or only occur, if treatments have a real population effect.

Both Type I and Type II errors are conditional events. That is, it is not possible to make a Type I error unless there is truly no treatment effect in the population. If treatments have any effect whatsoever, it is not possible to make a Type I error when testing the nil hypothesis. Similarly, it is impossible to make a Type II error unless there is a real treatment effect. As we will see later, the conditional nature of Type I errors has very important consequences for testing the traditional nil hypothesis.

Effects of sensitivity, effect size, and decision criterion on power. The power of a statistical test is a function of its sensitivity, the size of the effect in the population, and the standards or criteria used to test statistical hypotheses. Tests have higher levels of statistical power when:

1. *Studies are highly sensitive.* Researchers can increase sensitivity by using better measures or using study designs that allow them to control for unwanted sources of variability in their data (for the moment, we define *sensitivity* in terms of the degree to which

sampling error introduces imprecision into the results of a study; a fuller definition will be presented later in this chapter). The simplest method of increasing the sensitivity of a study is to increase its sample size (N). As N increases, statistical estimates become more precise and the power of statistical tests increase.

2. *Effect sizes (ES) are large.* Different treatments have different effects. It is easiest to detect the effect of a treatment if that effect is large (e.g., when treatment outcomes are very different or when treatments account for a substantial proportion of variance in outcomes; we discuss specific measures of effect size later in this chapter and in the chapters that follow). When treatments have very small effects, these effects can be difficult to reliably detect. As ES values increase, power increases.

3. *Criteria for statistical significance are lenient.* Researchers must make a decision about the standards that are required to reject H_0. It is easier to reject H_0 when the significance criterion, or alpha (α) level, is .05 than when it is .01 or .001. As the standard for determining significance becomes more lenient, power increases.

Power is highest when all three of these conditions are met (i.e., sensitive study, large effect, lenient criterion for rejecting the null hypothesis). In practice, sample size (which affects sensitivity) is probably the more important determinant of power. Effect sizes in the social and behavioral sciences tend to be small or moderate (if the effect of a treatment is so large that it can be seen with the naked eye, even in small samples, there may be little reason to test for it statistically), and researchers are often unwilling to abandon the traditional criteria for statistical significance that are accepted in their field (usually alpha levels of .05 or .01; Cowles & Davis, 1982). Thus, effect sizes and decision criteria tend to be similar across a wide range of studies. In contrast, sample sizes vary considerably, and they directly impact levels of power.

With a sufficiently large N, virtually any test statistic will be "significantly" different from zero, and virtually any nil hypothesis can be rejected. Large N makes statistical tests highly sensitive, and virtually any specific point hypothesis (e.g., the difference between two treatments is zero, the difference between two reading programs is 6 points) can be rejected if the study is sufficiently sensitive. For example, suppose you are testing a new medicine that will result in a .0000001% increase in success rates for treating cancer. This increase is larger than zero, and if researchers include enough subjects in a study evaluating this treatment, they will almost certainly conclude that the new treatment is statistically different from existing treatments. On the other hand if very small samples are used to evaluate a treatment that has a real and substantial effect, statistical power might be so low that they incorrectly conclude that the new treatment is not different from existing treatments.

Studies can have very low levels of power (i.e., are likely to make Type II errors) when they use small samples, when the effect being studied is a small one, or when stringent criteria are used to define a "significant" result. The worst case occurs when a researcher uses a small sample to study a treatment that has a very small effect, *and* he or she uses a very strict standard for rejecting the null hypothesis. Under those conditions, Type II errors may be the norm. To put it simply, studies that use small samples and stringent criteria for statistical significance to examine treatments that have small effects will almost always lead to the wrong conclusion about those treatments (i.e., to the conclusion that treatments have no effect whatsoever).

The Mechanics of Power Analysis

When a sample is drawn from a population, the exact value of any statistic (e.g., the mean or difference between two group means) is uncertain, and that uncertainty is reflected by a statistical distribution. Suppose, for example, that you evaluate a treatment that you expect has no real effect (e.g., you use astrology to advise people about career choices) by comparing outcomes in groups who receive this treatment with outcomes in groups who do not receive it (control groups). You will *not* always find that treatment and control groups have exactly the same scores, even if the treatment has no real effect. Rather, some range of values can be expected for any test statistic in a study like this, and the standards used to determine statistical significance are based on this range or distribution of values. In traditional null hypothesis testing, a test statistic is "statistically significant" at the .05 level if its actual value is outside of the range of values you would observe 95% of the time in studies where the treatment had no real effect. If the test statistic is outside of this range, the usually inference is that the treatment *did* have some real effect.

For example, suppose that 62 people are randomly assigned to treatment and control groups, and the *t*-statistic is used to compare the means of the two groups. If the treatment has no effect whatsoever, the *t*-statistic should usually be near zero, and will have a value less than or equal to approximately 2.00 95% of the time. If the *t*-statistic obtained in a study is larger than 2.00, you can safely infer that treatments are very likely to have some effect; if there was no real treatment effect, values greater than 2.00 would be a very rare event.

Understanding Sampling Distributions

In the example above, 62 people are randomly assigned to groups that either receive astrology-based career advice or who do not receive such advice. Even though you might expect that the treatment has no real effect, you would probably not expect that the difference between the average level of career success of these two groups will always be exactly zero. Sometimes the astrology group might do better and sometimes it might do worse.

Suppose you repeated this experiment 1,000 times and noted the difference between the average level of career success in the two groups. The distribution of scores would look something like Figure 1.2 below.

This distribution is referred to as a "sampling distribution," and it illustrates the extent to which differences between the means of these two groups might be expected to vary as a result of chance or sampling error. Most of the time, the differences between these groups should be near zero, because we expect that advice based on astrology has no real systematic effect. The variance of this distribution illustrates the range of differences in outcomes you might expect if your hypothesis is that astrology has no real effect. In this case, about 95% of the time, you expect the difference between the astrology and the no-astrology groups to be about 2 points or less. If you find a bigger difference between groups (suppose the

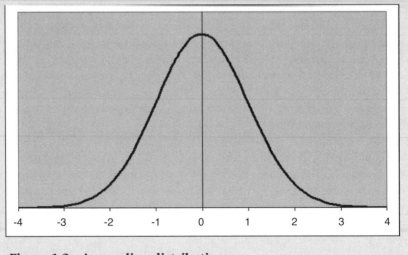

Figure 1.2 A sampling distribution.

average success score for the astrology group is 5 points higher than the average for the no-astrology group), you should reject the null hypothesis that the career advice has no systematic effect.

You might ask why anyone in their right mind would repeat this study 1,000 times. Luckily, statistical theory allows us to estimate sampling distributions on the basis of a few simple statistics. Virtually all the statistical tests discussed in this book are conducted by comparing the value of some test statistic with its sampling distribution, so understanding the idea of a sampling distribution is essential to understanding hypothesis testing and statistical power.

As the example above suggests, if treatments have no effect whatsoever in the population, you should not expect to always find a difference of precisely zero between samples of those who receive the treatment and those who do not. Rather, there is some range of values that might be found for any test statistic in a sample (e.g., in the example cited earlier, you expect the value of the difference in the two means to be near zero, but you also know it might range from approximately −2.00 to +2.00). The same is true if treatments have a real effect. For example, if a researcher expects that the mean in a treatment group that receives career advice based on valid measures of work interests will be 10 points higher than the mean in a control group (e.g., because this is the size of the difference in the population), that researcher should also expect some variability around that figure. Sometimes, the difference between two samples might be 9 points, and sometimes it might be 11 or 12. The key to power analysis is estimating the range of values one might reasonably expect for some test statistic if the real effect of treatments is small, or medium, or large. Figure 1.3 illustrates the key ideas in statistical power analysis.

Suppose you use a *t*-test to determine whether the difference in average reading test scores of 3,000 pupils randomly assigned to two different types of reading instruction is statistically significant. You do not make any specific prediction about which reading program will be better and, therefore, test the two-tailed hypothesis that the two programs lead to systematically different outcomes. To be "statistically significant," the value of this test statistic must be 1.96 or larger. As Figure 1.3 suggests, the likelihood you will reject the null hypothesis that there is no difference between the two groups depends substantially on whether the true effect of treatments is small or large.

If the null hypothesis that there is no real effect was true, you would expect to find values of 1.96 or greater for this test statistic in 5 tests out of

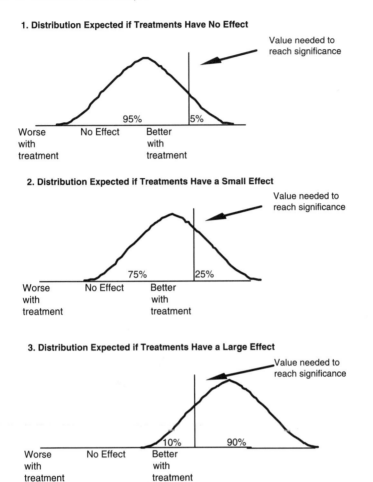

Note. Depending on the test statistic in question, the distributions might take different forms, but the essential features of this figure would apply to any test statistic.

Figure 1.3   Essentials of power analysis.

every 100 performed (i.e., $\alpha = .05$). This is illustrated in graph 1 of Figure 1.3. Graph 2 of Figure 1.3 illustrates the distribution of test statistic values you might expect if treatments had a small effect on the dependent variable. You might notice that the distribution of test statistics you would expect to find in studies of a treatment with this sort of effect has shifted a bit, and that in this case 25% of the values you might expect to find are greater than or equal to 1.96. That is, if you run a study under the scenario illustrated in graph 2 of this figure (i.e., treatments have a small effect), the probability you will reject the null hypothesis is .25. Graph 3 of Figure 1.3 illustrates the distribution of values you might expect if the true effect of treatments is large. In this distribution, 90% of the values are 2.00 or greater, and the probability you will reject the null hypothesis is .90. *The power of a statistical test is the proportion of the distribution of test statistics expected for a study like this that is above the critical value used to establish statistical significance.* The qualifier "for a study like this" is important because the distribution of test statistics you should reasonably expect in a particular study depends on both the population effect size and the sample size. If the power of a study is .80, that is the same thing as saying that if you draw a distribution of the test statistic values you expect to find based on the population effect size and the sample size, 80% of these will be equal to or greater than the critical value needed to reject the null hypothesis.

No matter what hypothesis you are testing, or what statistic you are using to test that hypothesis, power analysis always involves three basic steps that are listed in Table 1.1. First, a criterion or critical value for "statistical significance" must be established. For example, the tables found in the back of virtually any statistics textbook can be used to determine such critical values for testing the traditional null hypothesis. If the test statistic a researcher computes exceeds this critical value, the researcher will reject the null hypothesis. However, these tables are not the only basis for setting such a criterion. Suppose you wanted to test the hypothesis that the effects of treatments are so small that they can safely be ignored. This might involve specifying some range of effects that would be designated as "negligible," and then determining the critical value of a statistic needed to reject this hypothesis. Chapter 2 shows how such tests are performed and lays out

Table 1.1   The Three Steps to Determining Statistical Power

1. Establish a criterion or critical value for statistical significance.
   - What is the hypothesis that is being tested (e.g., traditional null hypothesis, minimum-effect tests)?
   - What level of confidence is desired (e.g., $\alpha = .05$ versus $\alpha = .01$)?
   - What is the critical value for your test statistic? (These critical values are determined on the basis of the degrees of freedom [df] for the test and the desired confidence level.)
2. Estimate the effect size (ES).
   - Are treatments expected to have large, medium, or small effects?
   - What is the range of values researchers expect to find for the test statistic, given this ES?
3. Determine where the critical value lies in relationship to the distribution of test statistics expected if the null hypothesis is true (i.e., the sampling distribution).

the implications of such hypothesis testing strategies for statistical power analysis.

> The power of a statistical test is the proportion of the distribution of test statistics expected for a study (based on the sample size and the estimated ES) that is above the critical value used to establish statistical significance.

Power analysis requires researchers to make their best guess of the size of effect treatments are likely to have on the dependent variable(s); methods of estimating effect sizes are discussed later in this chapter. As we noted earlier, if there are good reasons to believe that treatments have a very large effect, it should be quite easy to reject the null hypothesis. On the other hand, if the true effects of treatments are small and subtle, it might be very hard to reject the hypothesis that treatments have no real effect.

Once you have estimated ES, it is also possible to use that estimate to describe the distribution of test statistics that should be expected. We describe this process in more detail in Chapter 2, but a simple example will show what we mean. Suppose you are using a *t*-test to assess the difference in the mean scores of those receiving two different treatments. If there was no real difference between the treatments, you would expect to find *t*-values near zero most of the time, and you can use statistical theory to tell how much these *t*-values might depart from zero as a result of sampling error. The *t*-tables in most statistics textbooks tell you how much variability you might expect with samples of different sizes, and once the mean (here, zero) and the standard deviation of this distribution are known, it is easy to estimate what proportion of the distribution falls above or below any critical value. If there is a large difference between the treatments (e.g., the dependent variable has a mean of 500 and a standard deviation of 100, and the mean for one treatment is usually 80 points higher than the mean for another), large *t*-values should be expected most of the time.

The final step in power analysis is a comparison between the values obtained in the first two steps. For example, if you determine that a *t*-value of 1.96 is needed to reject the null hypothesis, and also determine that because the treatments being studied have very large effects you are likely to find *t*-values of 1.96 or greater 90% of the time, the power of this test (i.e., power is .90).

Sensitivity and power. Sensitivity refers to the precision with which a statistical test distinguishes between true treatment effects and differences in scores that are the result of sampling error. As noted above, the sensitivity of statistical tests is largely a function of the sample size. Large samples provide very precise estimates of population parameters, whereas small samples produce results than can be unstable and untrustworthy. For example, if 6 children in 10 do better with a new reading curriculum than with the old one, this might reflect nothing more than simple sampling error. If 600 out of 1,000 children do better with the new curriculum, this is powerful and convincing evidence that there are real differences between the new curriculum and the old one.

In a study with low sensitivity, there is considerable uncertainty about statistical outcomes. As a result, it might be possible to find a large treatment effect in a sample, even though there is no true treatment effect in the population. This translates into both substantial variability in study outcomes and the need for relatively demanding tests of "statistical significance." If outcomes can vary substantially from study to study, researchers need to observe relatively large effects to be confident that they represent true treatment effects and not mere sampling error. As a result, it is often difficult to reject the hypothesis that there is no true effect when small samples are used, and many Type II errors should be expected.

In a highly sensitive study, there is very little uncertainty or random variation in study outcomes, and virtually any difference between treatment and control groups is likely to be accepted as an indication that the treatment has an effect in the population.

Effect size and power. Effect size is a key concept in statistical power analysis (Cohen, 1988; Rosenthal, 1991; Tatsuoka, 1993a). At the simplest level, effect size measures provide an index of how much impact treatments actually have on the dependent variable; if H_0 states that treatments have no impact whatsoever, the effect size can be thought of as an index of just how wrong the null hypothesis is.

One of the most common ES measures is the standardized mean difference, d, defined as $d = (M_t - M_c)/SD$, where M_t and M_c are the treatment and control group means, respectively, and SD is the pooled standard deviation. By expressing the difference in group means in standard deviation units, the d-statistic provides a simple metric that allows one to compare treatment effects from different studies, areas of research, etc., without having to keep track of the units of measurement used in different studies or areas of research. For example, Lipsey and Wilson (1993) cataloged the effects of a wide range of psychological, educational, and behavioral treatments, all expressed in terms of d. Examples of interventions in these areas that have relatively small, moderately large, and large effects on specific sets of outcomes are presented in Table 1.2.

For example, worksite smoking cessation/reduction programs have a relatively small effect on quit rates ($d = .21$). The effects of class size on achievement or of juvenile delinquency programs on delinquency outcomes are similarly small. Concretely, a d-value of .20 means that the difference between the average score of those who receive the treatment and those who do not is only 20% as large as the standard deviation of the outcome measure within each of the treatment groups. This standard deviation

Table 1.2   Examples of Effect Sizes Reported in Lipsey and Wilson (1993) Review

	Dependent Variable	d
Small Effects (d = .20)		
Treatment programs for juvenile delinquents	Delinquency outcomes	.17
Worksite smoking cessation/reduction programs	Quit rates	.21
Small versus large class size, all grade levels	Achievement measures	.20
Medium Effects (d = .50)		
Behavior therapy versus placebo controls	Various outcomes	.51
Chronic disease patient education	Compliance and health	.52
Enrichment programs for gifted children	Cognitive, creativity, affective outcomes	.55
Large Effects (d = .80)		
Psychotherapy	Various outcomes	.85
Meditation and relaxation techniques	Blood pressure	.93
Positive reinforcement in the classroom	Learning	1.17

measures the variability in outcomes, independent of treatments, so d = .20 indicates that the average effect of treatments is only 1/5th as large as the variability in outcomes among people who receive the same treatments. In contrast, interventions such as psychotherapy, meditation and relaxation, or positive reinforcement in the classroom have relatively large effects on outcomes such as functioning levels, blood pressure, and learning (d-values range from .85 to 1.17).

It is important to keep in mind that "small," "medium," or "large" effect refers to the size of the effect, but not necessarily to its importance. For example, a new security screening procedure might lead to a small change in rates of detecting threats, but if this change translates into hundreds of lives saved at a small cost, the effect might be judged to be both important and worth paying attention to.

When the true treatment effect is very small, it might be hard to accurately and consistently detect this effect in successive samples. For example, aspirin can be useful in reducing heart attacks, but the effects are relatively small (d =.068; see, however, Rosenthal, 1993). As a result, studies of 20 or 30 patients taking an aspirin or a placebo will not consistently detect the true and life-saving effects of this drug. Large sample studies, however, provide compelling evidence of the consistent effect of aspirin on heart attacks. On the other hand, if the effect is relatively large, it is easy to detect, even with a relatively small sample. For example, cognitive ability has a strong influence on performance in school (d is approximately 1.10), and the effects of individual differences in cognitive ability are readily noticeable even in small samples of students.

Decision criteria and power. Finally, the standard or decision criteria used in hypothesis testing has a critical impact on statistical power. The standards that are used to test statistical hypotheses are usually set with a goal of minimizing Type I errors; alpha levels are usually set at .05, .01, or some other similarly low level, reflecting a strong bias against treating study outcomes that might be due to nothing more than sampling error as meaningful (Cowles & Davis, 1982). Setting a more lenient standard makes it easier to reject the null hypothesis, and while this can lead to Type I errors in those rare cases where the null is actually true, anything that makes it easier to reject the null hypothesis also increases the statistical power of the study.

As Figure 1.1 shows, there is always a tradeoff between Type I and Type II errors. If you make it very difficult to reject the null hypothesis, you will minimize Type I errors (incorrect rejections), but you will also increase the number of Type II errors. That is, if you rarely reject the null, you will often incorrectly dismiss sample results as mere sampling error, when they may in fact indicate the true effects of treatments. Numerous authors have noted that procedures to control or minimize Type I errors can substantially reduce statistical power and may cause more problems (i.e., Type II errors) than they solve (Cohen, 1994; Sedlmeier & Gigerenzer, 1989).

Power analysis and the general linear model. In the chapters that follow, we describe a simple and general model for statistical power analysis. This model is based on the widely used *F* statistic. This statistic and variations on the *d* are used to test a wide range of statistical hypotheses in the context of the general linear model (Cohen & Cohen, 1983; Horton, 1978; Tatsuoka, 1993b). The general linear model provides the basis for correlation, multiple regression, analysis of variance, discriminant analysis, and all of the variations of these techniques. The general linear model subsumes a large proportion of the statistics that are widely used in the behavioral and social sciences, and by tying statistical power analysis to this model, we will show how the same simple set of techniques can be applied to an extraordinary range of statistical analyses.

Statistical Power of Research in the Social and Behavioral Sciences

Research in the social and behavioral sciences often shows shockingly low levels of power. Starting with Cohen's (1962) review of research published in the *Journal of Abnormal and Social Psychology*, studies in psychology, education, communication, journalism, and other related fields have routinely documented power in the range of .20 to .50 for detecting small to medium treatment effects (Sedlmeier & Gigerenzer, 1989). Despite decades of warnings about the consequences of low levels of statistical power in the behavioral and social sciences, the level of power encountered in published studies is lower than .50 (Mone, Mueller, & Mauland, 1996). In other words, it is typical for studies in these areas to have less than a 50% chance of rejecting the null hypothesis. If you believe that the null hypothesis is virtually always wrong (i.e., that treatments have at least *some* effect, even if it is a very small one), this means that at least half of all studies in the social and behavioral sciences (perhaps as many as 80%) are likely to reach the wrong conclusion by making a Type II error when testing the null hypothesis.

These figures are even more startling and discouraging when you realize that these reviews have examined the statistical power of *published research*. Given the strong biases against publishing methodologically suspect studies or studies reporting null results, it is likely that the studies that survive the editorial review process are better than the norm, that they show stronger effects than similar unpublished studies, and that the statistical power of unpublished studies is even lower than the power of published studies.

Studies that do not reject the null hypothesis are often regarded by researchers as failures. The levels of power reported above suggest that "failure," defined in these terms, is quite common. If a treatment effect is small, and a study is designed with a power level of .20 (which is depressingly common), researchers are 4 times as likely to fail (i.e., fail to reject the null) as to succeed. Power of .50 suggests that the outcome of a study is basically like the flip of a coin. A researcher whose study has power of .50 is just as likely to fail to reject the null hypothesis as he or she is to succeed. It is likely that much of the apparent inconsistency in research findings is due to nothing more than inadequate power (Schmidt, 1992). If 100 studies are conducted, each with power of .50, approximately half of them will reject the null and approximately half will not. Given the stark implications of low power, it is important to consider *why* research in the social and behavioral sciences is so often conducted in a way in which failure is more likely than success.

The most obvious explanation for low level of power in the social and behavioral sciences is the belief that social scientists tend to study treatments, interventions, etc., that have small and unreliable effects. Until recently, this explanation was widely accepted, but the widespread use of meta-analysis in integrating scientific literature suggests that this is not necessarily the case. There is now ample evidence from literally hundred of analyses of thousands of individual studies that the treatments, interventions, and the like studied by behavioral and social scientists have substantial and meaningful effects (Haase, Waechter, & Solomon, 1982; Hunter & Hirsh, 1987; Lipsey, 1990; Lipsey & Wilson, 1993; Schmitt, Gooding, Noe, & Kirsch, 1984); these effects are of a similar magnitude as many of the effects reported in the physical sciences (Hedges, 1987).

A second possibility is that the decision criteria used to define "statistical significance" are too stringent. We argue in several of the chapters that follow that researchers are often too concerned with Type I errors and insufficiently concerned with statistical power. However, the use of overly stringent decision criteria is probably not the best explanation for low levels of statistical power.

The best explanation for the low levels of power observed in many areas of research is many studies use samples that are much too small to provide accurate and credible results. Researchers routinely use samples of 20, 50, or 75 observations to make inferences about population parameters. When sample results are unreliable, it is necessary to set some strict standard to distinguish real treatment effects from fluctuations in the data that are due to simple sampling error, and studies with these small samples often fail to reject null hypotheses, even when the population treatment effect is fairly large.

On the other hand, very large samples will allow you to reject the null hypothesis even when it is very nearly true (i.e., when the effect of treatments is very small). In fact, the effects of sample size on statistical power are so profound that it is tempting to conclude that a significance test is little more than a roundabout measure of how large the sample is. If the sample is sufficiently small, you will virtually never reject the null hypothesis. If the sample is sufficiently large, you will virtually always reject the null hypothesis.

Using Power Analysis

Statistical power analysis can be used for both planning and diagnosis. Power analysis is frequently used in designing research studies. The results of power analysis can help in determining how large your sample should be, or in deciding what criterion should be used to define "statistical significance." Power analysis can also be used as a diagnostic tool, to determine whether a specific study has adequate power for specific purposes, or to identify the sort of effects that can be reliably detected in that study.

Because power is a function of the sensitivity of your study (which is essentially a function of N), the size of the effect in the population (ES), and the decision criterion that is used to determine statistical significance, we can solve for any of the four values (i.e., power, N, ES, α), given the other three. However, none of these values is necessarily known in advance, although some values may be set by convention. The criterion for statistical significance (i.e., α) is often set at .05 or .01 by convention, but there is nothing sacred about these values. As we note later, one important use of power analysis is in making decisions about what criteria *should* be used to describe a result as "significant."

The Meaning of Statistical Significance

Suppose a study leads to the conclusion that "there is a statistically significant correlation between the personality trait of conscientiousness and job performance." What does *statistically significant* mean?

Statistically significant clearly does *not* mean that this correlation is large, meaningful, or important (although it might be all of these). If the sample size is large, a correlation that is quite small will still be "statistically significant." For example, if $N = 20,000$, a correlation of $r = .02$ will be significantly ($\alpha = .05$) different from zero. The term *statistically significant* can be thought of as shorthand for the following statement:

> In this particular study, there is sufficient evidence to allow the researcher to reliably distinguish (with a level of confidence defined by the alpha level) between the observed correlation of .02 and a correlation of zero.

In other words, the term *statistically significant* does not describe the result of a study, but rather describes the sort of result this particular study can reliably detect. The same correlation will be statistically significant in some studies (e.g., those that use a large N or a lenient alpha) and not significant in others. In the end, "statistically significant" usually says more about the design of the study than about the results. Studies that are designed with high levels of statistical power will, by definition, usually produce significant results. Studies that are designed with low levels of power will not yield significant results. A significant test usually tells you more about the study design than about the substantive phenomenon being studied.

The ES depends on the treatment, phenomenon, or variable you are studying, and is usually not known in advance. Sample size is rarely set in advance, and N often depends on some combination of luck and resources on the part of the investigator. Actual power levels are rarely known, and it can be difficult to obtain sensible advice about how much power you should have. It is important to understand how each of the parameters involved is determined when conducting a power analysis.

Determining the effect size. There is a built-in dilemma in power analysis. In order to determine the statistical power of a study, ES must be known.

But if you already knew the exact strength of the effect the particular treatment, intervention, etc., you would not need to do the study! The whole point of doing a study is to find out what effect the treatment has, and the true ES in the population is unlikely to ever be known.

Statistical power analyses are always based on *estimates* of ES. In many areas of study, there is a substantial body of theory and empirical research that will provide a well-grounded estimate of ES. For example, there are literally hundreds of studies of the validity of cognitive ability tests as predictors of job performance (Hunter & Hirsch, 1987; Schmidt, 1992), and this literature suggests that the relationship between test scores and performance is consistently strong (corrected correlations of approximately .50 are common). Even where there is no extensive literature available, researchers can often use their experience with similar studies to realistically estimate effect sizes.

When there is no good basis for estimating effect sizes, power analyses can still be carried out by making a conservative estimate. A study that has adequate power to reliably detect small effects (e.g., a d of .20 or a correlation of .10) will also have adequate power to detect larger effects. On the other hand, if researchers design studies with the assumption that effects will be large, they might have insufficient power to detect small but important effects. Earlier, we noted that the effects of taking aspirin to reduce heart attacks are relatively small, but that there is still a substantial payoff for taking the drug. If the initial research that led to the use of aspirin for this purpose had been conducted using small samples, the researchers would have had little chance of detecting the life-saving effect of aspirin.

Determining the desired level of power. In determining desired levels of power, researchers must weigh the risks of running studies without adequate power against the resources needed to attain high levels of power. Researchers can always achieve high levels of power by using very large samples, but the time and expense required may not always justify the effort.

There are no hard-and-fast rules about how much power is enough, but there does seem to be consensus about two things. First, if at all possible, power should be greater than .50. When power drops to less than .50, a study is more likely to fail (i.e., it is unlikely to reject the null hypothesis) than succeed. It is hard to justify designing studies in which failure is the most likely outcome. Second, power of .80 or greater is usually judged to be adequate. The .80 convention is arbitrary (in the same way that significance criteria of .05 or .01 are arbitrary), but it seems to be widely accepted, and it can be rationally defended.

Power of .80 means that success (rejecting the null) is 4 times as likely as failure. It can be argued that some number other than 4 might represent a more acceptable level of risk (e.g., if power = .90, success is 9 times as likely as failure), but it is often prohibitively difficult to achieve power much in excess of .80. For example, to have a power of .80 in detecting a small treatment effect (where the difference between treatment and control groups is $d = .20$), a sample of approximately 775 subjects is needed. If power of .95 is desired, a sample of approximately 1,300 subjects will be needed. Most power analyses specify .80 as the desired level of power to be achieved, and this convention seems to be widely accepted.

Applying power analysis. There are four ways to use power analysis: (1) in determining the sample size needed to achieve desired levels of power, (2) in determining the level of power in a study that is planned or has already been conducted, (3) in determining the size of effect that can be reliably detected by a particular study, and (4) in determining sensible criteria for "statistical significance." The chapters that follow will lay out the actual steps in doing a power analysis, but it is useful at this point to get a preview of the four potential applications of this method:

1. Determining sample size. Given a particular ES, significance criterion, and a desired level of power, it is easy to solve for the sample size needed. For example, if researchers think the correlation between a new test and performance on the job is .30, and they want to have at least an 80% chance of rejecting the null hypothesis (with a significance criterion of .05), they need a sample of approximately 80 cases. When planning a study, researchers should routinely use power analysis to help make sensible decisions about the number of subjects needed.

2. Determining power levels. If N, ES, and the criterion for statistical significance are known, researchers can use power analysis to determine the level of power for that study. For example, if the difference between treatment and control groups is small (e.g., $d = .20$), there are 50 subjects in each group, and the significance criterion is $\alpha = .01$, power will be only .05! Researchers should certainly expect that this study will fail to reject the null, and they might decide to change the design of this study considerably (e.g., use larger samples or more lenient criteria).

3. Determining ES levels. Researchers can also determine what sort of effect could be reliably detected, given N, the desired level of power, and α. In the example above, a study with 50 subjects in both the treatment and control groups would have power of .80 to detect a very large effect (approximately $d = .65$) with a .01 significance criterion, or a large effect ($d = .50$) with a .05 significance criterion.

4. Determining criteria for statistical significance. Given a specific effect, sample size, and power level, it is possible to determine the

significance criterion. For example, if you expect a correlation coefficient to be .30, $N = 67$, and you want power to equal or exceed .80, you will need to use a significance criterion of $\alpha = .10$ rather than the more common .05 or .01.

Hypothesis Tests Versus Confidence Intervals

Null hypothesis testing has been criticized on a number of grounds (e.g., Schmidt, 1996), but perhaps the most persuasive critique is that null hypothesis tests provide so little information. It is widely recognized that the use of confidence intervals and other methods of portraying levels of uncertainty about the outcomes of statistical procedures have many advantages over simple null hypothesis tests (Wilkinson et al., 1999).

Suppose a study is performed that examines the correlation between scores on an ability test and measures of performance in training. The authors find a correlation of $r = .30$, and on the basis of a null hypothesis test, decide that this value is significantly (e.g., at the .05 level) different from zero. That test tells them something, but it does not really tell them whether the finding that $r = .30$ represents a good or a poor estimate of the relationship between ability and training performance. A confidence interval (CI) would provide that sort of information.

Staying with this example, suppose researchers estimate the amount of variability expected in correlations from studies such as this and conclude that a 95% CI ranges from .05 to .55. This confidence interval would tell researchers exactly what they learned from the significance test (i.e., that they could be quite sure the correlation between ability and training performance was not zero). A confidence interval would also tell them that $r = .30$ might not be a good estimate of the correlation between ability and performance; the confidence interval suggests that this correlation could be much larger or much smaller than .30. Another researcher doing a similar study using a larger sample might find a much smaller confidence interval, indicating a good deal more certainty about the generalizability of sample results.

As the previous paragraph implies, most of the statements that can be made about statistical power also apply to confidence intervals. That is, if you design a study with low power, you will also find that it produces wide confidence intervals (i.e., there will be considerable uncertainty about the meaning of sample results). If you design studies to be sensitive and powerful, these studies will yield smaller confidence intervals. Although the focus of this book is on hypothesis tests, it is important to keep in mind that the same facets of the research design (N, the alpha level) that cause power to go up or down also cause confidence intervals to shrink or grow. A powerful study will not always yield precise results (e.g., power can be high in a poorly designed study that examines a treatment that has very strong effects), but in most instances, whatever researchers do to increase power will also lead to smaller confidence intervals and to more precision in sample statistics.

Summary

Power is defined as the probability that a study will reject the null hypothesis when it is in fact false. Studies with high statistical power are very likely to detect the effects of treatments, interventions, etc., whereas studies with low power can lead researchers to dismiss potentially important effects as sampling error. The statistical power of a test is a function of the size of the treatment effect in the population, the sample size, and the particular criterion used to define statistical significance. Although most discussions of power analysis are phrased in terms of traditional null hypothesis testing, where the hypothesis that treatments have no impact whatsoever is tested, power analysis can be fruitfully applied to any method of statistical hypothesis testing.

Statistical power analysis has received less attention in the behavioral and social sciences than it deserves. It is still routine in many areas for researchers to run studies with disastrously low levels of power. Statistical power analysis can and should be used to determine the number of subjects that should be included in a study, to estimate the likelihood that a study will reject the null hypothesis, to determine what sorts of effects can be reliably detected in a study, or to make rational decisions about the standards used to define "statistical significance." Each of these applications of power analysis is taken up in the chapters that follow.

2

A Simple and General Model
for Power Analysis

▼   ▼   ▼   ▼   ▼

This chapter develops a simple approach to statistical power analysis that is based on the widely used F-statistic. The F-statistic (or some transformation of F) is used to test statistical hypotheses in the general linear model (Horton, 1978; Tatsuoka, 1993b), a model that includes all of the variations of correlation and regression analysis (including multiple regression), analysis of variance and covariance (ANOVA and ANCOVA), t-tests for differences in group means, and tests of the hypothesis that the effect of treatments takes on a specific value or a value different from zero. Most of the statistical tests that are used in the social and behavioral sciences can be treated as special cases of the general linear model.

Analyses based on the F-statistic are not the only approach to statistical power analysis. For example, in the most comprehensive work on power analysis, Cohen (1988) constructed power tables for a wide range of statistics and statistical applications, using separate effect size (ES) measures and power calculations for each class of statistics. Kraemer and Thiemann (1987) derived a general model for statistical power analysis based on the intraclass correlation coefficient and developed methods for evaluating the power of a wide range of test statistics using a single general table based on the intraclass r. Lipsey (1990) used the t-test as a basis for estimating the statistical power of several statistical tests.

The idea of using the F distribution as the basis for a general system of statistical power analysis is hardly an original one; Pearson and Hartley (1951) proposed a similar model over 50 years ago. It is useful, however, to explain the rationale for choosing the F distribution in some detail because the family of statistics based on *F* have a number of characteristics that help to take the mystery out of power analysis.

Basing a model for statistical power analysis on the *F* statistic provides a nice balance between applicability and familiarity. First, the *F* statistic is familiar to most researchers. This chapter and the one that follows show how to transform a wide range of test statistics and effect size measures into *F* statistics, and how to use those *F* values in statistical power analysis. Because such a wide range of statistics can be transformed into *F* values, structuring power analysis around the *F* distribution allows one to cover a great deal of ground with a single set of tables.

Second, the approach to power analysis developed in this chapter is flexible. Unlike other presentations of power analysis, we do not limit ourselves to tests of the traditional null hypothesis (i.e., the hypothesis that treatments have no effect whatsoever). Traditional null hypothesis tests have been roundly criticized (Cohen, 1994; Meehl, 1978; Morrison & Henkel, 1970), and there is a need to move beyond such limited tests. Our discussions of power analysis consider several methods of statistical hypothesis testing and show how power analysis can be easily extended beyond the traditional null hypothesis test. In particular, we show how the model developed here can be used to evaluate the power of "minimum-effect" hypothesis tests (i.e., tests of the hypothesis that the effects of treatments exceed some predetermined minimum level).

Recently, researchers have devoted considerable attention to alternatives to traditional null hypothesis tests (e.g., Murphy & Myors, 1999; Rouanet, 1996; Serlin & Lapsley, 1985, 1993), focusing in particular on tests of the hypothesis that the effect of treatments falls within or outside of some range of values. For example, Murphy and Myors discuss alternatives to tests of the traditional null hypothesis that involve specifying some range of effects that would be regarded as negligibly small, and then testing the hypothesis that the effect of treatments either falls within this range (H_0) or is greater than this range (H_1).

The *F* statistic is particularly well suited to tests of the hypothesis that effects fall within some range that can be reasonably described as "negligible" versus falling above that range. The *F* statistic ranges in value from zero to infinity, with larger values indicating stronger effects. As we show in sections that follow, this property of the *F* statistic makes it easy to adapt familiar testing procedures to evaluate the hypothesis that effects exceed some minimum level, rather than simply evaluating the possibility that treatments have no effect.

Finally, the *F* distribution explicitly incorporates one of the key ideas of statistical power analysis (i.e., that the range of values that might reasonably be expected for a variety of test statistics depends in part on the size of the effect in the population). As we note below, the concept of ES is reflected very nicely in one of the three parameters that determines the distribution of the F statistic (i.e., the noncentrality parameter).

The General Linear Model, the F Statistic, and Effect Size

Before exploring the F distribution and its use in power analysis, it is useful to describe the key ideas in applying the general linear model as a method of structuring statistical analyses, to show how the F statistic is used in testing hypotheses according to this model, and to describe a very general index of whether treatments have large or small effects.

Suppose 200 children are randomly assigned to one of two methods of reading instruction. Each child receives instruction that is either accompanied by audio-visual aids (computer software that "reads" to the child while showing pictures on a screen) or given without the aids. At the end of the semester each child's reading performance is measured.

One way to structure research on the possible effects of reading instruction is to construct a mathematical model to explain why some children read well and others read poorly. This model might take a simple additive form:

$$y_{ijk} = a_i + b_j + ab_{ij} + e_{ijk} \qquad (2.1)$$

where

y_{ijk} = The score for child k, who received instruction method i and audio-visual aid j

a_i = The effect of the method of reading instruction

b_j = The effect of audio-visual aids

ab_{ij} = The effect of the interaction between instruction and audio-visual aids

e_{ijk} = The part of the child's score that cannot be explained by the treatments received

When a linear model is used to analyze a study of this sort, researchers can ask several sorts of questions. First, it makes sense to ask whether the effect of a particular treatment or combination of treatments is large enough to rule out sampling error as an explanation for why people receiving one treatment obtain higher scores than people not receiving it. As we explain below, the F statistic is well suited for this purpose.

Second, it makes sense to ask whether the effects of treatments are relatively large or relatively small. There are a variety of statistics that might be used in answering this question, but one very general approach is to estimate the percentage of variance (PV) in scores that is explained by various effects included in the model. Regardless of the specific approach taken in statistical testing under the general linear model (e.g., analysis of variance, multiple regression, *t*-tests), the goal of the model is always to explain variance in the dependent variable (e.g., to help understand why some children obtained higher scores than others).

Linear models such as the one above divide the total variance in scores into variance that can be explained by methods and treatment effects (i.e., the combined effects of instruction and audio-visual aids) and variance that cannot be explained in terms of the treatments received by subjects. The percentage of variance associated with each effect in a linear model provides one very general measure of whether treatment effects are large or small (i.e., whether they account for a lot of the variance in the dependent variable or only a little). The value of *PV* is closely linked to *F*.

There are a number of specific statistics that are used in estimating *PV*, notably eta-squared and R^2, which are typically encountered in the contexts of the analysis of variance and multiple regression, respectively. We prefer to use the more general term *PV* because it describes a general index of the effects of treatments or interventions and is not limited to any specific statistic or statistical approach. As we show later, estimates of *PV* are extremely useful in structuring statistical power analyses for virtually any of the specific applications of the general linear model.

Understanding Linear Models

Linear models combine simplicity, elegance, and robustness, but for people who are the least bit math-phobic, they can seem intimidating. Consider the model illustrated in Equation 2.1 (presented earlier in this chapter). The mathematical form of this model is

$$y_{ijk} = a_i + b_j + ab_{ij} + e_{ijk}$$

This model is easier to understand if we rewrite it as a story or an explanation. This equation says

> In order to understand why some children perform better than others in reading (y_{ijk}), it is important to consider three things. First, the type of instruction (a_i) matters. Second, it makes a different whether the child gets audio-visual aids (b_j). Third, these two variables might interact; the effects of methods of instruction might be different for children who receive audio-visual aids than for those who do not (ab_{ij}). Finally, all sorts of other variables might be important, but the effects of these variables were not measured and cannot be estimated in this experiment. The combined effects of all of the other things that affect performance

> introduce some error (e_{ijk}) into the explanation of why some children end up performing better than others.
>
> Linear models are easiest to understand if you think of them as an answer to the question: "Why do the scores people receive on the dependent variable (Y) vary?" All linear models answer that question by identifying some systematic sources of variance (here, $a_i + b_j + ab_{ij}$); whatever cannot be explained in terms of these systematic sources is explained in terms of error (e_{ijk}).

The *F* Distribution and Power

If you take the ratio of two independent estimates of the variance in a population (e.g., s^2_1 and s^2_2), this ratio is distributed as F, where:

$$F = s^2_1/s^2_2 \qquad (2.2)$$

The distribution of this F-statistic depends of the degrees of freedom for the numerator (s^2_1) and the denominator (s^2_2). The F ratio can be used to test a wide range of statistical hypotheses (e.g., testing for the equality of means or variances). In the general linear model, the F-statistic is used to test the null hypothesis (e.g., that means are the same across treatments) by comparing a measure of the variability in scores due to the treatments with a measure of the variability in scores you might expect as a result of sampling error. In its most general form, the F test in general linear models is as follows:

$$F = \text{Variability due to treatments/Variability due to error} \qquad (2.3)$$

The distribution of the F-statistic is complex, and it depends in part on the degrees of freedom of the hypothesis or effect being tested (df_{hyp}) and the degrees of freedom for the estimate of error used in the test (df_{err}). If treatments have no real effect, the expected value of F is very close to 1.0 [$E(F) = df_{err}/(df_{err} - 2)$]. That is, if the traditional null hypothesis is true, the F ratios will usually be approximately 1.0. Sometimes, the F ratio might be a bit greater than 1.0 and sometimes it might be a bit less; depending on the degrees of freedom (df_{hyp} and df_{err}), the F values that are expected if the null hypothesis is true might cluster closely around 1.00, or they might vary considerably. The F tables shown in most statistics textbooks provide a sense of how much F values might vary as a function of sampling error, given various combinations of df_{hyp} and df_{err}.

The *F* and chi-squared distributions are closely related. The ratio of two chi-squared variables, each divided by its degrees of freedom, is distributed as *F*, and both distributions are special cases of a more general form (the gamma distribution). Similarly, the *t*-distribution is closely related to the *F* distribution; when the means of two groups are compared, the value of *t* is identical to the square root of *F*.

The noncentral F. Most familiar statistical tests are based on the central *F* distribution (i.e., the distribution of *F*-statistics expected when the traditional nil hypothesis is true). However, interventions or treatments normally have at least some effect, and the distribution of *F* values expected in any particular study is likely to take the form of a singly noncentral *F* distribution. The power of a statistical test is defined by the proportion of that singly noncentral *F* distribution that exceeds the critical value used to define "statistical significance."

The shape and range of values in this noncentral *F* distribution is a function of both the degrees of freedom (df_{hyp} and df_{err}) and the "noncentrality" parameter (λ). One way to think of the noncentrality parameter is that it is a function of just how wrong the traditional null hypothesis is. When $\lambda = 0$, the traditional null hypothesis is true and the noncentral *F* is identical to the central *F* that is tabled in most statistics texts.

The exact value of the noncentrality parameter is a function of both ES and the sensitivity of the statistical test (which is largely a function of the number of observations, *N*). For example, in a study where *n* subjects are randomly assigned to each of four treatment conditions, $\lambda = [n\Sigma(\mu_j - \mu)^2]/\sigma^2_e$, where μj and μ represent the population mean in treatment group *j* and the population mean over all four treatments, and σ^2_e represents the variance in scores due to sampling error. Horton (1978) noted that in many applications of the general linear model:

$$\lambda_{est} = SS_{hyp}/MS_{err} \qquad (2.4)$$

where λ_{est} represents an estimate of the noncentrality parameter, SS_{hyp} represents the sum of squares for the effect of interest, and MS_{err} represents the mean square error term used to test hypotheses about that effect. Using *PV* to designate the proportion of the total variance in the dependent variable explained by treatments (which means that $1 - PV$ refers to the proportion not explained), the noncentrality parameter can be estimated using the following equation:

$$\lambda_{est} = df_{err} [PV/(1 - PV)] \qquad (2.5)$$

Equations 2.4 and 2.5 provide a practical method for estimating the value of the noncentrality parameter in many of the most common applications of the general linear model.[1] A more general form of Equation 2.5 that is useful from complex analyses of variance is:

$$\lambda_{est} = [N - p] \cdot [PV/(1 - PV)] \tag{2.6}$$

where

N = Number of subjects
p = Number of terms in the linear model

The noncentrality parameter reflects the positive shift of the F distribution as the size of the effect in the population increases (Horton, 1978). For example, if N subjects are randomly assigned to one of k treatments, the mean of the noncentral F distribution is approximately $(N - k)(k + \lambda - 1)/(k - 1)(N - 3)$ as compared with an approximate mean of 1.0 for the central F-distribution. More concretely, assume that 100 subjects are assigned to one of four treatments. If the null hypothesis is true, the expected value of F is approximately 1.0, and the value of F needed to reject the null hypothesis ($\alpha = .05$) is 2.70. However, if the effect of treatments is in fact large (e.g., $PV = .25$), you should expect to find F values substantially greater than 1.0 most of the time; given this effect size, the mean of the noncentral F distribution is approximately 11.3, and more than 99% of the values in this distribution exceed 2.70. In other words, the power of this F test, given the large effect size of $PV = .25$, is greater than .99. If the population effect is this large, a statistical test comparing k groups and using a sample of $N = 100$ is virtually certain to correctly reject the null hypothesis.

The larger the effect, the larger the noncentrality parameter and the larger the expected value of F. The larger the F, the more likely it is that H_0 will be rejected. Therefore, all other things being equal, the more noncentrality (i.e., the larger the effect or the larger the N), the higher the power.

---

[1] Equations 2.4 and 2.5 are based on simple linear models in which there is only one effect being tested and the variance in scores is assumed to be due to either the effects of treatments or to error (e.g., this is the model that underlies the t-test or the one-way analysis of variance). In more complex linear models, df_{err} does not necessarily refer to the degrees of freedom associated with variability in scores of individuals who receive the same treatment (within-cell variability in the one-way ANOVA model), and a more general form of Equation 2.5 ($\lambda_{est} = [(N - k) \cdot (PV/(1 - PV)]$, where N represents the number of observations and k represents the total number of terms in the linear model) is needed. When N is large, Equation 2.5 yields very similar results to those of the more general form shown above.

Using the Noncentral *F* Distribution to Assess Power

Chapter 1 laid out the three steps in conducting a statistical power analysis, determining the critical value for significance, estimating ES, and estimating the proportion of test statistics likely to exceed critical value. Applying these three steps here, it follows that power analysis involves the following:

1. *Deciding the value of F that is needed to reject H_0.* As we will see later in this chapter, this depends in part on the specific hypothesis being tested.
2. *Estimating the ES and the degree of noncentrality.* Estimates of *PV* can be used to estimate the noncentrality parameter of the *F* distribution.
3. *Estimating the proportion of the noncentral F that lies above the critical F from step 1.*

In the chapters that follow, we present a simple method of conducting power analyses that is based on the noncentral *F* distribution. This method can be used with a wide variety of statistics and can be used for testing both nil hypotheses and null hypotheses that are based on specifications of negligible versus important effects. Methods of approximating the singly noncentral *F* distribution are presented in subsequent chapters. Appendix A presents a table of *F* values obtained by estimating the noncentral *F* distribution over a range of df_{hyp}, df_{err}, and ES values.

The table presented in Appendix A saves you the difficulty of estimating noncentral *F* values, and more importantly, of directly computing power estimates for each statistical test. This table can be used to test both traditional and minimum-effect null hypotheses, and to estimate the statistical power of tests of both types of hypotheses.

Approximations. The methods described in this book are simple and general, but are not always precise to the last decimal place. There are many statistical procedures that fall under the umbrella of the "general linear model," and some specific applications of this model may present unique complications, or distributional complexities. However, the methods described in this book provide acceptably accurate approximations for the entire range of statistical tests covered under this general model.

Approximations are particularly appropriate for statistical power analysis because virtually all applications of this technique are themselves approximations. That is, because the exact value of the population effect size is rarely known for certain, power analyses usually depend on approximations and conventions rather than working from precise knowledge of critical parameters. Thus, in power analysis good approximations are usually quite acceptable.

For example, power analysis might be used to guide the selection of sample sizes or significance criteria in a study. Power analysis typically functions as a decision aid rather than as a precise forecasting technique, and it is rare that different decisions will be reached when exact versus approximate power values are known. That is, users of power analysis are likely to reach the same decisions if they know that power is approximately .80 in a particular study as they would reach if they knew that the power was precisely .815.

Statistical power analysis is an area where precision is not of sufficient value to justify the use of cumbersome methods in pursuit of the last decimal place. It is possible to use the general method presented in this book to closely approximate the more specific findings that are obtained when power analyses are tailored to specific analytic techniques (see Cohen, 1988, for discussions of power analysis for each of several types of statistical tests). Our approach allows researchers to estimate statistical power for statistical tests in the general linear model by translating specific test statistics or effect size measures into their equivalent F values.

Translating Common Statistics and ES Measures Into F

The model developed here is expressed in terms of the F-statistic, which is commonly reportetd in studies that employ analysis of variance or multiple regression. However, many studies report results in terms of statistics other than the F value. It is useful to have at hand formulas for translating common statistics and effect size measures (e.g., d) into their F equivalents. Table 2.1 presents a set of formulas for doing just that.

Suppose a study compared the effectiveness of two smoking cessation programs, using a sample of 122 adults, who were randomly assigned to treatments. The researchers used an independent-groups t-test to compare scores in these two treatments and reported t-value of 2.48. This t-value would be equivalent to an F value of 6.15, with 1 and 120 degrees of freedom. The tabled value for F with 1 and 120 degrees of freedom ($\alpha = .05$) is 3.91, and the researchers would be justified in rejecting the null hypothesis.

Suppose another study ($N = 103$) reported a squared multiple correlation of $R^2 = .25$ between a set of four vocational interest tests and an occupational choice measure. Applying the formula shown in Table 2.1, this R^2 value would yield an F value of 8.33, with 4 and 100 degrees of freedom. The critical value of F needed to reject the traditional null hypothesis ($\alpha = .05$) is 2.46; the reported R^2 is significantly different from zero.

Table 2.1 Translating Common Statistics Into *F* Equivalent Values

Statistic	*F* Equivalent	Degrees of Freedom df_{hyp}	df_{err}
t-Test for difference between means	$F(1, df_{err}) = t^2$	—	$N - 2$
Correlation coefficient	$F(1, df_{err}) = \dfrac{r^2\, df_{err}}{1 - r^2}$	—	$N - 2$
Multiple R^2	$F(df_{hyp}, df_{err}) = \dfrac{R^2\, df_{err}}{(1 - R^2)\, df_{hyp}}$	p	$N - p - 1$
Hierarchical regression	$F(df_{hyp}, df_{err}) = \dfrac{(R^2_F - R^2_R)/df_{hyp}}{(1 - R^2_F)/df_{err}}$	k	$N - p - 1$
Chi-squared (χ^2)	$F(df_{hyp}, df_{err}) = \chi^2/df_{hyp}$	df_{hyp}	∞
Standardized mean difference (*d*)	$F(1, df_{err}) = \dfrac{d^2\, df_{err}}{4}$	—	$N - 2$
d (repeated measures)	$F(1, df_{err}) = \dfrac{d^2\, df_{err}}{4\sqrt{1 - r_{ab}}}$	—	$N - 2$

Note: p = number of *X* variables in multiple regression equation. R^2_F and R^2_R represent the full and reduced model R^2 values, respectively, where the k represents the difference in the number of *X* variables in the two models. A χ^2 variable with df = df_{hyp} is distributed as *F* with df of df_{hyp} and infinity. When *d* is used to describe the difference between two measures obtained from the same sample, r_{ab} refers to the correlation between the two measures being compared.

Suppose that in another study, hierarchical regression is used to determine the incremental contribution of several new predictor variables over and above the set of predictor variables already in an equation. For example, in a study with $N = 250$, two spatial ability tests were used to predict performance as an aircraft pilot; scores on these tests explained 14% of the variability in pilots' performances (i.e., $R^2 = .14$). Four tests measuring other cognitive abilities were added to the predictor battery, and this set of six tests explained an additional 15% of the variance in performance (i.e., when all six tests are used to predict performance, $R^2 = .29$). The *F*-statistic that corresponds to this increase in R^2 is $F(4, 243) = 12.83$.

Worked Example: Hierarchical Regression

In Table 2.1, we presented a formula that can be used to calculate the *F* equivalent of the increase in R^2 reported in a study that used hierarchical regression. The formula is as follows:

$$F(df_{hyp}, df_{err}) = \frac{(R^2_F - R^2_R)/df_{hyp}}{(1 - R^2_F)/df_{err}}$$

In this study ($N = 250$), the researchers started with two predictors and reported $R^2 = .15$, then added four more predictors and reported $R^2 = .29$. It follows that:

$df_{hyp} = 4$ This is the number of predictors that is added to the original set of two predictors. The null hypothesis is that adding these four predictors leads to no real increase in R^2.

$df_{err} = 250 - 6 - 1 = 243$

$R^2_F = .29$ The full model containing all six tests explains 29% of the variance in performance.

$R^2_R = .14$ The restricted model that contains only the first two tests explains 14% of the variance.

$F(4, 243) = [(.29 - .14)/4]/[(1 - .29)/243]$

$F(4, 243) = .0375/.00292 = 12.84$

Most *F* tables will not report critical values for 4 and 243 degrees of freedom, but if you interpolate between the critical values of *F* ($\alpha = .05$) for 4 and 200 degrees of freedom and for 4 and 300 degrees of freedom, you will find that *F* values of 2.41 or greater will allow you to reject the null hypothesis. With $F(4, 243) = 12.84$, you can easily reject the null hypothesis and conclude that adding these four predictors does lead to a change in R^2.

As Table 2.1 shows, χ^2 values can be translated into *F* equivalents. For example, if a researchers found a χ^2 value of 24.56 with 6 degrees of freedom, the equivalent *F* value would be 4.09 (i.e., 24.56/6), with $df_{hyp} = 6$ and df_{err} being infinite. Because the *F* table asymptotes as df_{err} grows larger, $df_{err} = 10,000$ (which is included in the *F* table listed in Appendix B) represents an excellent approximation to infinite degrees of freedom for the error term. The critical value of F ($\alpha = .05$) needed to reject the null hypothesis in this study is 2.10, so once again, the null hypothesis will be rejected.

Table 2.1 also includes the ES measure d. This statistic is not commonly used in hypothesis testing per se, but it is widely used in describing the strength of effects, particularly when the scores of those receiving a treatment are compared with scores in a control group. This statistic can also be easily transformed into its F equivalent using the formulas shown in Table 2.1.

Finally, a note concerning terminology. In the section above, and in several sections that follow, we use the term "F equivalent." We find this term to be explicit in recognizing that even when the results of a statistical test in the general linear model are reported in terms of some statistic other than F (e.g., r, t, d), it is nevertheless usually possible to transform these statistics into the F value that is equivalent in meaning.

Worked Examples: Using the d-Statistic

The d-statistic can be used to describe the strength of an effect in a single study. For example, if a researcher was comparing two treatments and reported $d = .50$, this would indicate that the difference between treatment means was one half as large as the standard deviation within each group. An even more common use of d is in meta-analysis, in which the results of several studies are summarized to estimate how large an effect is in the population.

Suppose, for example, that previous research suggests that the effect size d should be about .25. This ES measure would be extremely useful in conducting power analyses. Given this value of d, a study in which 102 subjects were randomly assigned to one of these two treatments would be expected to yield the following:

$$F(1, \text{df}_{\text{err}}) = \frac{d^2 \text{df}_{\text{err}}}{4}$$

where
$$d = .25$$
$$\text{df}_{\text{err}} = N - 2 = 102 - 2 = 100$$

and
$$F(1,100) = [.25^2 \cdot 100]/4$$
$$F(1,100) = [.0625 \cdot 100]/4 = 1.56$$

The calculations above are based on the independent groups t, in which participants are randomly assigned to one of two treatments. Suppose you used a repeated measures design (e.g., one in which scores of 102 subjects on a pre-test and a post-test were compared, with a correlation of .60 between these scores). If you expect that $d = .25$, the formula for transforming repeated-measures t yields the following:

$$F(1, \text{df}_{err}) = \frac{d^2 \text{df}_{err}}{4\sqrt{1-r_{ab}}}$$

where

$$d = .25$$
$$\text{df}_{err} = N - 2 = 102 - 2 = 100$$
$$r_{ab} = .60$$

and

$F(1,100) = [.25^2 \cdot 100]/[4 \cdot .632]$ [the square root of $(1 - .60)$ is .632]

$F(1,100) = [.0625 \cdot 100]/2.529 = 2.47$

The critical value for F ($\alpha = .05$) when the degrees of freedom are 1 and 100 is 3.93, suggesting that the studies described above would not have sufficient power to allow you to reject the traditional null hypothesis.

As you may have noticed, in the examples above we included the sample size. The reason for this is that the value and the interpretation of the F-statistic depends in part on the size of the sample (in particular, on the degrees of freedom for the error term, or df_{err}). In the preceding paragraph, a d value of .25 in a sample of 102 would yield $F(1, 100) = 1.56$. In a study that randomly assigned 375 participants to treatments, the same d would translate into $F(1, 373) = 5.82$, which would be statistically significant. This reflects the fact that the same difference between means is easier to statistically detect when the sample (and therefore df_{err}) is large than when the sample is small. Small samples produce unstable and unreliable results, and in a small sample it can be hard to distinguish between true treatment effects and simple sampling error.

Transforming From F to PV. Table 2.1 shows how to transform commonly used statistics and effect size estimates into their equivalent F values. Table 2.1 can also often be used to transform from *F* values into ES measures. For example, suppose you randomly assigned participants into four different treatments and used analysis of variance to analyze the data. You reported a significant *F* value [$F(3, 60) = 2.80$], but this does not provide information about the strength of the effect. Equation 2.7 allows you to obtain an estimate of the proportion of variance in the dependent variable explained by the linear model (i.e., *PV*), given the value of *F*:

$$PV = (df_{hyp} \cdot F)/[(df_{hyp} \cdot F) + df_{err}] \qquad (2.7)$$

which yields

$$PV = (3 \cdot 2.80)/[(3 \cdot 2.80) + 60] \qquad (2.8)$$

$$PV = 8.4/68.4 = .12^3$$

In other words, the *F* value reported in this study allows you to determine that treatments accounted for 12% of the variance in outcomes.

Equation 2.7 cannot be used in complex, multifactor analyses of variance because the *F*-statistic for any particular effect in a complex ANOVA model and its degrees of freedom do not contain all of the information needed to estimate *PV*. In Chapters 7 and 8, we discuss the application of power analyses to these more complex designs and will show how information presented in significance tests can be used to estimate ES.

Defining Large, Medium, and Small Effects

Cohen's books and papers on statistical power analyses (e.g., Cohen, 1988) have suggested a number of conventions for describing treatment effects as "small," "medium," or "large." These conventions are based on surveys of the literature and seem to be widely accepted, at least as approximations. Table 2.2 presents conventional values for describing large, medium, and small effects, expressing these effects in terms of a number of widely used statistics.

For example, a small effect might be described as one that accounts for about 1% of the variance in outcomes, or one where the treatment mean is about one fifth of a standard deviation higher in the treatment group than in the control group, or as one where the probability that a randomly selected member of the treatment group will have a higher score than a randomly selected member of the control group is about .56.

Table 2.2 Some Conventions for Defining Effect Sizes

	PV	*r*	*d*	*f²*	**Probability of a Higher Score in Treatment Group**
Small effects	.01	.10	.20	.02	.56
Medium effects	.10	.30	.50	.15	.64
Large effects	.25	.50	.80	.35	.71

Note: Cohen's $f^2 = R^2/(1 - R^2) = \eta^2/(1 - \eta^2) = PV/(1 - PV)$, where $\eta^2 = SS_{treatments}/SS_{total}$.

Sources: Cohen (1988), Grissom (1994).

The values in Table 2.2 are approximations and nothing more. In fact, a few minutes with a calculator shows that they are not all exactly equivalent (e.g., if you square an *r* value of .30, you get an estimate of $PV = .09$, not $PV = .10$). Although they are not exact or completely consistent, the values in Table 2.2 are nevertheless very useful. These conventions provide a starting point for statistical power analysis, and they provide a sensible basis for comparing the results in any one study with a more general set of conventions.

Nonparametric and Robust Statistics

The decision to anchor our model for statistical power analysis to the *F* distribution is driven primarily by the widespread use of statistical tests based on that distribution. The *F*-statistic can be used to test virtually any hypothesis that falls under the broad umbrella of the "general linear model." There are, however, some important statistics that do not fall under this umbrella, and these are not easily transformed into a form that is compatible with the *F* distribution.

For example, a number of robust or "trimmed" statistics have been developed in which outliers are removed from observed distributions prior to estimating standard errors and test statistics (Wilcox, 1992; Yuen, 1974). Trimming outliers from data can sometimes substantially reduce the effects of sampling error, and trimmed statistics can have more power than their normal-theory equivalents (Wilcox). The power tables developed in this book are not fully appropriate for trimmed statistics and can substantially underestimate the power of these statistics when applied in small samples.

A second family of statistics that are not easily accommodated using the model developed here are those statistics referred to as "nonparametric" or distribution-free statistics. Nonparametric statistics do not require a priori assumptions about distributional forms and tend to use little information about the observed distribution of data in constructing statistical tests.

The conventional wisdom has long been that nonparametric tests have less power than their parametric equivalents (Siegel, 1956), but this is not always the case. Nonparametric tests can have more power than their parametric equivalents under a variety of circumstances, especially when conducting tests using distributions with heavy tails (i.e., more extreme scores than would be expected in a normal distribution; Zimmerman & Zumbo, 1993). The methods developed here do not provide accurate estimates of the power of robust or nonparametric statistics.

From *F* to Power Analysis

Earlier in this chapter, we noted that statistical power analysis involves a three-step process. First, you must determine the value of *F* that is needed to reject the null hypothesis (i.e., the critical value of *F*). Virtually any statistics text is likely to include a table of critical *F* values that can be used to test the traditional null hypothesis. The great advantage of framing statistical power analysis in terms of the noncentral *F* distribution is that this approach makes it easy to test a number of alternatives to the nil hypothesis. As we show in Chapter 3, this approach to statistical power analysis makes it easy to evaluate the power of tests of the hypothesis that treatments have effects that are not only greater than zero, but that are also sufficiently large that they are substantively meaningful. Like tests of the traditional null hypothesis, these minimum-effect tests start with the identification of critical values for the *F* statistic.

Once the critical value of *F* is established for any particular test, the assessment of statistical power is relatively easy. As we noted in Chapter 1, *the power of a statistical test is the proportion of the distribution of test statistics expected for a particular study that is above the critical value used to establish statistical significance.* If you determine that the critical value for the *F* statistic that will be used to test hypotheses in your study is equal to 6.50, all you need to do to conduct a power analysis is to determine the noncentral *F* distribution that corresponds with the design of your study (which determines df_{hyp} and df_{err}) and the ES you expect in that study, which determines the degree of noncentrality of the *F* distribution. If the critical value of *F* is equal to 6.50, power will be defined as the proportion of this noncentral *F* distribution that is equal to or greater than 6.50.

A number of methods can be used to carry out statistical power analyses. For the mathematically inclined, it is always possible to analytically estimate the noncentral *F* distribution; we discuss analytic methods below. However, most users of power analysis are likely to want a simpler set of methods. We discuss the use of power tables and power calculators in the section below.

Analytic and Tabular Methods of Power Analysis

Analytic methods of power analysis are the most flexible and the most exact, but also the most difficult to implement. Power tables or graphs provide good approximations of the statistical power of studies under a wide range of conditions. Our preference is to work with tables; in part the type of graphs needed to plot a variable (i.e., power) as a function of three other variables (i.e., N, α, and ES) strike us as complicated and difficult to use. Software and calculators that can be used to estimate statistical power combine the flexibility and precision of analytic methods with the ease of use of power tables.

Analytic methods. The most general method for evaluating statistical power involves estimating the noncentral F distribution that corresponds with the design of your study and the ES you expect. While this analytic method is both precise and flexible, it is also relatively cumbersome and time consuming. That is, the direct computation of statistical power involves (1) determining some standard for statistical or practical significance, (2) estimating the noncentral F distribution that corresponds to the statistic and study being analyzed, and (3) determining the proportion of that noncentral F distribution that lies above the standard. Even with a relatively powerful computer, the processes can be time consuming and may be daunting to many consumers of power analysis; for readers interested in analytic approaches, Appendix A presents several methods for estimating the necessary distributions. A more user-friendly approach is to develop tables or calculators that contain the essential information needed to estimate statistical power.

Power tables. A number of excellent books present extensive tables describing the statistical power of numerous tests; Cohen (1988) is the most complete source currently available. The approach presented here is simpler (although it provides slighty less information) and is considerably more compact. Unlike Cohen (1988), who developed tables for many different statistics, our approach involves translating different statistics into their F equivalents. This allows us to present virtually all the information needed to perform significance tests and power analyses for statistical tests in the general linear model in a single table.

Appendix B contains a table we call the "One-Stop F Table." This is called a "one-stop" table because each cell contains the information needed for (1) conducting traditional significance tests, (2) conducting power analyses at various key levels of power, (3) testing the hypothesis that the effect in a study exceeds various criteria used to define negligibly small or small to moderate effects, and (4) estimating power for these "minimum-effect" tests. Minimum-effects tests are explained in detail in Chapter 3; at this point we focus on the use of the One-Stop *F* Table for testing the traditional null hypothesis and for evaluating the power of these tests.

Using the One-Stop *F* Table

Each cell in the One-Stop *F* Table contains 12 pieces of information. The first four values in each cell are used for testing significance and estimating power for traditional null hypothesis tests. The next eight values in each cell are used for testing significance and estimating power when testing the hypothesis that treatment effects are negligible, using two different operational definitions of a "negligible" effect (i.e., treatments account for 1% or less of the variance, or they account for 5% or less of the variance). In this chapter, we focus on the first four pieces of information presented for each combination of df_{hyp} and df_{err}.

This table presents the critical value of *F* for testing the traditional null hypothesis, using α values of .05 and .01, respectively. We label these "nil .05" and "nil .01." For example, consider a study in which 54 subjects are randomly assigned to one of four treatments, and the analysis of variance is used to analyze the data. This study will have df_{hyp} and df_{err} values of 3 and 50, respectively. The critical values of *F* for testing the nil hypothesis will be 2.79 when α equals .05; the critical value of *F* for testing the nil hypothesis will 4.20 when α equals .01. In other words, in order to reject the nil hypothesis (α = .05), the value of the mean square for treatments will have to be at least 2.79 times as large as the value of the mean square for error (i.e., $F = MS_{treatments}/MS_{err}$).

The next two values in each cell are *F* equivalents of the effect size values needed to obtain power of .50 and power of .80 (we label these "pow .50" and "pow .80"), given an α level of .05 and the specified df_{hyp} and df_{err}. The values of pow .50 and pow .80 for 3 and 50 degrees of freedom in the table are 1.99 and 3.88, respectively. That is, a study designed with 3 and 50 degrees of freedom will have power of .50 for detecting an effect that is equivalent to *F* = 1.99. It will have power of .80 for detecting an effect that is equivalent to *F* = 3.88. *F* equivalents are handy for creating tables, but in order to interpret these values, it is necessary to translate them into ES measures.

Because subjects are randomly assigned to treatments and the simple analysis of variance is used to analyze the data, we can use Equation 2.7, presented earlier in this chapter, to transform these *F* values into equivalent *F* values (i.e., $PV = (df_{hyp} \cdot F)/[(df_{hyp} \cdot F) + df_{err}]$). Applying this formula, you will find that in a study with df_{hyp} and df_{err} values of 3 and 50, you will need a moderately large ES to achieve power of .50. Translating the *F* value of 2.16 into its equivalent *PV*, you will find:

$$PV = (3 \cdot 1.99)/[(3 \cdot 1.99) + 50] = 5.97/55.97 = .106 \qquad (2.9)$$

That is, in order to achieve power of .50 with df_{hyp} and df_{err} values of 3 and 50, you will need to be studying treatments that account for at least 10% of the variance in outcomes. Applying the same formula to the *F* needed to achieve power of .80 (i.e., *F* = 3.88), you will find that you need an effect size of *PV* = .188. In other words, in order to achieve power of .80 with this study, you will need to study a truly large effect, in which treatments account for approximately 19% or greater of the variance in outcomes.

Suppose that on the basis of your knowledge of the scientific literature, you expect the treatments being studied to account for about 15% of the variance in outcomes. This ES falls between *PV* = .10 and *PV* = .19, which implies that power of this study will fall somewhere between .50 and .80. As we show in the section that follows, it is easy to estimate where in this range the power of this study actually falls (in this example, power is approximately .65).

Interpolating between tabled values. As with all *F* tables, our One-Stop *F* Table is incomplete, in that it does not table all possible values of df_{hyp} and df_{err}. Fortunately, relatively good approximations to all of the values in this table can be obtained by linear interpolation. For example, our table includes df_{err} values of 50 and 60. If you wanted to find appropriate *F* values for df_{err} = 55, these would lie about halfway between the values for df_{err} = 50 and df_{err} = 60. Thus, the approximate *F* needed to reject the traditional null hypothesis (α = .05) with df_{hyp} = 2, df_{err} = 55 would be 3.165 (i.e., halfway between 3.15 and 3.18). Similarly, if df_{err} = 48, you could estimate the appropriate *F* values by computing the value that *F* was 80% of the distance between the tabled *F* for df_{err} = 40 and the tabled *F* for df_{err} = 50. In general, the value of the interpolated *F* can be obtained using the formula below:

$$F_{interpolated} = F_{below} + \frac{(df_{int} - df_{below})}{(df_{above} - df_{below})}(F_{above} - F_{below}) \qquad (2.10)$$

where

F_{below} = Tabled *F* below the value to be calculated
F_{above} = Tabled *F* above the value to be calculated
df_{below} = df_{err} for tabled *F* below the value to be calculated
df_{above} = df_{err} for tabled *F* above the value to be calculated
df_{int} = df_{err} for *F* value to be calculated

It is important to keep in mind that linear interpolation will yield approximate values only. For the purposes of statistical power analyses, these interpolations will virtually always be sufficiently accurate to help you to make sensible decisions about the design of studies, the choice of criteria for defining "statistical significance," etc.

Worked Example: Interpolating Between Values for Power of .50 and .80

A second application of linear interpolation is likely to be even more useful. Our table includes F equivalents for the effect size values needed to obtain power levels of .50 and .80, respectively. In the example described earlier, where $df_{hyp} = 3$ and $df_{err} = 50$, F values of 1.99 and 3.88 are equivalent to the population PV values that would be needed to obtain power levels of .50 or .80. These F values translated into PV values in a study such as this are .10 and .19, respectively. Here, you expected treatments to account for 15% of the variance. If you translate this figure into its F equivalent (using formulas presented in Table 2.1), you obtain F of 2.94. You can use linear interpolation to estimate the power of this study, using a formula that closely parallels the formula used to interpolate F values:

$$\text{Power}_{\text{interpolated}} = .50 + \left[\left(\frac{F_{\text{hypothesized}} - F_{.50}}{F_{.80} - F_{.50}} \right) \times .30 \right] \quad (2.11)$$

where
$\qquad F_{\text{hypothesized}} = F$ equivalent for hypothesized size of the effect
$\qquad F_{.50} = F$ equivalent of the PV needed to obtain power of .50 ($\alpha = .05$)
$\qquad F_{.80} = F$ equivalent of the PV needed to obtain power of .80 ($\alpha = .05$)

In the example discussed above $df_{hyp} = 3$ and $df_{err} = 50$. If you expect treatments to account for 15% of the variance, the equivalent F value is 2.94. In terms of Equation 2.11, $F_{\text{hypothesized}} = 2.94$, $F_{.50} = 1.99$, and $F_{.80} = 3.88$, which means that the power of this study for rejecting the null hypothesis ($\alpha = .05$) is .64.

The One-Stop *F* Calculator

It is often easier and more convenient to use a computer program rather than a set of tables to estimate statistical *power*. The One-Stop *F* Calculator program distributed with this book is the computer program analog for all tables at the back of this book, including the One-Stop *F* Table and the One-Stop *PV* Table. The One-Stop *F* Calculator program is written in Visual Basic and uses subroutines based on programs developed by Reeve (1986a, 1986b, 1986c).

Figure 2.1 illustrates the screen that opens when the One-Stop *F* Calculator is installed on a computer. This calculator contains five options for power analysis: "Significance Testing," "Power Analysis," "Sample Size (df Error) Determination," "Calculate Alpha and Power for a Completed Study," and "Calculate Power for a Completed Study." The calculator allows you to directly enter the information needed to complete each type of power analysis, or to go to a help screen that explains what information is needed and why. The calculator also gives you a quick way of looking up the various methods used to translate test statistics into their equivalent *F* and *PV* values. To use the calculator, simply select the option you want to explore, enter the requested information in the white text boxes and hit "Calculate."

To use this calculator, several decisions must be made. First, what hypothesis is being tested? The most common statistical test involved the nil hypothesis (i.e., the hypothesis that treatments have no effect). To test the traditional null hypothesis, enter the null hypothesis that treatments account for some negligible amount of variance (e.g., 1% or less of the variance), versus the alternate hypothesis that treatments have effects that are large enough to care about. These hypotheses can be easily tested by entering the appropriate effect size (e.g., .01 for 1% of the variance, .05 for 5%) in the "Effect Size" text box.

Depending on the option you choose (e.g., "Significance Testing"), you may need to enter the alpha level, df_{hyp}, df_{err}, *PV*, *d*, or *F*. For example, suppose 120 subjects are randomly assigned to one of four treatments. You are interested in significance testing, using an alpha level of .05. In the "Significance Testing" section, enter values of 0, .05, 3, and 116 in the "Effect Size," "Alpha," "df_{hyp}" and "df_{err}" boxes and press "Calculate." The One-Stop *F* Calculator will show that you will need an *F* value of 2.68 to achieve statistical significance, which is equivalent to a *PV* of .064.

To determine the effect size needed to achieve power of .80 for this same study, go to the "Power Analysis" option and enter values of 0, .80, .05, 3, and 116 in the "Effect Size," "Power," "Alpha," "df_{hyp}" and "df_{err}" boxes and press "Calculate." The One-Stop *F* Calculator will show that you will need a moderately large effect size (*PV* = .087) to achieve this level of power.

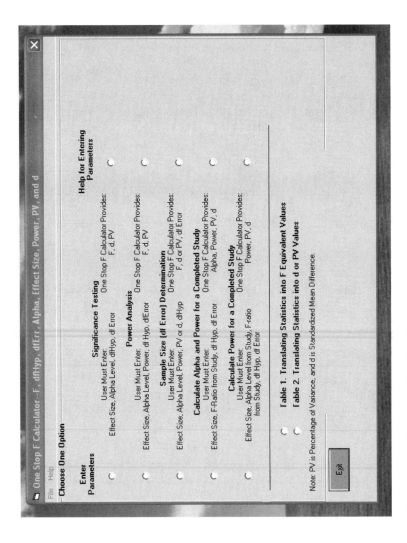

Figure 2.1   One-stop F calculator.

Suppose you expected a somewhat smaller ES (e.g., *PV* = .05), and you want to determine the sample size needed to achieve power of .80. Go to the "Sample Size (df$_{err}$) Determination" option and enter values of 0, .80, .05, 3 and .05 in the "Effect Size," "Power," "Alpha," "df$_{hyp}$" and "*PV*" boxes and press "Calculate." The One-Stop *F* Calculator will show that you will need a df$_{err}$ of 203 to achieve this level of power. In the one-way analysis of variance, the total sample size is given by $N = df_{hyp} + df_{err} + 1$, which means that you will need a sample of 207 to achieve power of .80.

Suppose you calculate the value of *F* and find $F = 2.50$. The "Calculate Alpha and Power for a Completed Study" option allows you to determine the confidence with which you could reject the null hypothesis. Enter values of 0, 2.50, 3, and 116 in the "Effect Size," "*F*," "df$_{hyp}$" and "df$_{err}$" boxes and and press "Calculate." The One-Stop *F* Calculator shows you could reject the traditional null hypothesis at the .06 level with power of .638. In many cases, it is difficult to convince researchers to use alpha levels other than the traditional values of .05 or .01. If you select the "Calculate Power for a Completed Study with a Selected Alpha Level" option and enter values of 0, .05, 2.5, 3, and 116 in, you will find that power in this study is .600 when alpha is .05.

The "Help" menu for the One-Stop *F* Calculator provides a primer on power analyses, references to relevant articles and books, and a discussion of the information needed to implement each of the options, as well as a discussion of the meaning of the results provided under each of the five options.

Summary

The statistics that are most widely used in the social and behavioral sciences are either interpreted in terms of, or easily translated into, the *F* statistic. Our model for power analysis uses the noncentral *F* distribution to estimate the power of a wide range of statistics (compare with Patnaik, 1949). This noncentral *F* represents the distribution of outcomes you expect to find in any particular study (given an effect size, df$_{hyp}$, and df$_{err}$); the degree of noncentrality (λ) is a direct function of the effect size of interest. The statistical power of your study is simply the proportion of this noncentral *F* distribution that lies above whatever criterion you use to define "statistical significance." This model of power analysis is not limited to tests of the traditional null hypothesis (i.e., that treatments had no effect whatsoever), but rather can be easily generalized to tests of substantively meaningful hypotheses (e.g., that the treatment effect exceeds some specific value).

We discuss both analytic and tabular methods of statistical power analysis. In particular, we introduce the "One-Stop *F* Table," which contains all of the information needed to test the null hypothesis and estimate statistical power. We also discuss a parallel table that lists *PV* values that are equivalent to the *F* values shown in the One-Stop *F* Table. This table allows researchers to conduct analyses in terms of effect size estimates rather than in terms of their *F* equivalents. Both tables contain the same basic information, but different users might find one form or the other more convenient to use. Finally, we discuss the "One-Stop *F* Calculator" program, which is included with this book. This program gives you a simple interface for carrying out virtually all of the analyses discussed in this book.

3

Power Analyses for
Minimum-Effect Tests

▼ ▼ ▼ ▼ ▼

The traditional null hypothesis is that treatments, interventions, etc., have no effect; in Chapters 1 and 2, we use the term *nil hypothesis* to describe this particular version of H_0. The nil hypothesis is so common and so widely used that most researchers assume that the hypothesis that treatments have no effect, or that the correlation between two variables is zero, *is* the null hypothesis. This is wrong. The null hypothesis is simply the specific hypotheses that is being tested (and that might be nullified by the data), and there are an infinite number of null hypotheses researchers might test. One researcher comparing two treatments might test the hypothesis that there is no difference between the mean scores of people who receive different treatments. A different researcher might test the hypothesis that one treatment yields scores that are, on average, 5 points higher than those obtained using another treatment. Yet another researcher might test the hypothesis that treatments have a very large effect, accounting for at least 25% of the variance in outcomes. These are all null hypotheses. Knowing that there are so many null hypotheses that might be tested, it is useful to understand why one special form (i.e., the nil hypothesis) is the one that actually *is* tested in most statistical analyses.

There are two advantages to testing the nil hypothesis: (1) it is easy to test this hypothesis—tests of this hypothesis represent the standard method presented in statistics textbooks, data analysis packages, etc., and the derivation of test statistics designed to evaluate the nil hypothesis is often comparatively simple and (2) if a researcher rejects the hypothesis that treatments have no effect, he or she is left with the alternative that treatments have *some* effect. If H_0 states that nothing happened as a result of treatments, the alternative hypothesis (H₁) is that *something* happened as a result of treatments. In contrast, tests of many specific alternatives to the nil hypothesis can lead to confusing results.

Suppose a researcher tests and rejects that hypothesis that the difference between treatment means is 5.0. The alternative hypothesis (H₁) is that the difference in treatment means is *not* 5.0, and this includes quite a wide range of possibilities. Treatments might lead to differences greater than 5.0. They might have no effect whatsoever. They might have some effect, but lead to differences less than 5.0. They might even have the opposite effect than the researchers expected (i.e., a new treatment might lead to worse outcomes than the old one). All the researcher learns by rejecting this null hypothesis is that the difference is not 5.0.

As we noted in Chapters 1 and 2, nil hypothesis testing has increasingly come under attack (Cohen, 1994; Meehl, 1978; Morrison & Henkel, 1970; Murphy, 1990; Schmidt, 1992, 1996. For discussions of the advantages of this approach, see Chow, 1988; Cortina & Dunlap, 1997; Hagen, 1997). The most general criticism of the traditional approach to null hypothesis testing is that very few researchers actually believe that the nil hypothesis is correct. That is, it is rare to encounter serious treatments or interventions that have no effect whatsoever which is the traditional null hypothesis. In a later section, we discuss in detail why the nil hypothesis is almost always false. Here, we simply note that if the null hypothesis to be tested is known in advance to be false, or is very likely to be false, tests of that hypothesis have very little value (Murphy, 1990).

The second critique of nil hypothesis testing is that the outcomes of tests of the traditional null hypothesis are routinely misinterpreted. As we show below, the outcomes of standard statistical tests probably reveal more about the power of your study than about the phenomenon you are studying. If you design a study with sufficient power, you will almost always reject the nil hypothesis. If you design a study with insufficient power, you will usually fail to reject the nil hypothesis. These facts are well understood by most researchers, but it is still common to find that when researchers fail to reject the null hypothesis, they end up drawing conclusions about the treatments or about the relationships being studied. In particular, researchers who fail to reject the null hypothesis all too often conclude that the treatments or interventions being studied did not work, or that the variables being studied are not correlated. Similarly, researchers who *do* reject the null hypothesis often conclude that there are meaningful treatment effects or that the intervention being studied worked. It should be clear by now that the outcomes of nil hypothesis tests are not driven solely, or even mainly, by the substantive phenomenon being studied. The outcomes of nil hypothesis tests usually tell researchers more about the study than they do about the substantive phenomenon being studied.

A third criticism of the traditional null hypothesis is that showing that a result is "significant" at the .05 level does not necessarily imply that it is important nor that it is especially likely to be replicated in a future study (Cohen, 1994). This significance test merely shows that the results reported in a study probably would not have been found if the true effect of treatments was zero. Unfortunately, researchers routinely misinterpret the results of significance tests (Cohen; Cowles, 1989; Greenwald, 1993). This is entirely understandable; most dictionary definitions of *significant* include synonyms such as "important" or "weighty." However, these tests do not directly assess the size or importance of treatment effects, nor do they assess the likelihood that future studies will find similar effects.

Tests of the traditional nil hypothesis are more likely to tell you about the sensitivity of your study than about the phenomenon being studied. With large samples, statistical tests of the traditional nil hypothesis become so sensitive that they can detect the slightest difference between a sample result and the specific value that characterized the null hypothesis, even if this difference is negligibly small. With small samples, on the other hand, it is difficult to establish that *anything* has a statistically significant effect. The best way to get an appreciation of the limitations of traditional null hypothesis tests is to scan the tables in any power analysis book (Cohen, 1988). What you will find is that, regardless of the true strength of the effect, the likelihood of rejecting the traditional null hypothesis is very small when samples are small, and the likelihood of rejecting this hypothesis is extremely high when samples are large. Clearly, there is a need for approaches to significance testing that tells researchers more about the phenomenon being studied than about the size of their samples. Alternatives to traditional nil hypothesis tests are described later in this chapter.

Is the Nil Hypothesis Almost Always Wrong?

There are several reasons to believe that the nil hypothesis is, by definition, almost always wrong. That is, regardless of the treatments interventions, correlations, etc., being studied, it is very unlikely that the true population effect (the difference between two means, the correlation between two variables) is precisely zero. First, the hypothesis is in theory usually wrong because is it is a point hypothesis. That is, the hypothesis being tested is that the effect of treatments is exactly zero, even to the millionth decimal place or beyond. The traditional nil hypothesis represents a convenient abstraction, similar to the mythical "frictionless plane" encountered by freshmen in solving physics problems, in which potentially small effects are treated as zero for the sake of simplicity. There are many real-world phenomena that seem to mirror the traditional nil hypothesis, the most obvious being flipping a coin (see Fick, 1995, for examples that seem to show how the traditional null could be correct). However, even in studies that involved repeated flips of a fair coin, the hypothesis that there is no difference whatsoever in the probability of getting a head or a tail is simply not true. It is impossible to mill a coin that is so precisely balanced that the likelihood of getting heads or tails is exactly equivalent; imbalance at the ten-billionth of the ounce will lead you to favor heads or tails if you flip the coin a sufficient number of times.

Notice that there is nothing special about the hypothesis that the difference between two treatments is zero. All point hypotheses (e.g., that the difference between two treatments is 5.0) suffer from the same problem. In the abstract, they might be true, but in reality, there is no way to ever demonstrate that they are true. Because the nil hypothesis is infinitely precise, none of the real-world phenomena it is designed to test can possibly be assessed at that level of precision. Therefore, if you showed that there was no difference in two treatments, even at the billionth decimal place, the possibility that some difference might emerge with a finer grained analysis could never be completely dismissed.

A third argument for the conclusion that the nil hypothesis is almost always wrong is best conveyed using a spatial analogy. Suppose you used a standard football field to represent all of the outcomes that could possibly occur when you compare the means of two populations, each of which received different treatments. One possibility is that there is no difference. Another possibility is that one treatment mean is .01 units higher than the other. Another possibility is that one treatment mean is .02 units higher than the other, and so on. Divide the football field so that H_0 represents the one outcome (no difference) that corresponds to the nil hypothesis and H_1 represents all the other outcomes. How much space do you think you would devote to H_0 versus H_1? The most optimistic proponent of nil hypothesis testing would only devote a tiny patch of dirt to H_0. Virtually the entire football field would have to be devoted to H_1 because there is an effectively infinite number of outcomes that could happen in this experiment. H_0 represents one of these outcomes, and H_1 represents all of the rest. In spatial terms, the solution space that represents H_0 is essentially infinitely small, whereas the solution space that represents H_1 is infinitely large.

The argument against the traditional null is not only a philosophical one; there are also abundant data to suggest that treatments in the social and behavioral sciences virtually always have at least some effect (Lipsey & Wilson, 1993; Murphy & Myors, 1999). In fact, it may not be possible to devise a real treatment that has no effect whatsoever. To be sure, there is no shortage of crackpot interventions, junk science, and treatments that have no meaningful effect (e.g., wearing magnetized bracelets as a way of treating cancer). However, if your goal is to evaluate serious treatments devised by someone who had a sensible reason to believe that they might work, the likelihood that treatments will have no effect whatsoever is so low that tests of the nil hypothesis may be pointless (Murphy, 1990).

Implications of Believing That the Nil Hypothesis Is Almost Always Wrong

The fact that the traditional nil hypothesis should almost always be rejected has important implications for thinking about Type I and Type II errors. In fact, we would argue that tests of the traditional nil hypothesis make sense *only* if you believe that the nil hypothesis is often correct, and we know of no researchers who actually believe this. It is very important to understand why assumptions about the likelihood that the nil hypothesis is true. Consider Figure 3.1 which illustrates two ways of making errors in a nil hypothesis test. First, it is possible that H_0 is really true and that researchers will wrongly conclude that treatments do have some effect (i.e., a Type I error). There is a large and robust literature detailing methods for controlling Type I errors (e.g., Wilkinson et al., 1999; Zwick & Marascuilo, 1984). As Figure 3.1 makes clear, the likelihood of making a Type I error depends first and foremost on whether the nil hypothesis that treatments have no effect is actually true (Murphy, 1990). If you believe that the nil hypothesis is never true, it follows that Type I errors are impossible—these errors can occur if and only if H_0 is true. If you believe that the nil hypothesis is almost always wrong, it follows that Type I errors are at best very rare. Unless you believe that the nil hypothesis is often right, it is unlikely that you will ever have much reason to be concerned about Type I errors.

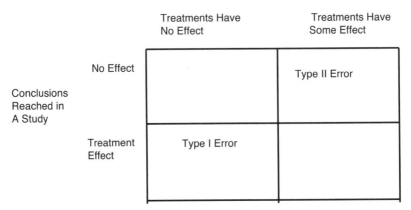

Figure 3.1   Errors in statistical tests.

Polar Bear Traps: Why Type I Error Control Is a Bad Investment

A simple analogy helps to drive home the importance of the low likelihood that the nil hypothesis is true. Suppose you are a homeowner and a salesman comes to the door selling Polar Bear Traps. He makes a compelling case that a polar bear attack would be very unpleasant and that these are good traps. Would you buy traps? We would not. The likelihood that a polar bear will attack is so small that purchasing the traps strikes us as a waste of money.

You should think of any and all procedures designed to control or reduce Type I errors as Polar Bear Traps. They give you a means of controlling or limiting something that you know is highly unlikely in the first place. More important, these traps cost something. Virtually anything you do to control Type I errors will increase the likelihood of Type II errors. For example, the common rationale for using a stringent alpha level, such as $\alpha = .01$, rather than a less demanding criterion (e.g., $\alpha = .05$) in defining statistical significance is that the stricter alpha will lead to fewer Type I errors. If you think that Type I errors are virtually impossible in the first place, you are unlikely to believe that the loss of power implied by the more stringent alpha is worthwhile. In general, steps you take to control Type I errors usually lead to reduced levels of power. If you think about Type I error control as a Polar Bear Trap, you are unlikely to see it as a wise investment.

Throughout this book, we show how the conclusion that the traditional nil hypothesis is rarely true undermines many familiar methods of statistical analysis. If you believe that the nil hypothesis is never true, it follows that tests of that hypothesis never tell you anything about the substantive questions your study is trying to answer (although they may tell you some things about the design of the study). If you accept our argument that the null hypothesis is almost always wrong in serious research studies, it follows that tests of this hypothesis have very little value and that alternatives are needed to solve some of the problems inherent in this method of hypothesis testing. If you truly believe that the nil hypothesis is so often true that tests of this hypothesis have any real probative value, you are in a very small minority. Most researchers who routinely use nil hypothesis tests simply do not understand that they are using procedures that make sense only in the unlikely case where H_0 is actually likely to be true.

The Nil May Not Be True, but It Is Often Fairly Accurate

The conclusion that the nil hypothesis is almost always wrong is not the same as the conclusion that most treatments, interventions, etc., actually work. On the contrary, it is reasonable to believe that many treatments and interventions have very small effects, and the statement that they had no effect at all is often fairly close to the truth. As we noted in Chapters 1 and 2, most studies you read in the literature are likely to deal with treatments, interventions, etc., that have small (but perhaps important) effects. If the effects of treatments were large and obvious, there would not be much demand for further studies testing the nil hypothesis. Many of the most important and interesting studies you are likely to read will deal with new treatments, novel interventions, and innovative approaches—most of these just will not work very well. As a point hypothesis, the nil hypothesis is almost always wrong; but as a general description of what researchers expect might happen, it is often a good approximation. What is needed is an approach that captures the worrisome possibility that many treatments, interventions, etc., might have very small effects, without all the problems that accompany tests of point hypotheses. A method that overcomes many of the limitations of traditional nil hypothesis tests is presented in the section that follows.

Minimum-Effect Tests as Alternatives
to Traditional Null Hypothesis Tests

The criticisms of nil hypothesis tests outlined above have led some critics to call for abandoning null hypothesis testing altogether (e.g., Schmidt, 1992, 1996). Rather than take this drastic step, we think it is better to reform the process. The problem with most null hypotheses tests is that the specific hypothesis being tested (i.e., that treatments have no effect whatsoever) is neither credible nor informative (Murphy, 1990). There are several alternatives to testing the nil hypothesis, and all of these are a marked improvement over the standard procedure of testing the hypothesis that the effect of treatments is precisely zero.

Serlin and Lapsley (1993) show how researchers can test the hypothesis that the effect of treatments falls within or outside of some range of values that is "good enough" to establish that one treatment is meaningfully better than the other. Rouanet (1996) shows how Bayesian methods can be used to assert the importance or negligibility of treatment effects. Both of these methods allow researchers to directly test credible and meaningful hypotheses.

The method described in this book involves testing "minimum-effect" hypotheses (Murphy & Myors, 1999). The traditional nil hypothesis involves a choice between the following:

H_0—Treatments have no effect.

versus

H_1—Treatments have some effect.

Minimum-effect hypotheses involve a choice between the following:

H_0—Treatments have an effect that is so small that it can be described as negligible.

versus

H_1—Treatments have an effect that is so large that they should be described as meaningful or important.

Minimum-effect tests require researchers to make a decision about what sort of treatment effect is so small that it should be labeled as negligible. This decision may be a difficult one, but if a reasonable standard for defining effects that are negligibly small can be defined, it is quite easy to develop the appropriate tests, using the same noncentral F-based model we have used in presenting power analysis.

The central assumption of minimum-effect tests is that there is some range of possible effect size values that are so small that they might as well be zero. For example, if there is a substantive reason to believe that a treatment effect that accounts for less than 1% of the variance is simply too small to care about, it does not matter whether the true treatment effect is $PV = 0.0$, $PV = .001$, $PV = .002$, etc. Anything that falls below $PV = .01$ will be regarded as too small to be meaningful or important, and the null hypothesis in this minimum-effect test is that the population treatment falls somewhere within this range. A researcher who can reject this null hypothesis is left with the alternative hypothesis that effects are large enough to be important.

Minimum-effect tests have many advantages over traditional nil hypothesis tests. First, both H_0 and H_1 are substantively meaningful and intrinsically interesting to most researchers. Second, the minimum-effect null hypothesis, that treatments have effects so small that they are negligible, is one that might actually be true. Third, these tests can be developed in ways that allow researchers to apply virtually all of the procedures, standards, and metrics they have learned in the context of nil hypothesis testing to tests that the effects of treatments are either negligibly small or large enough to be of interest.

Minimum-effect tests are meaningful. There is much to be learned by conducting minimum-effect tests of null hypothesis that effects of treatments are negligibly small (e.g., they account for 1% or less of the variance in outcomes). In contrast to tests of the traditional null, tests of this sort are far from trivial. First, researchers do not know in advance whether H_0 is right or wrong. Second, these tests involve questions that are of real substantive interest. Because these include some range of values rather than a single exact point under the "null umbrella," the results of these tests are not a foregone conclusion. Although it might be impossible to devise a treatment, intervention, etc., that had no effect whatsoever, there are any number of treatments whose effects fall somewhere between zero and whatever point you choose to designate as a negligible effect. The possibility that your treatments will have a negligibly small effect is both real and meaningful (whereas the possibility that they will have no effect whatsoever is not), and researchers can learn something important about their treatments by testing this hypothesis.

The minimum-effect might actually be true. In an earlier section of this chapter, we noted that when testing the traditional null hypothesis, a researcher can guarantee the outcome if the sample is sufficiently large. That is, with a sufficiently sensitive study, the statistical power of tests of the traditional null hypothesis will reach 1.00. The reason it is possible to reach power levels of 1.00, regardless of the substantive question being examined in a study, is that traditional models of power analysis are based on the entirely realistic assumption that H_0 is virtually never true.

As we noted above, the assumption that H_0 is virtually never true also means that Type I errors are virtually impossible and that significance tests will rarely tell you anything meaningful about the substantive questions being studied. In contrast to the nil hypothesis, the minimum-effect null hypothesis is often a realistic possibility. That is, there certainly are treatments, interventions, etc., that turn out to have truly small effects. Because there is a real possibility that the effect of treatments will turn out to be negligible, H_0 might really be true, and Type I errors might really occur.

Because there is a very real possibility that the effects of treatments will turn out to be negligibly small, the upper bound of the power of minimum-effects tests will generally be less than 1.00. No matter how sensitive the study, researchers can never be certain in advance of the result of a minimum-effect test. We regard this as a good thing. One major criticism of tests of the traditional nil hypothesis is that they are literally pointless (Murphy, 1990). Because researchers know in advance that the traditional H_0 is almost certainly wrong, they are unlikely to learn anything new about H_0, regardless of the outcome of the significance test. Minimum-effect tests, on the other hand, can be informative, particularly if these tests are conducted with acceptable levels of statistical power. If a researcher designs a study that has a great deal of power and still fails to reject the hypothesis that the effects of treatments are negligible, this failure to reject the null hypothesis can be interpreted as strong evidence that the treatment effect truly *is* negligible.

Minimum-effect tests produce meaningful information. Tests of the nil hypothesis do not necessarily tell researchers anything useful about the phenomenon being studied. Consider a study comparing two different methods of mathematics instruction. Students are randomly assigned to one of these two methods, and at the end of the year, they all take the same final examination. A study reports a significant difference ($\alpha < .05$) between the mean test scores in these two treatments. What have we really learned?

Without additional information (e.g., sample size), the result presented above does not necessarily tell us anything meaningful about the two treatments. For example, it is possible that there is a miniscule difference in the mean scores of students who receive these two treatments, and that the researcher used a sufficiently large sample to detect that difference. It is possible that the difference is large, but the significance test does not, by itself, tell you that.

Suppose another researcher fails to reject the null hypothesis. Does this mean that there is literally no difference between the two treatments? Again, in the absence of additional information, it is impossible to say what this study tells us about the treatments. If the sample was very small, the researcher will not reject H_0—even if one method is truly much better than another.

Suppose another researcher examines these same two treatments and determines that treatment effects that account for 1% of the variance or less can safely be labeled as negligible. If this researcher rejects the null hypothesis that treatment effects are negligible (i.e., the population effect falls somewhere between $PV = 0.0$ and $PV = .01$), this researcher has learned something meaningful about the treatments. In particular, this study has presented evidence that there is a meaningful difference between the two methods of mathematics instruction.

Testing the Hypothesis That Treatment Effects Are Negligible

The best way to describe the process of testing a minimum-effect hypothesis is to compare it with the process used in testing the traditional nil hypothesis. The significance of the F-statistic is usually assessed by comparing the value of the F obtained in a study to the value listed in a standard F table. The tabled values presented in virtually every statistics text correspond to specific percentiles in the central F distribution. For example, if $df_{hyp} = 2$ and $df_{err} = 100$, the tabled values of the F-statistic that is used in testing the nil hypothesis are 3.09 and 4.82, for $\alpha = .05$ and $\alpha = .01$, respectively. In other words, if the nil hypothesis is true and there are 2 and 100 degrees of freedom, you should expect to find F values of 3.09 or less 95% of the time, and values of 4.82 or less 99% of the time. If the F in a particular study is greater than these values, the researcher can reject the null hypothesis and conclude that treatments probably do have some effect.

Tests of minimum-effect hypotheses proceed in exactly the same way, the only difference being that they use a different set of tabled F values (Murphy & Myors, 1999). The F tables found in the back of most statistics texts are based on the central F distribution, or the distribution of the F-statistic that would be expected if the traditional nil hypothesis were true. Tests of minimum-effect hypotheses are based on a noncentral F distribution rather than the central F that is used in testing the nil hypothesis.

For example, suppose a researcher decides that treatments that account for 1% or less of the variance in outcomes have a "negligible" effect. It is then possible to estimate a noncentrality parameter (based on $PV = .01$), and to estimate the corresponding noncentral F distribution for testing the hypothesis that treatment effects are at best negligible. If $PV = .01$, $df_{hyp} = 2$, and $df_{err} = 100$, 95% of the values in this noncentral F distribution will fall at or below 4.49, and 99% of the values in this distribution will fall at or below 6.76 (as we note below, F values for testing minimum-effect hypotheses are listed in Appendix B). In other words, if the observed F in this study is greater than 4.49, the researcher could be confident ($\alpha = .05$) in rejecting the hypothesis that treatments accounted for 1% or less of the variance. Later in this chapter, we discuss standards that might be used in designating effects as "negligible."

You might notice that minimum-effect hypotheses involve specifying a range of values as "negligible." In the example above, effects that account for 1% or less of the variance in the population were designated as negligible effects, and if a researcher can reject the hypothesis that the effects are negligibly small, he or she is left with the alternative hypothesis that they are *not* negligibly small (i.e., that treatment effects are large enough to consider).

You might wonder how a single critical *F* value allows you to test for a whole range of null possibilities. If you remember, one characteristic of the *F*-statistic is that it ranges from zero to infinity, with larger *F* values indicating larger effects. Therefore, if you can be 95% confident that the observed *F* is larger than the *F* you would have obtained if treatments accounted for 1% of the variance, you can also be at least 95% confident that the observed *F* would be larger than that which would have been obtained for any *PV* value between .00 and .01. If the observed *F* is larger than the *F* values expected 95% of the time when *PV* = .01, it must also be larger than 95% of the values expected for any smaller *PV* value.

An example. Suppose 125 subjects are randomly assigned to one of five treatments. You find $F(4, 120) = 2.50$, and in this sample, treatments account for 7.6% of the variance in the dependent variable. This *F* is large enough to allow you to reject the traditional null hypothesis ($\alpha = .05$; the critical value of *F* for testing this nil hypothesis is $F = 2.45$). This significant *F* allows the researcher to reject the nil hypothesis, but since the nil hypothesis is almost always wrong, rejecting it in this study does not really inform the researcher much about the treatments.

Suppose also that treatments of this sort that account for less than 1% of the variance in the population have effects that can sensibly be labeled as "negligible." To test the hypothesis that the effects observed in this study came from a population in which the true effect of treatments is negligibly small, all the researcher needs to do is to consult the noncentral *F* distribution with $df_{hyp} = 4$, $df_{err} = 120$, and $\lambda = 1.21$ (i.e., a good estimate of the noncentrality parameter λ is given by $[120 \cdot .01]/[1 - .01]$). In this noncentral *F* distribution, 95% of the values in this distribution are 3.13 or less. The obtained *F* was 2.50, which is smaller than this critical value. This means that the researcher cannot reject this minimum-effect null hypothesis. That is, although the researcher can reject the hypothesis that treatments have no effect whatsoever (i.e., the traditional null), the researcher cannot reject the hypothesis that the effects of treatments are negligibly small (i.e., a minimum-effect hypothesis that treatments account for less than 1% of the variance in outcomes).

Defining a minimum effect. The main advantage of the traditional nil hypothesis is that it is simple and objective. If a researcher rejects the hypothesis that treatments have no effect, he or she is left with the alternative that they have some effect. On the other hand, testing minimum-effect hypotheses requires value judgments and requires that some consensus be reached in a particular field of inquiry. For example, the definition of a "negligible" effect might reasonably vary across areas, and there may be no set convention for defining which effects are so small that they can be effectively ignored and which cannot. An effect that looks trivially small in one discipline might look reasonably large in another. However, it is possible to offer some broad principles for determining when effects are likely to be judged "negligible."

First, the importance of an effect should depend substantially on the particular dependent variables involved. For example, in medical research it is common for relatively small effects (in terms of the percentage of variance explained) to be viewed as meaningful and important (Rosenthal, 1993). One reason is that the dependent variables in these studies often include quality of life, and even survival (i.e., mortality rates). A small percentage of variance might translate into many lives saved.

Second, decisions about what effects should be labeled as "negligible" might depend on the relative likelihood and relative seriousness of Type I versus Type II errors in a particular area. As we note in a section that follows, the power of statistical tests in the general linear model decreases as the definition of a "negligible" effect expands. In any particular study, power is higher for testing the traditional nil hypothesis that treatments have no effect than for testing the hypothesis that they account for 1% or less of the variance in outcomes, and higher for tests of the hypothesis that treatments account for 1% or less of the variance than for tests of hypothesis that treatments account for 5% or less of the variance in outcomes. If Type II errors are seen as especially serious in a particular area of research, it might make sense to choose a very small figure as the definition of a "negligible" effect.

On the other hand, there are many areas of inquiry in which numerous well-validated treatments are already available (see Lipsey & Wilson, 1993, for a review of numerous meta-analyses of treatment effects), and in these areas, it might make sense to "set a higher bar" by testing a more demanding hypothesis. For example, in the area of cognitive ability testing (where the criterion is some measure of performance on the job or in the classroom), it is common to find that tests account for 20% to 25% of the variance in the criterion (Hunter & Hunter, 1984; Hunter & Hirsch, 1987). Tests of the traditional null hypothesis (i.e., tests that have no relationship whatsoever to these criteria) are relatively easy to reject; if $r^2 = .25$, a study with $N = 28$ will have power of .80 for rejecting the traditional null hypothesis (Cohen, 1988). Similarly, the hypothesis that tests account for 1% or less of the variance in these criteria is easy to reject; if $r^2 = .25$, a study with $N = 31$ will have power of .80 for rejecting this minimum-effect hypothesis (Murphy & Myors, 1999). In this context, it might make sense to define a "negligible" relationship as one in which tests account for 10% or less of the variance in these criteria.

Utility analysis has been used to help determine whether particular treatments have effects that are large enough to warrant attention (Landy, Farr, & Jacobs, 1982; Schmidt, Hunter, McKenzie, & Muldrow, 1979; Schmidt, Mack, & Hunter, 1984). Utility equations suggest another important parameter that is likely to affect the decision of what represents a negligible versus a meaningful effect (i.e., the standard deviation of the dependent variable, or SD_y). When there is substantial and meaningful variance in the outcome variable of interest, a treatment that accounts for a relatively small *percentage* of variance might nevertheless lead to practical benefits that far exceed the costs of the treatment.

For example, suppose a training program costs \$1,000 per person to administer, and that it is proposed as a method of improving performance in a setting where the current SD_y (i.e., the standard deviation of performance) is \$10,000. Utility theory can be used to determine whether to compare the costs with the expected benefits of this method of training. Depending on the effectiveness of the training program, researchers might conclude that benefits exceed costs (if the training is highly effective) or that costs exceed benefits (if the training is not very effective). Utility theory equations can also be used to determine the level of effectiveness the training program needs to meet so that benefits will at least equal costs, and it can be argued that this effectiveness level represents a very good definition of a minimum effect. That is, training programs that lead to more costs than benefits are not likely to be seen as effective, whereas training programs that lead to benefits that exceed their costs will be seen as effective. This break-even point represents a sensible definition of a minimally effective program.

Landy, Farr, and Jacobs (1982) discuss the application of utility theory in evaluating performance improvement programs. They note that the overall benefit of such interventions can be estimated using the equation:

$$\Delta U = (r_{xy} \cdot SD_y) - C \qquad (3.1)$$

where

ΔU = The projected gain in productivity associated with training
r_{xy} = The correlation between training and performance
C = The cost of the training program

In this example, SD_y = \$10,000 and C = \$1,000, so Equation 3.1 can be restated as:

$$\Delta U = (r_{xy} \cdot \$10,000) - \$1,000 \qquad (3.2)$$

A minimally effective training program will produce benefits that are equal to costs. The benefits of this training program depend on its effectiveness (i.e., the benefits are estimated by $[r_{xy} \cdot \$10,000]$). Therefore, in defining the minimum level of training effectiveness that will allow benefits to offset costs, all we need to do is to determine the value of r_{xy} at which predicted benefits equal costs.

Benefits equal costs when $(r_{xy} \cdot SD_y)$ equals C. Rearranging the terms in Equation 3.1, this break-even point is defined as:

$$(r_{xy} \cdot SD_y) = C \text{ when } r_{xy} = C/SD_y \qquad (3.3)$$

That is, benefits equal costs when the effectiveness of training (r_{xy}) is equal to C/SD_y. In our example, benefits equal costs when r_{xy} is equal to .10 (i.e., \$1,000/\$10,000). If this value of r_{xy} is squared, the point at which the benefits of training at least equal costs is when PV = .01. In other words, if training accounts for at least 1% of the variance in performance, benefits will at least offset costs, and this strikes us as a sensible definition of a minimum effect.

In many of the examples presented in this chapter and chapters that follow, we use conventions similar to those described in Cohen (1988), describing treatments that have less than 1% of the variance as having small effects, and those that account for less than 5% of the variance in outcomes as having small to medium effects. Many of the tables presented in this book are arranged according to these particular conventions. However, it is critical to note that the decision of what represents a "negligible" effect is one that is likely to vary across research areas, and that there will be many cases in which these particular conventions do not apply. Appendix A presents the information needed to determine critical F values for minimum-effect tests that employ some other operational definition of "negligible," and we urge researchers to carefully consider their reasons for choosing any particular value as a definition of the minimum effect of interest.

Power of minimum-effect tests. As this example suggests, researchers should expect less power when testing the hypothesis that effect exceeds some minimum value than when testing the hypothesis that the effect is exactly zero. Switching from a central to a noncentral distribution as the basis of your null hypothesis necessarily increases the F value needed to reach significance, thereby reducing power.

The traditional hypothesis that treatments have no effect whatsoever is almost always wrong (Murphy, 1990) and is therefore relatively easy to reject. If the sample is large enough, researchers will *always* reject the hypothesis that treatments have no effect, even if the true effect of treatments is extremely small. Tests of the hypothesis that treatment effects exceed the standard that is used to define *negligible* are more demanding than tests of the traditional nil hypothesis, in part because there is always a chance that the treatment effects *are* negligible. Therefore, there is no guarantee that a researcher will reject a minimum-effect hypothesis, no matter how sensitive the study. However, as we note in several of the chapters that follow, the lower power of minimum-effect tests is easily offset by the fact that these tests tell researchers something meaningful, regardless how large the sample size or how sensitive the study.

Using the One-Stop Tables to Assess Power to Test Minimum-Effect Hypotheses

In Chapter 2, we describe the use of the One-Stop *F* Table (Appendix B) and the One-Stop *PV* Table (Appendix C) in performing significance tests and power analyses for nil hypothesis tests. These same tables also include all the information you need to conduct significance tests and power analyses for tests of minimum-effect hypotheses, where negligible effects are defined as those that account for 1% or less of the variance or as those that account for 5% or less of the variance in outcomes.

Testing minimum-effect hypotheses (PV = .01). Rather than testing the hypothesis that treatments have no effect whatsoever, researchers might want to test the hypothesis that treatment effects are so small that they account for less than 1% of the variance in outcomes. If this *PV* value represents a sensible definition of a "negligible" effect in a particular area of research and researchers test and reject this hypothesis, they can be confident that effects are *not* negligibly small.

The fifth and sixth values in each cell of the One-Stop *F* Table are the critical *F* values needed to achieve significance (at the .05 and .01 levels, respectively) when testing the hypothesis that treatments account for 1% or less of the variance in outcomes. With $df_{hyp} = 3$ and $df_{err} = 50$, an *F* of 3.24 or larger (with $\alpha = .05$) is needed to reject the hypothesis that the treatment effect is negligibly small (defined as accounting for 1% or less of the variance in outcomes).

The seventh and eighth values in each cell are *F* equivalents of the effect size values needed to obtain particular levels of power (given an α level of

.05 and the specified df_{hyp} and df_{err}) for testing this minimum-effect hypothesis. The values in the table are 2.46 and 4.48 for power levels of .50 and .80, respectively. This translates into *PV* values of .13 and .21, respectively. That is, if treatments accounted for 13% of the variance in the population, a study that uses minimum-effect tests with $df_{hyp} = 3$, $df_{err} = 50$, and $\alpha = .05$ will have power of approximately .50 for detecting that effect. If treatments account for 21% of the variance in the population, the power of this study will be approximately .80.

Testing minimum-effect hypotheses (PV = .05). Many treatments routinely demonstrate moderate to large effects. For example, well-developed cognitive ability tests allow researchers to predict performance in school and in many jobs with a relatively high degree of success (correlations in the .30 to .50 range are common). Rather than testing the hypothesis that tests have no relationship whatsoever with these criteria (i.e., the traditional nil) or even that treatments account for 1% or less of the variance in outcomes, it might make sense to test a more challenging hypothesis (i.e., that the effect of this particular treatment is at least small to moderate in size). For reasons that are explained in the section that follows, there are many contexts in which it is useful to test the hypothesis that treatments explain 5% or less of the variance in the population. If a researcher can test and reject the hypothesis that effects explain 5% or less of the variance in outcomes, he or she is left with the alternative that treatments explain greater than 5% of the variance. In most contexts, effects this large are likely to be treated as meaningful, even if smaller effects (i.e., those accounting for 1% of the variance) are not.

The ninth and tenth values in each cell of the One-Stop *F* Table represent the critical *F* values needed to achieve significance (at the .05 and .01 levels, respectively) when testing the hypothesis that treatments account for 5% or less of the variance in outcomes. With $df_{hyp} = 3$ and $df_{err} = 50$, an *F* of 4.84 or greater (with $\alpha = .05$) is needed to reject the hypothesis that treatments account for 5% or less of the variance in the population.

The eleventh and twelfth values in each cell are *F* equivalents of the effect size values needed to obtain particular levels of power (given an α level of .05 and the specified df_{hyp} and df_{err}) for tests of this minimum-effect hypothesis. The values in the table are 4.08 and 6.55 for power levels of .50 and .80, respectively. This translates into *PV* values of .20 of and .28, respectively. In other words, in order to have power of .50 for testing the hypothesis that treatments account for 5% or less of the variance in outcomes in a study with $df_{hyp} = 3$ and $df_{err} = 50$, the true population effect size will have to be fairly large (*PV* = .20). In order to achieve power of .80, the population effect will have to be quite large (*PV* = .28).

Worked Example: Minimum-Effect Testing

A researcher randomly assigns 125 participants to one of five treatments and reports $F(4, 120) = 3.50$, and that treatments account for 10% of the variance (if applying Equation 2.7 from Chapter 2 confirms this transformation of F to PV, i.e., $PV = (\text{df}_{hyp} \cdot F)/[(\text{df}_{hyp} \cdot F) + \text{df}_{err}]$). What conclusions can be drawn from this study?

First, it is possible to reject the nil hypothesis at both the .05 and .01 levels; the critical values shown in Appendix B for $\text{df}_{hyp} = 4$ and $\text{df}_{err} = 120$ are 2.45 and 3.48, respectively. If the observed value of PV (i.e., $PV = .10$) is taken as a reasonable estimate of the population PV, the study has more than adequate power for these nil hypothesis tests. As Appendix C shows, a population PV of .09 would be large enough to provide power of .80 for tests of the nil hypothesis when $\text{df}_{hyp} = 4$ and $\text{df}_{err} = 120$.

Second, it is possible to reject the null hypothesis ($\alpha = .05$) that treatments account for 1% or less of the variance. Appendix B shows that an F value of 3.13 or greater would be needed to reject this null hypothesis. If a more stringent alpha level (e.g., $\alpha = .01$) is set, the observed F will be smaller than the critical value of F (i.e., $F = 4.40$). In other words, the researcher will not be able to reject, with a 99% level of confidence, the hypothesis that treatments account for 1% or less of the variance.

Appendix C shows that population effect sizes of $PV = .07$ and $PV = .11$ will be needed to achieve power levels of .50 and .80, respectively, in tests of this minimum-effects hypothesis. The observed PV falls between these two values, and if this observed effect is used as an estimate of the population effect, this suggests that power is slightly less than .80.

Finally, the results of this study would not allow researchers to reject the hypothesis ($\alpha = .05$) that treatments account for 5% or less of the variance. The critical value of F for this null hypothesis test is 5.45. Appendix C shows that in order to have power of .80 for testing this hypothesis with $\text{df}_{hyp} = 4$ and $\text{df}_{err} = 120$, the population treatment effect would have to be quite large (i.e., $PV = .18$).

You might note that our One-Stop F Table does not contain a set of rows corresponding to relatively large effects (i.e., effects accounting for more than 5% of the variance in outcomes). As we noted in Chapter 1, when the effect of treatments is known or thought to be large, there is often no point to conducting the research. Large effects are usually so obvious that a study confirming their existence is unlikely to make much of a contribution. More to the point, when the effects under consideration are large, statistical power is unlikely to be a problem unless samples are extremely small. When samples are this small, researchers have problems that are much more severe than statistical power (e.g., lack of generalizability), and power analyses for large effects strike us as very limited in value.

Using the One-Stop *F* Calculator for Minimum-Effect Tests

Both the One-Stop *F* Table and the One-Stop *PV* Table (Appendices B and C) are designed to support both nil hypothesis tests and minimum-effect tests. In particular, these tables provide the information needed to carry out significance tests and power analyses when the hypothesis being tested is that treatments account for 1% or less of the variance or that treatments account for 5% or less of the variance in outcomes. The One-Stop *F* Calculator is also designed to support both nil hypothesis and minimum-effect tests. Unlike the tables presented in Appendices B and C, this calculator allows researchers to conduct significance tests and power analyses for all possible minimum-effect tests.

Suppose the working definition of a negligible effect in a particular area of research was an effect that accounted for less than 2.5% of the variance in outcomes. There is nothing sacred about values of 1% or 5% of the variance as definitions of *negligible*, and any other value might be chosen. It would be possible to conduct minimum-effect tests for this particular definition of *negligible* by calculating noncentral *F* that corresponds to the test. A simpler method is to use the One-Stop *F* Calculator, which is designed to make the process of minimum-effects testing every bit as easy as testing the traditional nil hypothesis.

Suppose you randomly assign 102 participants to either a training program that requires active learning or a training program based on traditional lectures. You find a significant difference between the mean test scores of these two groups, $t = 3.66$, $PV = .118$. The first step in applying the models described in this chapter is to transform this t-value into an *F*. Since $F = t^2$, this translates into $F = 13.39$ with $df_{hyp} = 1$ and $df_{err} = 100$.

To test for statistical significance ($\alpha = .05$), using a minimum-effects test in which effects accounting for 2.5% or less of the variance are treated as negligible, choose the "Significance Testing" option of the One-Stop *F* Calculator and enter values of .025, .05, 1, and 100 in the "Effect Size," "Alpha," "df_{hyp}," and "df_{err}" boxes. The calculator indicates that the critical value of *F* for testing this hypothesis is 10.87 (the corresponding *PV* is .10). The observed F is larger than the critical value, so you can be confident that in the population, treatments account for more than 2.5% of the variance.

The "Power Analysis" option of this calculator suggests that the power of this study is less than .80. If you enter values of .025, .80, .05, 1, and 100 in the "Effect Size," "Power," "Alpha," "df_{hyp}" and "df_{err}," boxes, you will find that a population PV of .146 would be needed to yield power of .80. The observed PV is .116, substantially smaller than the value needed to achieve power of .80.

If the researcher wanted to achieve power of .80, he or she would need a larger sample. The "Sample Size (df Error) Determination" option of the calculator allows the researcher to determine sample size requirements. Enter .025, .80, .05, 1, and .116 in the "Effect Size," "Power," "Alpha," "df_{hyp}," and "PV" boxes, and you will find that df_{err} must be at least 143 ($df_{err} = N - 2$, so N must be 145) to achieve power of .80 for testing this null hypothesis.

Summary

Tests of the traditional nil hypothesis, that treatments or interventions have no effect, have been criticized by methodologists. The most important criticism is that the nil hypothesis is, by definition, almost always wrong. As a result, tests of that hypothesis have little real value, and some of the procedures that are widely used in statistical analysis (e.g., adopting a stringent alpha level to control for Type I errors) are illogical and costly.

This chapter describes an alternative to the traditional nil hypothesis test, in which the null hypothesis describes a range of possible outcomes. In particular, it is often possible to define a range of effect sizes that would, by any reasonable standard, be defined as negligible. One possibility is to define any treatment effect that accounts for less than 1% of the variance in treatments as negligible (another possibility is to use 5% of the variance as a cutoff). Tests of the null hypothesis either that treatment effects fall within some range defined as negligible or that the effects of treatments are large enough to be of real interest to the researcher are easy to perform and they offer numerous advantages. First, the results of these tests are not trivial. If a researcher can confidently reject the hypothesis that treatments had a negligibly small effect, he or she is left with the conclusion that they had effects large enough to be important.

The minimum-effects tests described here are simple extensions of the familiar F test. The only difference between nil hypothesis F tests and minimum-effect F tests is that they use different F tables. Nil hypothesis tests are based on the hypothesis that treatments have no effect, a hypothesis that is extremely unlikely to be true. Minimum-effect tests have the advantage of being simple and informative. In the chapters that follow, we present minimum-effect tests as well as nil hypothesis tests. In our final chapter, we argue that the advantages of alternatives to nil hypothesis tests, such as the minimum-effects test, are so compelling that they call into question the continuing use of the traditional nil hypothesis test.

4

Using Power Analyses

▼　▼　▼　▼　▼

In Chapter 1, we noted that there are two general ways that power analysis might be used. First, power analysis is an extremely useful tool for planning research. Critical decisions, such as how many subjects are needed, whether multiple observations should be obtained from each subject, and even what criterion should be used to define *statistical significance* can be better made by taking into account the results of a power analysis. Decisions about whether to pursue a specific research question might even depend on considerations of statistical power. For example, if your research idea involves a small (but theoretical meaningful) interaction effect in a complex experiment, power analysis might show that thousands of subjects would be needed to have any reasonable chance of detecting the effect. If the resources are not available to test for such an effect, it is certainly better to know this before the fact than to learn it after collecting your data.

Second, power analysis is a useful diagnostic tool. Tests of the traditional null hypothesis often turn out to be little more than roundabout power analyses. If you conduct a study and all of the correlations among variables, as well as all of the planned and unplanned comparisons between treatments turn out to be statistically significant, this probably indicates that the sample was very large. If the sample is large enough, you will have tremendous power and any effect that is literally different from zero will also be statistically different from zero. On the other hand, if none of a researcher's well-conceived hypotheses are supported with significant results, that researcher might want to conduct a power analysis before asking what is wrong with his or her ideas. If the power is too low, a researcher might never reject the null hypotheses, even in cases where it is clearly and obviously wrong.

In this chapter, we discuss the major applications of power analysis. In Chapter 1, we noted that because statistical power is itself a function of three parameters—the number of observations (*N*), the criterion used to define statistical significance (α), and the effect size (ES)—it is possible to solve for any one of four values (i.e., power, *N*, ES, or α) given the other three. The effect size parameter may be the most problematic because it represents a real but unknown quantity (i.e., the real effect of your treatments). Before discussing practical applications of power analysis, it is useful to examine more closely the methods that might be used in estimating effect sizes.

Estimating the Effect Size

In Chapter 1, we noted that the exact effect size is usually unknown; if you knew precisely how treatment groups would differ, there would be little point in carrying out the research. There are three general methods that might be followed in estimating effect sizes in statistical power analysis. First, you might use inductive methods. If similar studies have been carried out previously, you might use the results from these studies to estimate effect sizes in your own studies. Twenty years ago, this inductive method might have relied heavily on personal experience (i.e., whatever studies a particular researcher had read and remembered); but with the rapid growth of meta-analysis, it is often easy to find summaries of the results of large numbers of relevant studies (see, for example, Hunter & Hirsh, 1987; Lipsey & Wilson, 1993) already translated into a convenient effect size metric (e.g., *d*, r^2).

Second, you might use deductive methods, in which existing theory or findings in related areas are used to estimate the size of an effect. For example, suppose you want to estimate the effect of vitamin supplements on performance in long-distance races. Suppose further that you know that (a) the vitamin supplement has a strong and immediate effect on the efficiency with which your body uses oxygen, and (b) efficiency in using oxygen is strongly correlated with success in such a race. It seems reasonable in this context to deduce that the vitamin supplements should have a reasonably strong influence on race outcomes.

Third, you might use widely accepted conventions that define what represents a "large," "medium," or "small" effect to structure your power analysis. As we note below, analyses based on these conventions require very careful thought about what sort of effect you can realistically expect or what sort of information about statistical power you really need. Nevertheless, the use of these conventions can help in carrying out useful and informative power analyses, even if there is no basis for predicting with any accuracy the size of the treatment effect.

Inductive methods. Inductive methods are best where there is a wealth of relevant data. For example, there have been hundreds and perhaps thousands of studies on the validity of cognitive ability tests in predicting performance in school and on the job (Hunter & Hirsch, 1987; Hunter & Hunter, 1984). Similarly, Lipsey and Wilson (1993) review numerous meta-analyses of psychological and educational interventions. This method is not restricted to the behavioral and social sciences; meta-analytic procedures are being applied in areas such as cancer research (e.g., Himel, Liberati, Laird, & Chalmers, 1986); Lipsey and Wilson (1993) cite numerous meta-analyses of research on other medical topics.

Suppose you are doing research on the effectiveness of programs designed to help individuals quit smoking and you have sufficient resources to collect data from 250 subjects. Lipsey and Wilson (1993) cite two separate meta-analyses that suggest relatively small effects on quit rates (for physician-delivered and worksite programs, $d = .34$ and $d = .20$, based on eight and twenty studies, respectively). This body of research provides a reasonable starting point for estimating power; the average of the two d values in these two meta-analyses is .274. The F equivalent for this effect size estimate, given a study comparing quit rates in a treatment group ($n = 125$) with those in a control group ($n = 125$) is $F(1, 248) = 3.57$. Your power for testing the traditional null hypothesis ($\alpha = .05$) is therefore below .50 (the F equivalent for power of .50 from the One-Stop F Table is 3.81; see Appendix B). If you were testing the hypothesis that treatments accounted for 1% or less of the variance in outcomes in the population, your power would be well below .50 (the F equivalent for power of .50 is 10.33; in this study, power is less than .10).

Using the One-Stop F Calculator to Perform Power Analysis

Suppose you have 250 subjects available for a study. You can use the One-Stop F Calculator to carry out a range of analyses that are useful for understanding the statistical power of different studies that might be carried out and for understanding the limitations you might have to work with in planning and analyzing studies. For example, suppose you wanted to determine what sorts of effects could be detected in tests of the nil hypothesis with a power of .80.

Choose the Power Analysis option and enter 0.0 for ES, .05 for alpha, .80 for power, 1 for df_{hyp}, and 248 for df_{err}. This sets you up to test the traditional nil hypothesis, using $\alpha = .05$, in a study in which 250 subjects are divided into two groups (df_{hyp} = number of groups − 1, df_{err} = N − df_{hyp} − 1). You will find that with a sample this large, you can detect effects as small as $PV = .03$ ($d = .35$) with power of .80. You can use this same option to determine the effect size needed to achieve this same level of power in tests of minimum-effect hypotheses. For example, if treatments account for as little as 6% of the variance in outcomes, this sample will give you power of .80 for testing the hypothesis that treatments account for 1% or less of the variance in the population.

Suppose you expect a very small effect (e.g., treatments will account for 1.5% of the variance in outcomes). You probably will not have a great deal of power with a sample of 250; you can use the One-Stop F Calculator to determine how large the sample will need to be to achieve the desired level of power. Choose the Sample Size (df error) Determination option. Entering 0.0 as the ES, .8 as power, 1 as df_{hyp}, and .015 as the PV, you will find that a sample of $N = 495$ will be needed ($df_{err} = 493$, $N = df_{err} + 2$).

Finally, suppose you have a rough idea of the effect size you expect (e.g., treatments will explain 1.5% of the variance). You cannot afford to collect a sample of $N = 495$, and you would like to find out how much power you have with the sample of $N = 250$ that is available. There are a variety of ways to do this analysis, but the simplest approach involves an iterative process in which you estimate power, see how close you are, then continue to refine your estimate. This iterative process starts with a rough guess of the level of power your study is likely to have. It is never a bad idea to start with power = .50.

Choose the Power Analysis option and enter 0.0, .05, .50, 1, and 248 for ES, alpha, power, df_{hyp}, and df_{err}, respectively. If you hit Calculate, you will find that given $N = 250$, you will need to have a population effect of $PV = .04$ to achieve power of .50. You expect a much smaller population effect ($PV = .015$), so you should expect power to be less than .50. Your next guess might be that power will be .25. Entering 0.0, .05, .25, 1, and 248 for ES, alpha, power, df_{hyp}, and df_{err}, respectively, you will find that you can achieve power of .25 for population effects as small as $PV = .026$. This means that the power of your study is even less than .25. If you follow the strategy of cutting the assumed power value in half (i.e., entering .1275 for power), you will find that your estimate of power is *still* too high; you would need a population PV of .017 or greater to achieve power of .1275. The actual level of power in this study is roughly .10, which means that you are 9 times as likely to fail to reject the null hypothesis with this study as you are to reject it. This strikes us as a *very* low level of power.

Even though the study you have in mind has a relatively large sample ($N = 250$), power is low, even for testing the traditional null hypothesis. The reason for this is that the effects of smoking cessation programs on quit rates are small ($d = .24$ means that treatments account on average for about 1.4% of the variance in quit rates). The body of research in this area gives you good reason to expect small effects, and if you want to have adequate power for detecting these effects, you will need a much larger sample (e.g., you will need about 525 subjects to achieve power of .80 in tests of the traditional null hypothesis).

Deductive methods. Deductive methods are the best when there is a wealth of relevant theory or models; Newtonian mechanics is probably the best example of an area in which numerous effects can be deduced on the basis of a small set of theoretical statements and principles. However, there are areas in the social and behavioral sciences where the relevant theories or models are sufficiently well developed so that sound inferences could be made about effect sizes. For example, the models most commonly used to describe human cognitive abilities are hierarchical in nature, with specific abilities linked to broad ability factors, which in turn are linked to a single general cognitive ability (see Carroll, 1993, for a review of factor-analytic studies). If you wanted to estimate the validity of a new test measuring specific abilities as a predictor of performance in school, you could use what is known about the structure of abilities to make a reasonable estimate; tests that are strongly related to verbal or general cognitive ability factors are likely to show moderate to strong relationships to school performance.

Suppose you used existing models of cognitive ability to estimate test validity and obtained a figure of .40 (e.g., estimated correlation between test scores and school performance). If you used a sample of 65 subjects, an expected correlation of .40 would yield an F equivalent value of $F(1, 63) = 12.00$, and your power for testing the traditional null would be greater than .80; tests of the hypothesis that tests account for greater than 1% of the variance in the population would also have power in excess of .80. Because the expected effect is relatively large, it is easy to obtain adequate power, even with a small sample.

Worked Example: Calculating *F* equivalents and Power

If you expect the correlation between two variables to be .40, and you have 65 participants in your experiment, what level of power would you expect? There are several ways of attacking this question, but the most general of these involves transforming the correlation into its equivalent *F* value.

1. The formula shown in Table 2.1 (Chapter 2) for transforming r to F is

$$F(1, \text{df}_{err}) = \frac{r^2 \text{ df}_{err}}{1 - r^2}$$

2. $\text{df}_{err} = N - 2 = 65 - 2 = 63$; $r^2 = .40^2 = .16$, so $F(1, 63) = (.16 \cdot 63)/(1 - .16) = 12.0$.

3. Once again, you can use the same procedure illustrated in a previous example in which you make a rough guess at power then adjust up or down until you reach a point where the F value provided by the One-Stop F Calculator is approximately 12.0

4. Use the Power Analysis option of the One-Stop F Calculator and start by entering: ES = 0.0, power = 0.80 (a guess), alpha = 0.05, $\text{df}_{hyp} = 1$, and $\text{df}_{err} = 63$. The computer program responds with $F = 7.85$.

5. Try a higher power estimate. Enter power = .90, and the calculator will return $F = 10.19$, which is still less than $F = 12$

6. Keep raising the power estimate. Try a power estimate of .95. Enter power = .95, and the calculator will return $F = 12.3$, which is slightly above $F = 12$. If you try a slightly lower level, you will find that when power = .94, $F = 11.76$. In other words, the power of this study for detecting a correlation of .40 is between .94 and .95.

Effect size conventions. As we noted in the preceding section, there are some widely accepted conventions for defining "small," "medium," and "large" effects. For example, a "small" treatment effect has been described as one in which treatments account for approximately 1% of the variance in outcomes, as one in which the difference between treatment and control group means is about one fifth of a standard deviation, or as one in which a person randomly selected from the treatment group has a probability of .56 of having a higher score than a person randomly selected from the control group (see Table 2.2 in Chapter 2). None of these figures is sacred or exact (e.g., 2% of the variance might reasonably be described as a "small" effect"), but the conventions described in Table 2.2 do seem to be accepted as reasonable by many researchers, and they provide a basis for doing a power analysis even when the actual treatment effect cannot be estimated by inductive or deductive methods.

When conventions are used to estimate effect sizes, it is usually best to base power analyses on small or small to medium effect sizes. As we noted in Chapter 1, a study with sufficient power to detect a small effect will have sufficient power for detecting medium and large effects as well. If you plan your study with the assumption that the effect is a large one, you run the considerable risk of missing meaningful effects that did not reach quite the magnitude you optimistically hoped to achieve. Thus, if the data and theory in a particular field do not provide a firm inductive or deductive basis for estimating effect sizes, you can always follow the convention and base your analysis on the assumption that the effects might very well be small. A study that has sufficient power to reliably detect small effects runs little risk of making a serious Type I or Type II error, regardless of the actual size of the treatment effect.[1]

Four Applications of Statistical Power Analysis

The two most common application of statistical power analysis are in (1) determining the power of a study, given N, ES, and α and (2) determining how many observations will be needed (i.e., N), given a desired level of power, an ES estimate, and an α value. Both of these analysis are extremely useful in planning research and are usually so easy to do that they should be a routine part of designing a study. Power analysis may not be the *only* basis for determining whether to do a particular study or how many observations should be collected, but a few simple calculations are usually enough to help researchers make informed decisions in these areas. The lack of attention to power analysis (and the deplorable habit of placing too much weight on the results of small sample studies) is well documented in the research literature (Cohen, 1962; Haase, Waechter, & Solomon, 1982; Sedlmeier & Gigerenzer, 1989), and there is no good excuse to ignore power in designing studies.

Two other applications of power analysis are less common but no less informative. First, you can use power analysis to evaluate the sensitivity of your studies. That is, power analysis can tell you what sorts of effect sizes might be reliably detected in a study. If you expect the effect of a treatment to be small, it is important to know whether your study will detect that effect, or whether the study you have in mind only has sufficient sensitivity

---

[1] As we noted in Chapters 1 and 2, Type I errors are a concern only when there is some possibility that the null hypothesis is true, which is virtually never the case in tests of the traditional null. Type II errors are still possible if the treatment effect is extremely small, but we would not regard this type of error (i.e., concluding that treatments have no effect when in fact they have a completely trivial effect) as very serious.

to detect larger effects. Second, you can use power analysis to make rational decisions about the criteria used to define *statistical significance*.

Calculating Power

Chapters 1 and 2 were largely devoted to explaining the theory and procedures used in calculating the statistical power of a study, and we will not repeat here all of the details laid out in those two chapters. It is, however, useful to comment on problems or issues that arise in carrying out each of the steps of statistical power analysis.

As the examples presented in Chapter 2 suggest, in estimating the level of power expected in a study you do the following:

1. Estimate the size of the effect, expressed in terms of a common ES measure, such as *PV* or *d*;
2. Determine the degrees of freedom (i.e., df_{hyp} and df_{err}) for the statistical test you want to perform and the type of hypothesis (e.g., traditional null, minimum-effect hypothesis) you want to test;
3. Translate that effect size estimate into an *F* equivalent, given these df_{hyp} and df_{err} values; and
4. Use the One-Stop *F* Table to estimate power. If the *F* equivalent is greater than the *F* needed to obtain power of .80, you should have sufficient power for most purposes, and a more precise estimate is probably not necessary. If the *F* equivalent is less than the *F* needed to obtain power of .50, you will not have sufficient power for most purposes, and a more precise estimate is probably not helpful. If the *F* equivalent is between these two values on the One-Stop *F* Table, you can use the interpolation formulas in Chapter 2 (Equations 2.10 and 2.11) to estimate the power level of the study.

As we noted earlier, there are several ways to estimate the effect size. Regardless of the method chosen, it is usually better (or at least more prudent) to underestimate than to overestimate ES values; a study with enough power to detect a small effect will also have enough power to detect a larger effect. Second, when planning a study, some preliminary estimate of the sample size (and possibly of the research) design must be made. This estimate, which may be modified if the study yields either too much or too little power, helps in determining the degrees of freedom of the *F*-statistic. In most cases, power analyses are likely to lead you to increase the sample size, but it is certainly possible that a power analysis will lead you to conclude that adequate power can be obtained with a smaller sample than the one you had initially planned.

As we have emphasized in Chapters 1 and 2, power depends substantially on the precise hypothesis being tested. It is easier to obtain high levels of power for tests of the traditional null hypothesis than for tests of a minimum-effect hypothesis, at least in part because the traditional null is so easily rejected. Tests of minimum-effect hypotheses, while more difficult, are likely to be more informative.

Finally, you need to make a decision about the significance criteria. Later in this chapter, we discuss in detail the issues involved in making this choice. Here, it is sufficient to note that your choice is often practically limited to the conventional values of .05 versus 01. If you use any other value to define *statistical significance* (e.g., .02 might be a perfectly reasonable choice in some settings), you will have to fight convention and defend your choice to a potentially hostile set of reviewers, readers, and editors (Labovitz, 1968).

Determining Sample Sizes

Rather than calculating the level of power a particular study had or will have, it is often useful to determine the sample or research design needed to achieve specific levels of power. To do this, you must first decide how much power you want. As we noted in Chapter 2, it is hard to justify a study design that yields power less than .50; when power is less than .50, the study is more likely to lead to an incorrect conclusion (i.e., it will not reject H_0, even though you are virtually certain this hypothesis is wrong) than to a correct one. Power substantially greater than .80 might be desirable, but it is often prohibitively difficult to obtain; in most analyses, the desirable level of power is likely to be .80.

Once the desirable level of power is selected, determining sample sizes follows the same general pattern as the determination of power itself. That is, you need to take into account the research design, the estimated effect size, the nature of the hypothesis being tested, and the significance criteria being used. Appendix D can be used to determine sample sizes needed to detect a wide range of effects.

The rows of Appendix D correspond to effect sizes, described in terms of either the standardized mean difference (d) or the proportion of variance explained (PV), which represent the most common effect size estimates in the literature. Table 4.1 provides formulas for translating a number of other statistics, including F, into d and/or PV.

The values in Appendix D represent degrees of freedom (df_{err}) rather than exact sample sizes (N). Our reason for presenting a table of df_{err} values rather than a table of sample sizes is that N is a function of *both* df_{hyp} and df_{err}. In many applications, $N = df_{hyp} + df_{err} + 1$, but in complex multifactor designs (e.g., studies using factorial analysis of variance), the total sample size

Table 4.1 Translating Common Statistics Into Standardized Mean Difference (*d*) or Percentage of Variance (*PV*) Values

Standardized Mean Difference (*d*)

$$d = \frac{2r}{\sqrt{1 - r^2}}$$

$$d = \frac{2t}{\sqrt{df_{err}}}$$

Percentage of Variance (*PV*)

$$PV = \frac{t^2}{t^2 + df_{err}}$$

$$PV = \frac{df_{hyp}\ F}{df_{hyp}\ F + df_{err}}$$

$$PV = \frac{d^2}{d^2 + 4}$$

depends on the number of levels of all design factors, and without knowing the research design in advance, it is impossible to put together an accurate table for *N*. In most cases, however, the sample size needed to achieve power of .80 will be very close to the df_{err} value shown in Appendix D. Chapter 5 deals with applications of power analysis in multifactor studies.

Appendix D presents df_{err} needed when testing the traditional null hypothesis. Appendix E presents the df_{err} needed when testing the hypothesis that treatments account for 1% or less of the population variance in outcomes. As you can see, larger samples are needed when testing this minimum-effect hypothesis than when testing the traditional (but sometimes trivial) hypothesis that treatments have no effect whatsoever.

To illustrate the use of Appendix D and Appendix E, consider a study comparing the effectiveness of four diets. Suppose you expect a small to moderate effect (e.g., the choice of diets is expected to account for about 5% of the variance in weight loss). To achieve power of .80 in testing the traditional null hypothesis (with α = .05), you would look down the column of Appendix D that corresponds to df_{hyp} = 3 (i.e., with four diets, there are 3 degrees of freedom) and find that the df_{err} needed for *PV* = .05 would be approximately 209. You would therefore need a sample of about 214 subjects (i.e., *N* = 209 + 3 + 1) to achieve this level of power, or about 54 per group.

Appendix E shows the df_{err} needed to achieve power of .80 in testing the hypothesis that treatments account for 1% or less of the variance in outcomes. To achieve a power of .80 in testing this minimum-effect hypothesis, you would need a sample of approximately 409 (i.e., $N = 405 + 3 + 1$), or about 100 per group. This sample is almost twice as large as the one needed to reject the traditional null hypothesis that treatments have no effect. However, if you put together a study that allows you to reject the hypothesis that treatments have a negligibly small effect (i.e., they account for less than 1% of the variance in outcomes), you will not only know that treatments have *some* effect, but also have a formal test of the hypothesis that the effect is large enough to warrant your attention.

Determining the Sensitivity of Studies

It is often useful to know what sort of effect could be reasonably detected in a particular study. If a study can reliably detect only a large effect (especially in a context where you expect small effects to actually occur), it might be better to postpone that study until the resources needed to obtain adequate power are available. The process of determining the effect size that can be detected, given particular values for N and α, together with a desired level of power again closely parallels the procedures described above. In fact, Appendices D and E, which specify the df_{err} needed to achieve power of .80 in testing both traditional and minimum-effect hypotheses are also quite useful for determining the type of effect that could be reliably detected in a given study.

Suppose you are comparing two methods of mathematics instruction. There are 140 students available for testing (70 will be assigned to each method), and you decide to use an α level of .05 in testing hypotheses. Here, $df_{hyp} = 1$ (i.e., if two treatments are compared, there is one degree of freedom for this comparison) and $df_{err} = 138$ (i.e., $df_{err} = N - df_{hyp} - 1$). If you look down the $df_{hyp} = 1$ column of Appendix D, you find that 138 falls somewhere between the df_{err} needed to detect an the effect of treatments when $PV = .05$ and $PV = .06$ (or between $d = .46$ and $d = .51$). In other words, with 140 students, you would have power of .80 to detect a small to moderate effect, but you would not have this level of power for detecting a truly small (but perhaps important) effect.

Take another example. Suppose there are four cancer treatments and 44 patients. Here, $df_{hyp} = 3$ and $df_{err} = 40$. If you consult Appendix D, you will find that you have power of .80 to detect effects that are quite large (i.e., $PV = .24$); if the true effects of treatments are small or even moderate, your power to detect these effects will drop substantially.

Both the examples above are based on tests of the traditional null hypothesis. If you want to test the hypothesis that treatments account for 1% or less of the variance in outcomes (which corresponds to d values of

.20 or less), your sample of 140 students will given you power of .80 for detecting differences this large between the two treatments only if the true effect is relatively large (i.e., $PV = .09$ or $d = .63$; see Appendix D). You will have this level of power for detecting nontrivial differences among the four cancer treatments (with $N = 44$) only if the true differences between treatments are truly staggering (i.e., $PV = .26$; see Appendix E).

Using the One-Stop F Calculator to Evaluate Sensitivity

The most common application of power analysis is to determine sample sizes. Another very useful application is to determine what sorts of effects might reasonably be detected with a given sample size and significance criteria. Suppose, for example, that you are studying the effect of a new math curriculum in a small school. There are only 100 students, and you have the option of assigning half to one curriculum and half to another, but you cannot increase the sample size. You can use power analysis to determine what sorts of questions can sensibly be asked in this context.

If 100 students are randomly assigned to one of two groups, $df_{hyp} = 1$ and $df_{err} = 98$ (i.e., $N - 2$). If you go to the Significance Testing option of the One-Stop F Calculator and enter 0.0 for ES (this is a traditional null hypothesis test), .05 for alpha, 1 for df_{hyp}, and 98 for df_{err}, you will find that you will be able to detect a small to moderate effect ($PV = .038$).

Suppose you decide a traditional nil hypothesis test is not useful in this setting (e.g., you are almost certain H_0 is false). You can evaluate the sensitivity of minimum-effect tests by simply changing the ES entry to .01 (to test the hypothesis that treatments account for 1% of the variance or less in outcomes). With this relatively small sample, you will need a much larger effect ($PV = .068$) to reject the null hypothesis.

Determining Appropriate Decision Criteria

As we noted earlier, the choice of criteria for defining *statistical significance* is often practically limited to the conventional values of .05 versus .01 (occasionally, social scientists use .001 or .10 as significance levels, but these are rare exceptions). The choice of any other value (e.g., .06) is likely to be met with some resistance, and the battle is probably not worth the effort. Because the choice among significance levels is constrained by convention, the steps involved in making this choice do not exactly parallel the processes laid out in the three preceding sections of this chapter. Rather than describing specific steps in choosing between .05 and .01 as alpha levels, we discuss the range of issues that are likely to be involved in making this choice. This discussion leads us to the conclusion that *you should never use the .01 level (or any more stringent criterion, such as .001) when testing traditional null hypotheses, nor should you usually use other procedures designed to guard against Type I errors in testing this hypothesis.* As we show below, choice of the .01 significance criterion leads to a substantial reduction in statistical power, with virtually no meaningful gain in terms of protection against Type I errors. The same is true of most procedures designed to reduce Type I errors (see Zwick & Marascuilo, 1984, for a review of procedures used to control Type I error in testing multiple contrasts).

Balancing risks in choosing significance levels. In Chapter 1, we noted that when testing the traditional null hypothesis, two types of errors are possible. Researchers who reject the null hypothesis when in fact it is true make a Type I error (α is the probability of making this error if H_0 is in fact true). The practical effect of a Type I error is that researchers could come to believe that treatments have some effect when in fact they have no effect whatsoever. Researchers who fail to reject the null hypothesis when it is false make a Type II error (β is the probability of making this error when H_0 is in fact false, and power = $1 - \beta$). The practical effect of making a Type II error is that researchers might give up on treatments that in fact have some effect.

The most common strategy for reducing Type I errors is to make it difficult to reject the null hypothesis (e.g., by using .01 rather than .05 as a criterion for significance). Unfortunately, this strategy also substantially reduces the power of your tests. For example, suppose you are comparing two treatments (with 200 people assigned to each treatment) and you expect a small effect (i.e., $d = .20$). Using .05 as a significance criterion, your power would be .64; if $\alpha = .01$, power drops to .37 (Cohen, 1988). This tradeoff between Type I error protection and power suggests that in deciding which significance level to use, you must balance the risk and consequences of a Type I error with the risk and consequences of a Type II error. Nagel and Neff (1977) discuss a decision-theoretic strategy for choosing an alpha level that provides an optimum balance between the two errors.

Cascio and Zedeck (1983) suggest that Equation 4.1 can be used to estimate the apparent relative seriousness (ARS) of Type I versus Type II errors in statistical significance tests:

$$\text{ARS} = \frac{p(H_1)\beta}{[1 - p(H_1)]\alpha} \tag{4.1}$$

where $p(H_1)$ = Probability that H_0 is false

According to Equation 4.1, if the probability that treatments have *some* effect is .7, alpha is .05 and power is .80, your choice of the .05 significance criterion implies that a mistaken rejection of the null hypothesis (i.e., a Type I error) is 9.33 times as serious [i.e., (.7 ·.2)/(.3 · .05) = 9.33] as the failure to reject the null when it is wrong (i.e., a Type II error). In contrast, setting α at .10 leads to a ratio of 4.66 [i.e., (.7 · 2)/(.3 · .10) = 4.66], or to the conclusion that Type I errors are treated as if they are 4.66 times as serious as a Type II error (see also Lipsey, 1990).

The first advantage of Equation 4.1 is that it makes explicit values and preferences that are usually not well understood, either by researchers or by the consumers of social science research. In the scenario described above, an alpha level of .05 makes sense only if you think that Type I errors *are* over 9 times as serious as Type II errors. If you believe that Type I errors are only 4 or 5 times as serious as Type II errors, you should set your significance level at .10, not at .05.

The second advantage of Equation 4.1 is that it explicitly involves the probability that the null hypothesis is true. As we have noted in several other contexts, the traditional null hypothesis is virtually never true, which means that both null hypothesis testing and efforts to reduce Type I errors are sometimes pointless (Murphy, 1990). *If the null hypothesis is by definition false, it is not possible to make a Type I error.* Thus, the only circumstance in which you should use stringent significance criteria, adopt testing procedures that minimize Type I errors, and so forth are those in which the null hypothesis might actually be true. This virtually never happens when testing the traditional null hypothesis, but it might occur when testing a minimum-effect hypothesis.

Should you ever worry about Type I errors? In testing the traditional null hypothesis, it is often virtually impossible to make a Type I error, no matter how hard you try. If H_0 is known to be false, there simply is no way to make a Type I error, and your only concern should be maximizing power (and therefore minimizing Type II errors). In contrast, there are good reasons for concern over Type I errors when testing a minimum-effect hypothesis. It is virtually impossible to devise serious treatments or interventions that have *no* effect whatsoever, but there are many treatments, interventions, tests, etc., that have only negligible effects. If the hypothesis to be tested is that the effect of treatments falls under some sensible minimum, it is quite possible that the null *will* be true, and that you will in fact learn something by testing it.

As Equation 4.1 suggests, it is impossible to sensibly evaluate the relative emphasis given to Type I versus Type II errors unless the probability that the null hypothesis is in fact true can be estimated. Table 4.2 shows the relative seriousness with which Type I versus Type II errors are treated, as a function of both the alpha rate and the probability that the null hypothesis is true, in studies where power = .80. For example, if there is a 5% chance that

Table 4.2 Relative Seriousness of Type I Versus
Type II Errors as Function of Alpha and Probability
That the Null Hypothesis Is True (Power = .80)

Probability That H₀ Is True	Alpha		
	.01	**.05**	**.10**
.50	20.00	4.00	2.00
.30	46.66	9.33	4.66
.10	180.00	36.00	18.00
.05	380.00	76.00	38.00

treatments really do have a negligible effect (i.e., the probability that the min-imum-effect null hypothesis is true = .05), the decision to use an alpha level of .01 makes sense only if you believe that Type I errors are 380 times as seri-ous as Type II errors. As you can see from Table 4.2, as alpha increases (i.e., as it becomes easier to reject H₀), the relative seriousness attached to Type I versus Type II errors goes down. If you believe that Type II errors are at all serious, relative to Type I errors, the message of Table 4.2 is clear—i.e., you should use a more lenient criterion for determining statistical significance.

It is easy to rearrange the terms of Equation 4.1 to compute the alpha level you *should* use to reach an appropriate balance between Type I and Type II errors, a balance we describe as the *desired relative seriousness* (DRS).[2] For example, if you decide to treat Type I errors as twice as serious as Type II errors, the DRS is 2.00; if the probability that the null hypothesis was true is .30, power is .80, and you want to treat Type I errors as if they are twice as serious as Type II errors, you should use an alpha level of .23. The desired alpha level (i.e., level which will yield the appropriate balance between Type I and Type II errors) can be obtained from Equation 4.2.

$$\alpha_{desired} = \frac{p(H_1)\beta}{[1 - p(H_1)]}\left(\frac{1}{DRS}\right) \tag{4.2}$$

where
$\alpha_{desired}$ = Alpha level that will yield the desired relative seriousness of Type I and Type II errors
DRS = Desired relative seriousness of Type I and Type II errors

To repeat what we regard as a critical point, you should be concerned with Type I errors if and only if there is a realistic possibility that such an error can occur. One of the distinctions between the traditional null and minimum-

---

[2] Keep in mind, however, that using nonconventional alpha levels will often require you to vigorously defend your choice, even in contexts where the "conven-tional" choice (e.g., .05, .01) makes no sense whatsoever.

effect tests is that there is a realistic possibility that the minimum-effect null hypothesis *will* be true, which suggests that serious decisions must be made about the appropriate balance between Type I and Type II errors. Equations 4.1 and 4.2 can help you make those decisions.

Finding a Sensible Alpha

Suppose you truly believed that Type I errors were 10 times as serious as Type II errors. Using Equation 4.2, it is possible to design a study in such a way that the likelihood of making Type I versus Type II errors reflects their relative seriousness, which in this case will translate into designing a study in which the probability of making a Type I error is one-tenth the probability of making a Type II error. In order to do this, you need to determine what level of power you want to achieve, some estimate of the probability that the null hypothesis is *wrong* (i.e., $p(H_1)$). We have argued in several parts of this book that $p(H_1)$ will almost certainly be high (e.g., $p(H_1) = .90$) when testing the null hypothesis and have also argued that power should be high in most studies. If you assume that power $(1 - \beta) = .80$ (and therefore $\beta = .20$) and that Type I errors are 10 times as serious as Type II errors, Equation 4.2 translates into

$$\alpha_{desired} = [(.9 \cdot .2)/(1 - .9)) \cdot (1/10)] = .18$$

In other words, the alpha level that makes the most sense in this context is $\alpha = .18$.

If you think that the null hypothesis is almost always wrong, and that $p(H_1)$ should equal .99 rather than .90, Equation 4.2 translates into

$$\alpha_{desired} = [(.99 \cdot .2)/(1 - .99)) \cdot (1/10)] = 1.98$$

An alpha level greater than 1.0 is impossible, so what does this calculation tell you? If you really believe that the null hypothesis is almost always wrong and that Type I errors are 10 times worse than Type II errors, this calculation suggests that *you cannot set your alpha too high*. No matter what decision criteria you choose, performing significance testing when you know ahead of time that H_0 is almost certainly wrong will always cause you to run a risk of Type II errors, and that does not make sense, given your beliefs about the relative seriousness of the two errors.

Summary

Statistical power analysis can be used in planning future studies (e.g., determining how many subjects are needed) or in diagnosing studies that have already been carried out (e.g., calculation of power levels helps you sensibly interpret significance tests). All applications of statistical power analysis require at least an estimate of the true effect size; estimates can be obtained from literature reviews or from relevant theory. Even where little is known about the true effects of treatments, effect size conventions can be used to structure power analyses.

It is possible to use the methods described here to (1) determine the probability that a study will correctly reject the null hypothesis, (2) determine the number of subjects or observations needed to achieve adequate power, (3) determine the sort of effects that can be reliably detected in a particular study, or (4) make informed choices about the criteria that define *statistical significance*. As we have noted throughout this book, these applications of power analysis are not in any way limited to tests of the traditional null hypothesis, but rather can be easily adapted to more interesting and informative tests of the hypothesis that treatment effects exceed some minimum level.

The distinction between traditional and minimum-effect hypotheses is especially important when making decisions about criteria for defining a *significant* outcome. Simply put, when testing the traditional null hypothesis, there is rarely any justification for choosing a stringent alpha level (e.g., .01 rather than .05). Procedures designed to protect you against Type I errors (e.g., Bonferroni corrections) usually reduce your power and should only be applied if there is some realistic possibility that a Type I error can be made. This is unlikely when testing the traditional null hypothesis; this hypothesis is usually known to be incorrect, virtually by definition. Type I errors are a very real concern in tests of minimum-effect hypotheses, and the equations presented here allow you to rationally assess the relative emphasis placed on maximizing statistical power versus avoiding errors of this sort.

5

Correlation and Regression

▼　▼　▼　▼　▼

There is a clear link between correlation and regression analysis and the broader topic of power analysis because both are concerned fundamentally with effect sizes (ES). Throughout this book, we use the percentage of variance in the dependent variable that is explained by treatments, interventions, or other variables (i.e., *PV*) as our main ES measure. If you square the correlation between two variables, *X* and *Y*, what you get is *PV* (i.e., the proportion of variance in *Y* that is explained by *X*). Similarly, in multiple regression, where several *X* variables are used to predict scores on *Y*, the squared multiple correlation coefficient (i.e., R^2) is a measure of proportion of the variance of *Y* that is explained. One of the substantial advantages of framing statistical analyses under the general linear model in terms of correlation (e.g., both *t*-tests and analyses of variance are easily performed using correlational methods) is that it is virtually impossible to make one of the most common mistakes when testing the null hypothesis—i.e., forgetting to examine and report effect size measures. Correlations *are* effect size measures.

Power analysis is useful for both designing and understanding correlational studies. It provides a coherent framework for making decisions about sampling and about the interpretation of both significant and nonsignificant findings. As with other analytic methods discussed in this book, the general message of power analysis when applied to correlation is that large samples are usually needed to provide adequate power. However, as the example discussed below shows, large samples can lead to potentially confusing results, particularly when researchers depend on tests of the nil hypothesis to drive the interpretation of their results.

The Perils of Working With Large Samples

McDaniel (1988) used very large samples to study the validity measures of pre-employment drug use as predictors of job suitability in the military. Validity coefficients for pre-employment use of drugs such as marijuana, cocaine, various stimulants, and depressants were calculated in samples ranging in size from 9,224 to 9,355 subjects. As you might expect, the correlations were all "statistically significant," and an incautious reading of these "significance" tests might mislead readers when arriving at conclusions about the value of these tests.

Several of the validities reported by McDaniel (1988) are shown in Table 5.1. These results are almost beyond the scope of the One-Stop F Table, but interpolating between $df_{err} = 1,000$ and $df_{err} = 10,000$ allows us to reject the traditional null hypothesis in every case at the .01 level. The interpolated critical F value for $\alpha = .01$ at 1 and 9,224 degrees of freedom is 6.64, which is much smaller than any of these observed F values. However, as we note below, the tests are significant because of the enormous samples involved, not because of the size of the effect.

Although significant in the traditional sense, McDaniel's (1988) validities are probably not meaningful in any substantive sense, and as the author himself notes, employers would be better advised to base their employment decision on information other than applicant's previous history of drug use. This study is an excellent example of the pitfalls of relying on tests of the traditional null hypothesis. These correlations are all "significant," and it is all too easy to confuse "significant" with "meaningful." As we note below, these correlations are so small that they should probably be ignored altogether.

We titled this section "The Perils of Working With Large Samples" because significance tests can cause real problems for researchers who work with small samples (low power), but can also cause problems for researchers who work with large samples. In this study, all the correlations were significant, but none was very big. Large samples have many important advantages, notably their ability to provide more accurate estimates, but they

Table 5.1 Predictive Validity of Pre-Employment Drug Use Reported by McDaniel (1988)

Drug	N	Validity	PV	t	F
Marijuana	9,355	.07	.0049	6.79	46.06
Cocaine	9,224	.04	.0016	3.85	14.81
Stimulants	9,286	.07	.0049	6.76	45.73
Depressants	9,267	.07	.0049	6.76	45.63

can mislead researchers who rely on significance tests to tell whether their results are noteworthy and important.

Traditional versus minimum-effect tests. An examination of Table 5.1 shows just how small these validities are, accounting for less than half a percent of the variance in job suitability in each case. This fact is reflected in the One-Stop F Table as well. At 1 and 9,224 degrees of freedom, the interpolated critical F for rejecting the null hypothesis that the effect is negligibly small (i.e., 1% or less of the variance) at 126.1, well above any of the observed F values. In other words, none of the validities reaches the level we have designated as "trivial." Although they are significantly different from zero, it is clear that the relationship between these tests and job suitability is so weak that the variables could be treated as virtually independent.

This example illustrates an important feature of minimum-effect null hypotheses. Unlike the traditional null, you cannot necessarily reject a minimum-effect null simply by collecting more data. If an effect is genuinely negligible, it will continue to be negligible no matter how many subjects you test. This phenomenon is reflected in the One-Stop F Table by the fact that critical F values for the 1% and 5% minimum-effect nulls do not asymptote as df_{err} increases. As you can see, as df_{err} gets very large, the critical values for minimum-effect nulls keep pace with the increase and do not allow you to reject the minimum-effect null hypothesis unless the effect you are studying is genuinely meaningful. Herein lies another important advantage of minimum-effect null hypothesis testing over traditional null hypothesis testing. When testing a minimum-effect null hypothesis, you cannot guarantee rejection simply by collecting a large sample.

Power estimation. As we noted above, the large samples employed in this study give tremendous power in tests of the traditional null hypothesis. If we assume, for example, that pre-employment tests account for only one half of one percent of the variance in job suitability (i.e., $PV = .005$), we would still have power in excess of .80 for all of the tests of the traditional null hypothesis reported in Table 5.1. With $N = 9,224$ and an assumed effect of $PV = .005$, the F equivalent is 46.35, whereas the critical F for achieving power of .80 is 7.81. It is little wonder that the author of this study rejected the traditional null hypothesis. Even if the true effect of pre-employment drug tests is absolutely trivial, this study would still provide plenty of power for rejecting the hypothesis that there is no effect whatsoever.

In contrast, if the hypothesis to be tested is that these tests account for 1% or less of the variance in suitability, McDaniel's (1988) study does not achieve power of even .50; to reach this level of power for samples this large, you would need an F of greater than 120. As we noted above, if the samples included 90,000 rather than 9,000 individuals, you still would not have power for rejecting a minimum-effect null with data like these. The effect is much too small to be sensibly described as "meaningful," and no matter how large the sample, it will still be small. The fact that you can never attain the power needed to reject a minimum-effect hypothesis when the effect is in fact negligible is neatly illustrated with this study.

Multiple Regression

Students who apply for admission to college usually submit scores on several tests (e.g., SAT general and subject tests), high school transcripts, and other indicators of academic potential. One of the challenges faced by admissions officers is to put all of this information together to predict the applicants' future performance. One solution to this problem is to use multiple regression.

Multiple regression involves using several X variables to predict a criterion or outcome variable (Y). The X variables can be continuous (e.g., SAT scores) or discrete (e.g., membership in honor societies); multiple regression provides an analytic method of combining information from multiple predictors to do the best job possible predicting scores on Y.[1] In this particular context, multiple regression involves finding the weighted linear combination of test scores, high school grades, and other indicators that are most highly correlated with the criteria of success in college.

Power analysis can be easily applied to several types of regression. The examples below illustrate some of the possibilities.

Multiple regression models. Beaty, Cleveland, and Murphy (2001) examined the relationship between four personality factors (neuroticism, agreeableness, extroversion, and conscientiousness) and evaluations of organizational citizenship behaviors. Their results suggest that these four personality variables account for approximately 3% of the variance in ratings of citizenship. Because their sample was large ($N = 488$), this R^2 value was judged to be significantly different from zero.

It is important to keep in mind that multiple regression involves finding the best possible combination of variables for predicting Y. That means that no other possible weighted combination of these four personality variables will account for more than 3% of the variance in citizenship. This R^2 is significantly different from zero, but it is worth asking whether it is large enough to allow the conclusion that the relationship between personality and organizational citizenship is anything but trivial. As we noted in

---

[1] The "best" set of predictions is defined here as predictions that minimize the sum of the squared differences between actual and predicted Y variables (i.e., the least squares method).

our earlier discussions of minimum-effect hypotheses, it might be reasonable to define treatments, interventions, or predictors that account for 1% of the variance or less in the population as having effects that are trivially small. Either the One-Stop F Table or the One-Stop F Calculator can be used to test the hypothesis that the relationship between these four personality traits and evaluations of organizational citizenship is either trivially small (H_0) or large enough to be meaningful (H_1).

Testing Minimum-Effect Hypotheses in Multiple Regression

In this study, $N = 488$, $R^2 = .03$. This is a significant multiple correlation, but it is not clear whether it is large enough to be meaningful. One way to ask the question about whether this R^2 is large enough to be meaningful is to define the PV value that represents a trivial effect (e.g., one that accounts for 1% of the variance or less) and test the hypothesis that in the population, the percentage of variance accounted for is larger than 1%. To carry out this minimum-effect test, all you need to do is to determine the degrees of freedom and use them to either guide your search through the One-Stop F Table or enter them into the One-Stop F Calculator.

With a sample of 488 subjects and four predictor variables (i.e., $p = 4$), the degrees of freedom for the sample R^2 are 3 ($p - 1$) and 484 ($N - p - 1$). The One-Stop F Calculator (Significance Testing option) shows that in order to reach a .05 alpha level in tests of this minimum-effect hypothesis, R^2 must be .035, which is slightly higher than the observed R^2 of .03. In other words, you *cannot* reject the hypothesis ($\alpha = .05$) that the relationship between these four personality variables and evaluations of citizenship behavior is trivially small. However, you can nearly approximate the type of effect needed to reject this hypothesis.

If you enter .01, .80, .05, 3, and 484 for ES, power, alpha, df_{hyp}, and df_{err} under the Power Analysis option, you will find that you could achieve power of .80 for tests of the hypothesis ($N = 488$) that these four personality variables have a trivial versus a meaningful relationship with citizenship given a population PV as low as .045. In other words, if the percentage of variance explained had been .045 rather than .03, you would have had power of .80 for testing this minimum-effect hypothesis. With a population PV of .03, you would need a much larger sample ($df_{err} = 1143$, $N = 1148$) to achieve this same level of power.

One of the properties of multiple regression is that adding new predictor variables always increases the value of R^2. For example, adding *any* variable to the four personality characteristics discussed in the example above will lead to an increase in the percentage of variance explained. As a result, it is always important in regression to know and consider how many predictor variables are in the regression equation. Explaining 20% of the variance in some important criterion variable with four predictors is considerably more impressive than explaining 20% of the variance with 15 predictors. As a result, virtually all assessments of power in multiple regression will require information about both the number of subjects (N) and the number of predictor variables (p).

Hierarchical regression models. Bunce and West (1995) examined the role of personality factors (propensity to innovate, rule independence, intrinsic job motivation) and group climate factors (support for innovation, shared vision, task orientation, participation in decision making) in explaining innovation among health service workers. They carried out a 17-month, three-stage longitudinal study, and as with most longitudinal studies, suffered significant loss of data (subject mortality) across time. Their N dropped from 435 at stage 1 to 281 and 148 at stages 2 and 3. Incomplete data reduced the effective sample size for several analyses further; several critical analyses appear to be based on a set of 76 respondents.

One analysis used stage 1 innovation, personality factors, and group factors as predictors in a hierarchical regression model, where the dependent variable was innovation at stage 2. The results of this analysis are summarized in Table 5.2.

The principal hypotheses tested in this analysis were (1) personality accounts for variance in stage 2 innovation not explained by innovation at stage 1, and (2) group climate accounts for additional variance not accounted for by personality and stage 1 innovation. Because stage 1 innovation is entered first in the equation, you might interpret tests of the changes in R^2 after personality and climate are added to the equation as reflecting the influence of these factors on changes in innovation over time. The results suggest that personality has a significant effect, but that group climate

Table 5.2 Hierarchical Regression Results Reported in Bunce and West (1995)

Predictor	R^2	df	F	ΔR^2	df	F
Innovation (stage 1)	.18	1,75	16.73*			
Personality	.33	4,72	8.86*	.15	3,72	5.37*
Group Climate	.39	8,68	5.38*	.06	4,68	1.67

* $p < .05$ in tests of the traditional null hypothesis

does not account for variance above and beyond stage 1 innovation and personality.

Power estimation. The results in Table 5.2 show a pattern we have encountered in some of our previous examples, a relatively small sample combined with some reasonably large effects (e.g., stage 1 innovation accounts for 18% of the variance in stage 2 innovation), which makes it difficult to determine offhand whether the study will have enough power for its stated purpose. Some quick calculations suggests that this study does not possess sufficient power to test all of the hypotheses of interest.

Rather than starting from the reported R^2 and F values, suppose you used standard conventions for describing large, medium, and small effects to structure your power analysis. In hierarchical regression studies, the predictors are usually chosen to be relevant to the dependent variable (which means they should each be related to Y) and are therefore usually intercorrelated (i.e., several variables that are all related to Y are likely to also be related to one another). As a result, you will generally find that the first variable entered will yield a relatively large R^2 and that R^2 will not increase as quickly as more variables are entered (Cohen & Cohen, 1983). This might lead you to expect a large effect for the first variable you enter, a smaller change in R^2 for the next variable, and a smaller change in R^2 for the last variable. In Chapter 2, we noted that R^2 values of .25, .10, and .01 corresponded to conventional definitions of large, medium, and small effects (see Table 2.2). These values turn out to be reasonably similar to the actual R^2 and ΔR^2 values shown in Table 5.2 (i.e., .18, .15, and .06, respectively). Even more to the point, the overall R^2, which represents the sum of these conventional values (i.e., $R^2 = .36 = .25 + .10 + .01$) is very similar to the actual overall value (i.e., $R^2 = .39$) reported by Bunce & West (1995).

To estimate power for detecting R^2 values of .25, .10, and .01, given the degrees of freedom in this study, we first translate the R^2 values into F equivalents, using the equations shown in Table 2.1. The F equivalents are 25.0, 3.69, and .27, respectively. There is plenty of power for testing the hypothesis that $R^2 = .25$ [$F(1, 75) = 25.0$]; the critical tabled F for this level of power is 8.01. Even when testing the minimum-effect hypothesis that the first variable entered accounts for 5% or less of the variance, power far exceeds .80.

There is also a reasonable level of power for testing the hypothesis that the second variable entered into the regression equation will have a medium effect [i.e., $R^2 = .10$, $F(3, 72) = 3.69$]. Interpolating between values in the One-Stop F Table, you would achieve power of .80 with an F value of 3.79. The F here is quite close, and the power of this test is approximately .78.

If you assume that the third in a set of intercorrelated predictors will generally yield a small increment in R^2 (i.e., $\Delta R^2 = .01$), there is clearly not enough power to test that hypothesis. To achieve power of .50, you would need an F of 1.68; assuming a small effect here, F is only .27.

The conclusions reached by looking at these three conventional values closely mirror those that would be obtained if the actual R^2 values were used. The F values for the first predictor (stage 1 innovation), second predictor (personality), and third predictor (group climate) are 16.73, 5.37, and 1.67, respectively. Power easily exceeds .80 in tests of the hypothesis that stage 1 innovation is related to stage 2 innovation (the critical F for this level of power is 8.01). Power also exceeds .80 for testing the hypothesis that personality accounts for variance not explained by stage 1 innovation (the critical F is 3.79; the observed F is 5.37). Power is slightly less than .50 for testing the hypothesis that group climate accounts for variance not accounted for by the other two predictors (the critical F is 1.68; the observed F is 1.67).

Sample Size Estimation

The sample is certainly large enough to provide a powerful test of the hypothesis that stage 1 innovation predicts stage 2 innovation. Power is also reasonably high for testing the hypothesis that adding personality to the equation yields a significant increase in R^2. However, a *much* larger sample would be needed to provide a powerful test of the last hypothesis (i.e., that group climate explains additional variance). We used the Sample Size (df_{err}) Determination option of the One-Stop F Calculator to determine the number of subjects needed to attain power of .80 for a test of an increase in R^2 of .01. A sample of greater than 1,170 would be needed, nearly 15 times as large as the sample collected by Bunce and West (1995).

Power in Testing for Moderators

Many theories in the social behavior sciences take the form "X is related to Y, but the strength of this relationship depends on Z." This is a *moderated* relationship. For example, the relationship between cognitive ability and job performance is stronger for jobs that involve frequent and intense cognitive demands than for jobs that are relatively simple and not demanding (Gutenberg, Arvey, Osburn, & Jenneret, 1983). That is, job demands moderate the relationship between cognitive ability and job performance.

One of the most widely replicated findings in research on moderator effects is that studies that search for moderators often lack sufficient power to detect them (Osburn, Callender, Greener, & Ashworth, 1983; Sackett, Harris, & Orr, 1986). Once you understand how moderators are defined and assessed, it is easy to see why power can be so low in so many studies.

Suppose you think cognitive ability (X) is related to job performance (Y) and that this relationship is moderated by job complexity (Z). The best method of testing the hypothesis that Z moderates the relationship between X and Y is to first determine whether Y is related to both X and Z (e.g., is there a significant and meaningful correlation between ability and performance and between job complexity and performance?). Next, a series of regression models is compared. In particular, the test for moderation involves computing the cross-product between X and Z (i.e., multiply each person's ability score by his or her job complexity score—symbolized by $X \cdot Y$), then compare the following:

1. $R^2_{y.x, z}$ (i.e., the squared correlation between job performance and both ability and job complexity).
2. $R^2_{y.x, z.x\cdot z}$ (i.e., the squared correlation between job performance and ability, job complexity, and the cross-product between ability and job complexity).

If there is a real moderator effect, adding the cross-product to a regression equation that contains both ability and job complexity considered alone will lead to an increase in R^2. That is, considering ability and job complexity jointly will provide new information over and above what can be gained by considering these two factors separately; the statistical test for a moderator involves testing the hypothesis that adding cross-product terms leads to a significant and meaningful increase in R^2. For example, if $R^2_{y.x, z} = .30$ and $R^2_{y.x, z.x\cdot z} = .45$, this means that the joint consideration of ability and job complexity accounts for 15% of the variance in performance that cannot be accounted for by ability and job complexity considered alone.

The most compelling explanation for the traditionally low levels of power for testing moderator hypotheses is that large increases in R^2 when cross-products are added to a regression equation are rare, meaning that most moderator effects are fairly small. One of the recurring themes in power analysis, regardless of the statistical procedures being analyzed, is that small effects lead to low power unless samples are extremely large.

Why Are Most Moderator Effects Small?

There are statistical as well as substantive reasons to expect moderator effects to be small in most cases. In particular, the cross-product terms described above will almost always end up being highly correlated with the variables that were used to create this cross-product. For example, if the cross-product between ability and job complexity is used in testing for moderators, you should expect reasonably large correlations between ability and complexity considered alone and the cross-products between these two variables. If ability and complexity are positively correlated, the cross-product of these two variables *must* be highly correlated with the two variables considered alone.

As we noted in the preceding section, adding a new variable to a regression equation will always lead to some increase in R^2, but there is also a decreasing payoff in the sense each new variable that is added to a regression is likely to lead to increasingly small increases in R^2. In multiple regression, the increase in R^2 represents new information contributed by the variable added to the regression equation, and when the new variable to the regression (e.g., $x \cdot z$) is correlated with variables already in the regression equation (e.g., both x and z considered alone), it is quite unlikely that it will add a great deal of new information. Even in situations where there are very strong moderator effects (i.e., where the relationship between X and Y changes substantially depending on the value of Z), it is uncommon to find large increases in R^2.

Power Analysis for Moderators

Suppose you collected data from 500 employees in a range of jobs and correlated ability and performance scores. If you had highly reliable measures of ability and job performance, it would be reasonable to find ability–performance correlations in the range of .35 to .60, with an average of approximately .50. This translates into an R^2 value of .25. A sample of $N = 500$ provides plenty of power for testing the hypothesis that ability is related to performance. For example, if you enter 0, .05, .99, 1, and 498 into the ES, alpha, power, df_{hyp}, and df_{err} boxes of the Power Analysis section of the One-Stop F Calculator, you will find that you can achieve power of .99 with an R^2 value as low as .031. If you add job complexity to the regression equation, it is reasonable to expect an increase in R^2 of approximately .05 to .10. If you enter 0, .05, .99, 1, and 497 into the ES, alpha, power, df_{hyp}, and df_{err} boxes of the Power Analysis section of the One-Stop F Calculator, you will again find that you can achieve power of .99. If you add the cross-products of ability and job complexity into that regression equation, you might expect an increase in R^2 of approximately .005 to .01. The Sample Size

(df_{err}) Determination option of the One-Stop F Calculator suggests you would need a sample of well over 1,500 employees to detect a change of .005 in R^2. Even if the change is a large as .01, you would still need a sample of more than 750 employees.

A sample of $N = 500$ is relatively large, compared with the typical samples obtained in behavioral and social science research; depending on the topic, samples of 50 to 200 subjects are common. However, this sample is not large enough to provide a powerful test of the moderator hypothesis unless the moderator effect is an unusually strong one.

Implications of Low Power in Tests for Moderators

Sometimes the relationships between variables are truly simple, but many relationships are complicated by the existence of moderator variables. For example, as noted above, the complexity of jobs moderates the relationship between cognitive ability and job performance. Ability is always positively related to performance, but that relationship is stronger in complex jobs than in simpler jobs. As a result, the best answer to the question, "What is the correlation between ability and job performance?" is "It depends on the complexity of the job."

The low power of most tests for moderators has potentially important effects on research and applications of research in the behavioral and social sciences (Osburn et al., 1983; Sackett et al., 1986). In particular, lack of power in a search for moderators may lead researchers to underestimate the complexity of their data. For example, prior to Gutenberg et al.'s (1983) study showing that job complexity was a moderator of the ability–performance relationship, many researchers assumed that validity was invariant (i.e., that the validity of ability tests was identical across most if not all jobs). This was not necessarily because of the lack of variability in outcomes across jobs, but rather because of the lack of power in studies searching for moderators. Similarly, researchers sometimes assume that the tests they use are unbiased because tests of the hypothesis that sex, race, age, or other demographic characteristics of test takers do not moderate the relationships between test scores and important criteria. Unless very large samples are used, tests of the hypothesis that demographic variables moderate the effects of tests often have insufficient power, and the failure to identify moderators may say more about the quality of the study than about the lack of bias of the test. In general, the conclusion that any relationship between two variables in invariant may be difficult to test because it can be very demanding to put together powerful tests of the hypothesis that moderator variables exist.

Summary

Power analyses are easily applied to studies that use correlation and regression. The power of a statistical test always depends on three factors: sample size, alpha, and effect size. Because the squared correlation coefficient is an effect size measure (i.e., it is identical to *PV*), the process of applying power analysis in this context is unusually straightforward.

Our analysis of a correlational study that used very large samples illustrates the potential folly of using traditional nil hypothesis tests to evaluate the importance and meaning of study results. In the McDaniel (1988) study, all the correlations between pre-employment drug tests and employment outcomes were significant, but none was very large. This study also illustrates the advantages of testing a minimum-effects hypothesis. If you define a trivially small relationship between X and Y as one in which X accounts for less than 1% of the variance in Y (leaving at least 99% unexplained), none of the correlations examined in this section would be thought of as meaningful. If you test the null hypothesis that the relationship between pre-employment drug tests and employment outcomes is trivially small, you will find that you *cannot* reject this null hypothesis. These correlations *are* trivially small, at least by this definition.

Applications of power analysis to a variety of multiple regression applications suggest that it is often easy to test the hypothesis that one or two variables predict Y, but that it becomes increasingly difficult to test the hypothesis that other variables add new information once the first few reasonable predictors of Y are taken into account. Because most of the variables that are likely to be included in a regression equation are almost certain to be positively intercorrelated, it becomes increasingly hard for each new variable to add information to the prediction of Y over and above whatever information is already present in the regression equation. This has serious implications for tests of moderator hypotheses because the essence of the test for moderation is that the cross-product of two variables (e.g., X and Z) contains information that is not contained by X alone or Z alone. Because of the typically high levels of correlation between X, Z, and the cross-product of X and Z, it is unusual to find that adding the cross-product of X and Z to a regression equation that already contains both X and Z as individual variables will lead to large increases in R^2. In other words, moderator effects tend to be fairly small, and it is very difficult to achieve high levels of power in studies where small effects are expected.

6

t-Tests and the Analysis of Variance

▼ ▼ ▼ ▼ ▼

One of the most common applications of statistics in the behavioral and social sciences is the comparison of means obtained from different treatments, different groups, or different measurements. For example, there are thousands of studies published each year that involve comparisons between a treatment group that has received some sort of intervention or special treatment and a control group that has not received this intervention. Other comparisons might involve assessing differences between scores obtained prior to some treatment or intervention (pre-test) with scores obtained subsequent to that treatment (post-test). Still other comparisons might contrast the average scores across several groups that receive different treatments or combinations of treatments.

The *t*-Test

The *t*-test is commonly used to compare one group or one set of scores with another. For example, 200 subjects might be randomly assigned to treatment and control groups; the independent *t*-test can be used to statistically compare these average scores. Alternately, pre-test and post-test scores might be collected from the same set of 200 subjects; repeated measures or dependent *t*-tests can be used to compare these scores. Finally, this same *t*-statistic can be used to compare the mean in a sample with some fixed or reference value. For example, you might have the hypothesis that the average SAT Critical Reasoning score in a sample is equal to the population mean of 500. This one-sample *t*-test is rarely encountered in the behavioral and social sciences; therefore, our discussion will focus for the most part on the independent and the dependent *t*-tests.

Table 6.1 Degrees of Freedom for the *t*-Statistic

Type of Test	Test Compares	df
One-sample	Sample mean to some fixed value	$N - 1$
Independent *t*	Two sample means	$(n_1 - 1) + (n_2 - 1)$ or $N - 2$
Dependent *t*	Two scores from the same set of people	$N - 1$

N = Number of individuals in sample
n = Number of individuals in each independent group

As with other test statistics, the evaluation of a *t*-statistic involves comparing the observed value of *t* with the critical value of *t* for the null hypothesis being tested. The critical value of *t*, in turn depends on three things: the type of hypothesis being tested (e.g., traditional nil versus minimum-effect test), the alpha level, and the degrees of freedom.

The degrees of freedom for the three different types of *t*-tests are listed in Table 6.1.

It is not always clear why different tests have different degrees of freedom, but if you keep in mind what each test compares, it is easier to see why, for example, the one-sample test has different degrees of freedom from the two-sample test. In a one-sample test, the scores of N people are used to estimate a population mean. Using our previous example, if you compare the mean in a sample of N students who took the SAT Critical Reasoning test to the overall average score this test is designed to yield (i.e., a score of 500), the degrees of freedom are $N - 1$ because there is only one sample statistic being used to estimate its corresponding population parameter. That is, the hypothesis you are testing is that the mean score *in the population you sampled from* is 500. In the two-sample test, there are n subjects in both the treatment and control group, and scores in these samples are used to estimate the means in the populations each group represents, yielding $(n - 1)$ degrees of freedom within each group, or $(n - 1) + (n - 1) = N - 2$ degrees of freedom for the study. In a dependent *t*-test, where the same N people provide both sets of scores to be compared, the hypothesis being tested is that Post-test − Pre-test = 0. There are N measures of this pre/post difference, yielding $N - 1$ degrees of freedom for estimating the population difference between pre-tests and post-tests.

In very small samples, a *t*-table is often used in assessing statistical significance; for samples of 60 or more, the distribution of the *t*-statistic is very similar to a standard normal distribution. Thus, for example, the critical value for a two-tailed *t*-test with df = 100 is 1.96. Rather than relying on the *t*-distribution, it is both easy and useful to convert *t* to *F*, by simply squaring the value of *t*. In particular, $t^2(df_{err}) = F(1, df_{err})$. Throughout this text, we have noted that converting to F simplifies power analysis, something that is trivially easy to do when working with the t-test.

Suppose 100 subjects are randomly assigned to either a treatment designed to increase reading speed or a control group. A researcher compares the means for these two groups and reports $t(98) = 2.22$. This translates into $F(1, 98) = 4.94$; applying the F to PV conversion formula of Equation 2.7 $PV = (df_{hyp} \cdot F)/[(df_{hyp} \cdot F) + df_{err}]$ you find:

$$PV = (1 \cdot 4.94)/[(1 \cdot 4.94) + 98] = .05$$

This is both a relatively small sample and a relatively small effect, suggesting that the level of power in this study will be low. The One-Stop F Table confirms this. The F needed to achieve power levels of .50 and .80 are 3.85 and 7.95, respectively. The observed F is between these two values, and the level of power for this study is .58.

Independent Groups t-Test

Suppose a researcher is interested in comparing the outcomes of two different programs designed to help people quit smoking. The researcher thinks that a good study can be done using 50 subjects (25 randomly assigned to each treatment). Power analysis might lead this researcher to rethink that assumption.

Estimating power for this study. Suppose the researcher chooses to test a traditional null hypothesis, using an alpha level of .05. She is not sure whether there will be large or small differences between the programs, and performs a power analysis that assumes small treatment effect (e.g., $PV = .01$). In the t-test, there is 1 degree of freedom for the hypothesis being tested (i.e., df_{hyp}). The degrees of freedom for error (see Table 6.1) are:

$$df_{err} = n_1 + n_2 - 2$$
$$df_{err} = 25 + 25 - 2$$
$$df_{err} = 48$$

To determine whether the proposed study has sufficient power, use the "Power Analysis" frame on the One-Stop F Calculator and enter 0.0 for ES, .05 for alpha, 1 for df_{hyp}, and 48 for df_{err}. In order to achieve a power of .80, you would need fairly strong effect (i.e., $PV = .14$), much larger than the small effect that the researcher assumed. The study this investigator has planned has very low power. If you enter .50 for power in this section of the One-Stop F Calculator, you will find that you still need a moderately large effect (i.e., $PV = .079$) to achieve this low level of power. If you keep entering smaller estimates of power, you will eventually find that if there truly is a small effect in the population (i.e., $PV = .01$), a sample of $N = 50$ will achieve power of .105. That is, if there truly is a small difference between these two programs, the odds are about 1 in 10 that your study will find it, and about 9 in 10 that your study will miss it. If the investigator had reason to believe that PV was equal to .10 as opposed to .01, power would have been much higher (with $N = 50$ and $PV = .10$, power is .615); but if the assumption of a small effect is a reasonable one, this study is grossly under-powered.

Determining an Appropriate Sample Size

The power analysis conducted above shows that the researcher was much too optimistic about the possibility of detecting a small difference between two approaches to reducing smoking using a sample of $N = 50$. To determine the sample size needed for a study such as this, two different approaches might be followed. First, you can use the One-Stop F Calculator. Second, you can use the table presented in this book to estimate the sample size required to reach an acceptable level of power.

If you assume that there is a small difference between programs (i.e., $PV = .01$) and that you desire power of .80 for tests of the traditional null hypothesis, you can use the One-Stop F Calculator to determine the sample size that will be required. Using the Sample Size (df_{err}) determination section of the calculator, enter 0.0 for ES, .8 for power, .05 for alpha, 1 for df_{hyp}, and .01 for PV. You will find that you need a sample of 755 subjects to achieve this level of power (the calculator shows $df_{err} = 753$, which is equal to $N - 2$, so $N = 755$).

Alternately, you could use the df_{err} Table presented in Appendix D. This table shows that when $PV = .01$ and $df_{hyp} = 1$, the df_{err} required to achieve power of .80 is 775. You might note that this is not exactly the same value as the one provided by the One-Stop F Calculator in the example above, although it is quite close. As we noted earlier in this book, virtually all power calculations are estimates, usually based on broad assumptions (e.g., that $PV = .01$), and the precise assumptions of different calculations are not always identical. The small differences provided by alternate calculations are not important, in part because power analysis is almost always more concerned with providing useful rough estimates than with providing precise answers, and regardless of which value one used, the same conclusion would be reached (i.e., that a *much* larger sample would be needed to provide adequate power).

Traditional Versus Minimum-Effect Tests

Clapp and Rizk (1992) measured placental volumes in 18 healthy women who maintained a regular routine of exercise during pregnancy. Nine women engaged in aerobics, four ran, and five swam. The control group comprised 16 females who did not engage in such a regimen. Placental volumes were measured using modern ultrasound techniques at 16, 20, and 24 weeks gestation. Results of the study are reproduced in Table 6.2.

Two aspects of this study are especially noteworthy. First, the sample is small ($N = 34$). In most cases, this would mean very low power levels. However, in this study the effects are quite strong. In the three time periods studied, exercise accounted for between 29% and 47% of the variance in placental volume (d ranges from 1.71 to 2.41). Because the apparent effects of exercise were quite substantial, it should be easy to rule out the hypothesis that the treatment had no effect (traditional null), or even that the true effects of exercise are at best small (minimum-effect hypothesis).

The t-test in this study has 32 degrees of freedom; if it is squared, the statistic is distributed as F with 1 and 32 degrees of freedom. If you consult the the One-Stop F Table, you will find entries for 1 and 30 and 1 and 40 degrees of freedom, but none for 1 and 32 degrees of freedom, meaning that you must interpolate to analyze these results. As can be seen in the One-Stop F Table, critical F values for the traditional null hypothesis at 1 and 30 degrees of freedom for $\alpha = .05$ and $.01$ are 4.16 and 7.56, respectively. The corresponding values at 1 and 40 degrees of freedom are 4.08 and 7.31. Using Equation 2.10, the $\alpha = .05$ and $.01$ critical values for 1 and 32 degrees of freedom when testing the traditional null hypothesis are 4.14 and 7.51, respectively. All of the observed F values in Table 6.2 are greater than 7.51,

Table 6.2 Placental Volumes Reported by Clapp and Rizk (1992)

Week	Control (*N* = 16)	Treatment (*N* = 18)	*t*	*F*	*PV*	*d*
16	106 (18)	141 (34)	3.68	13.55	.29	1.94
20	186 (46)	265 (67)	3.96	15.66	.33	1.71
24	270 (58)	410 (87)	5.45	29.66	.47	2.41

Note: Volumes are expressed in cm³. Standard deviations are shown in parentheses. Note that in this table *d* represents the mean difference divided by the control group SD. Use of pooled SD values yields somewhat smaller *d* values, but they will nevertheless exceed conventional benchmarks for "large" effects.

so we can reject the traditional null at the .01 level and conclude that regular exercise has *some* impact on placental volume.

You can conclusively rule out the possibility that exercise has *no* effect, and the data suggest that the actual effect is quite large. However, it is always possible that the *true* effect is small and that the large *PV* and *d* values observed here represent chance fluctuations in a process that usually produces only a small effect. You can use the One-Stop *F* Table to test the hypothesis that the effects of treatments are negligible, or perhaps small to moderate. Again, using Equation 2.10 to interpolate, the critical *F* (α = .05) for the minimum-effect null hypothesis that the effect is small to medium in size (i.e., the null is that treatments account for no more than 5% of the variance in outcomes) is 9.52. All *F* values in Table 6.1 exceed 9.52, so we can reject the minimum-effect null hypothesis that the effects of treatments are no greater than small to moderate, with a 95% level of confidence. We can also reject this hypothesis at the .01 level for mean placental volumes at 20 and 24 weeks (critical *F* = 15.26; observed *F* = 15.66 and 29.44 at 20 and 24 weeks, respectively). That is, we can be at least 99% confident that the effects of treatments exceed our definition of *small to moderate*.

Power estimation. Assume, as the results of this study suggest, that the effects of maternal exercise on placental volume are substantial (e.g., exercise accounts for 25% of the variance in placental volume). If this assumption is true, this study possesses very high levels of power for rejecting the traditional null. With 1 and 32 degrees of freedom, an effect size of *PV* = .25 has an *F*-equivalent value of 10.66. The critical *F* for achieving a power of .80 at α = .05 in this study is 8.3. The power to reject the hypothesis that treatments account for less than 1% of the variance in the population is also well in excess of .80; the critical *F* for power of .80 in testing this minimum-effect hypothesis is 10.12. Using the Calculate Power for a Completed Study option in the One-Stop *F* Calculator, we estimate power to be at least .91 for these tests.

In addition to placental volume, Clapp and Rizk (1992) examined a range of other dependent variables for the women in this study. If exercise could function as a viable treatment of fetal under- or overgrowth, we might expect it to have some effect on the final birth weight of the babies as well. In this case, Clapp and Rizk reported the mean birth weight of babies for women in the control group as 3,553 g (SD = 309) compared with 3,408 g (SD = 445) for women in the treatment group. Reference to the One-Stop *F* Table shows that even when testing hypotheses about birth weight, you cannot reject the traditional null hypothesis [*F*(1, 32) = 1.19, *p* < .05].

One possible explanation for this finding is low power. If the true effect of exercise on birth weight (as opposed to placental volume) is small, power will be well less than .50 in this study. For example, if we assume that the true effect of exercise on birth weight meets the conventional definition for a small effect (i.e., $PV = .01$), the F equivalent in this study is less than .32, whereas the critical F for a power of .50 to reject the traditional null at the .05 level is 4.03. Thus the power of this study to detect traditionally significant differences in birth weight is much less than .50 (approximately .18 in fact). Of course the power to detect substantively meaningful differences is even lower.

Sample size estimation. How many subjects would be required to reliably detect differences in birth weight as a result of exercise during pregnancy? In order to answer this question you can refer to Appendices D and E, which allow you to determine sample sizes needed, given that $\alpha = .05$ and the desired level of power is .80. If you assume that the effect of exercise on birth weight is small ($PV = .01$, $d = .20$), you will need appromixmately 777 subjects in total (i.e., $N = df_{hyp} + df_{err} + 1$; for the t-test, $df_{hyp} = 1$) or appromixmately 389 subjects in each group (i.e., 777/2) to achieve this level of power in tests of the traditional null hypothesis.

The power analyses conducted here suggest that the Clapp and Rizk (1992) study was well suited for answering questions about the effect of exercise on placental volume, which was its major focus. Power exceeded .80 for tests of both traditional and minimum-effect null hypotheses. However, the sample size is quite inadequate for answering questions about the effects of exercise on birth weight. Because a small effect might reasonably be expected here, huge samples are probably needed to provide adequate power.

One-Tailed Versus Two-Tailed Tests

In the two examples above, the null hypothesis being tested was that there were no differences between treatments or conditions, or that the differences were trivially small (e.g., accounted for less than 1% of the variance in outcomes). This represents a two-tailed statistical test because differences in programs will lead you to reject the null regardless of the direction of the difference. For example, in Clapp and Rizk (1992), you would reject the null hypothesis if subjects in the treatment condition had higher scores than those in the control condition but would also reject the same null hypothesis if subjects in the control condition ended up with higher scores. This type of test is most common in the behavioral and social sciences, and it is called a two-tailed test because score differences at either end of the distribution (i.e., large positive differences or large negative differences) will cause you to reject the null hypothesis.

Sometimes, researchers have specific directional hypotheses (e.g., that scores in the treatment group are *higher* than scores in the control group). These one-tailed tests are more powerful than their two-tailed counterparts and are preferable in many circumstances. The key to working with one-tailed tests is that doubling the alpha level of a two-tailed test allows you to determine the critical values, power, sample size needed, etc., of a one-tailed test. That is, results you obtained from analysis of the power of two-tailed tests at the $\alpha = .10$ level would be identical to those obtained for one-tailed tests at the $\alpha = .05$ level. The One-Stop F Calculator is particularly useful for working with one-tailed tests because it allows you to enter in virtually any alpha value you want.

Re-Analysis of Smoking Reduction Treatments: One-Tailed Tests

The analyses presented earlier in this chapter were based on the assumption that two-tailed tests were being performed (i.e., that two interventions designed to reduce smoking were being compared), without specifying *a priori* which one was likely to work better. Suppose the researcher had a good reason to believe that one treatment was indeed better. There would be substantial advantages to using one-tailed rather than two-tailed tests.

First, with degrees of freedom of 1 and 48 for the hypothesis being tested, power analysis for one-tailed tests, with $\alpha = .05$ would be performed by using an alpha level of .10 when entering data into the One-Stop F Calculator. If the true differences between programs is small (e.g., assume that the true $PV = .01$), power would still be quite low with only 50 subjects. Choose the Power Analysis option and enter 0.0 for the ES, .10 for alpha, and 1 and 48 for df_{hyp} and df_{err}, respectively. If you enter .80 for the desired power level, you will find that a much larger effect ($PV = .11$) would be needed to reach that level of power. If you enter increasingly lower levels of desired power, you will eventually find that this study achieves power of about .18 in a one-tailed test (versus power of .11 for a two-tailed test). Using the Sample Size (df_{err}) Estimation option, you will find that you need a sample of $N = 585$ to achieve power of .80 in one-tailed tests of this null hypothesis (with a two-tailed test, $N = 755$ is required).

Repeated Measures or Dependent *t*-Test

Suppose 50 students take a pre-test designed to measure their knowledge of American history. They then go through a training program and complete a post-test measure of history knowledge three weeks later. One of the key

Table 6.3 Pre-Test and Post-Test Comparison

	Pre-Test	Post-Test
Mean	110	116
SD	20	18

Note: The correlation between pre-test and post-test scores is .40, $t = 3.14$, $d = .315$.

assumptions of the two-sample *t*-test is that the scores being compared are obtained from independent samples, and that certainly is not the case in studies that rely on the dependent *t*-test. Rather, it is best to assume that multiple scores obtained from the same people (either on pre- and post-versions of the same measure or on two distinct measures) are correlated, and this correlation affects both the structure of the significance test and the power of that test.

Table 6.3 presents the means and standard deviations for the pre- and post-test scores, as well as the correlation between pre and post. The formula for the dependent *t* is

$$t = \frac{\text{Mean } 1 - \text{Mean } 2}{\sqrt{\dfrac{\text{var } 1}{N} + \dfrac{\text{var } 2}{N} - \dfrac{2r_{12}SD_1SD_2}{N}}} \tag{6.1}$$

where

Mean 1, var 1, SD_1 are mean, variance, and standard deviation of first measure

Mean 2, var 2, SD_2 are mean, variance, and standard deviation of second measure

Equation 6.1 presents a general formula for the *t*-test. When the means of independent groups are compared, the correlation between scores is necessarily equal to zero, and Equation 6.1 reduces to the more familiar formula for *t* presented below:

$$t = \frac{\text{Mean } 1 - \text{Mean } 2}{\sqrt{\dfrac{\text{var } 1}{N} + \dfrac{\text{var } 2}{N}}} \tag{6.2}$$

In our example of pre-test/post-test comparisons, the difference between means is relatively small ($d = .315$), and the sample is also relatively small, but because of the increased power provided by a repeated-measures design, this difference is nevertheless statistically significant. In Chapter 7, we discuss repeated measures designs for comparing any number of scores (the dependent *t* can only be used to compare two different scores) and will show a more general version of the dependent *t*-test that is based directly on the analysis of variance and the *F*-statistic. We will hold our discussions of power analysis for research designs that involve repeated measures until that chapter. We will, however, note something that might be obvious from examining Equation 6.1. The larger the correlation between the two measures being compared, the smaller the standard error of the difference between means, and therefore the higher the power of statistical comparisons.

The Analysis of Variance

The analysis of variance (ANOVA) is widely used in the social and behavioral sciences and is often the method of choice for analyzing data from psychological experiments. Students sometimes find the term *analysis of variance*, confusing because this method is often used to test the null hypothesis that the means obtained from different groups or under different conditions are all identical, as opposed to the alternate hypothesis that some group means are different from others. This suggests that a more apt term might be *analysis of means*. In fact, *analysis of variance* is a very good term because the principal goal of this method of analysis it to help us understand why scores vary. In a traditional experiment, where subjects are randomly assigned to one of several treatments, ANOVA is used to determine how important differences between treatment means are for understanding the data obtained from an experiment. If treatments explain a substantial portion of the variance in scores, we might conclude that treatment effects are large and important. On the other hand, it is possible (particularly if the number of subjects is large) to conclude that there are significant differences between the means obtained in different treatments, even though the overall amount of variance explained by treatment effects is quite small.

The analysis of variance provides both significance tests and effect size measures. Significance testing is done using the *F* statistic, making the application of the models developed in this book (all of which are based on the noncentral *F* distribution) especially easy. Analysis of variance also provides an effect size measure, eta-squared, which represents the proportion of variance (i.e., *PV*) explained by differences between groups of treatments. Again, this effect size measure fits neatly and easily into the frameworks presented here, most of which revolve around *F* and *PV*.

The simplest application of ANOVA is called a one-way analysis of variance, in which there are two or more treatments or conditions that subjects might be assigned to and in which the main focus is to determine how much of the variability in scores can be explained by the different treatments. This one-way analysis of variance is closely related to the independent-groups t-test, in that the t-test is used to compare scores in two groups or conditions, whereas the analysis of variance is used to compare average scores in any number of treatments. When there are only two groups, the one-way analysis of variance can be used in place of the t-test; as we noted earlier, the F-statistic that is used in significance in ANOVA is obtained simply by squaring the value of t. More complex analyses, which are discussed later in this chapter and in the chapters that follow, will allow us to ask a wider array of questions, but there is often considerable utility in asking the simple question: "How important are the different treatments or conditions in explaining variability in subjects' scores?" The one-way analysis of variance asks this question.

Suppose an investigator randomly assigns 60 rats to one of three groups. All rats run through a straight alley (runway) once a day for a total of 30 days. Rats in the first group are given a small reward for each run through the runway. Rats in the second group are given a medium-sized reward for each run through the runway. Rats in the third group are given a large reward for each run through the runway. One hour after a given rat runs through the runway, each rat is given additional food. The total food per day for all rats is the same. That is, the additional food for the small-sized reward rats is more than the additional food for the medium-sized reward rats. The additional food for medium-sized reward rats is more than the additional food for large-sized reward rats.

At the end of 30 days, training is completed, and each rat is given one last trial running through the alley; the time it takes each rat to make it to the end of the alley is recorded. The question here is whether the magnitude of reward during training will affect the dependent variable (time to run).

Table 6.4 reports the results of an analysis of variance conducted on data from this experiment.

In this table, df represents the degrees of freedom for the hypothesis being tested and error (in one-way ANOVA, $df_{hyp} = k - 1$, where k represents the number of means being compared, and $df_{err} = N - k$), SS represents the sum of the squared deviations attributable to differences in treatment means and to variability within each of the treatment groups (which is used to estimate error), and MS represents mean squares (MS = SS/df) for treatment and error effects. These mean squares are sample estimates of variance in

Table 6.4 ANOVA Results for the Rat Running Study

Source	df	SS	MS	F	Eta²
Magnitude of reward	2	32	16.0	1.34	.045
Error	57	678	11.89		
Total	59	710			

the population that can be explained by group differences and by error (the variance is computed by taking the average of the squared deviations from the mean; hence, the term *mean square*).

Eta-squared (SS for the hypothesis divided by SS total) provides an estimate of the proportion of variance accounted for by differences between groups; the implication of finding that differences between groups account for 4.5% of the variance in scores is that the lion's share of variance (95.5%) is explained by something other than differences in the magnitude of rewards these rats received during training. The *F* ratio is calculated by dividing the mean square for differences between groups by the mean square for error (i.e., $F = MS_{hyp}/MS_{err} = 16.0/11.89 = 1.34$). In this study, an *F* value of approximately 3.15 would be needed to reject the null hypothesis that differences in reward have no effect whatsoever, meaning that the effect here is nonsignificant.

Power analysis. The sample was not very large, and one likely explanation for the nonsignificant finding is that power is low. Using the Calculate Power for a Completed Study option of the One-Stop *F* Calculator, enter 0.0 for ES (traditional null hypothesis), .05 for alpha, 1.34 for *F*, and 2 and 57 for df_{hyp} and df_{error}, respectively. You will find that this study has power of .26. Using the Sample Size (df_{err}) Determination option, if you enter .80 as the desired power level and .045 as the *PV* value, you will find that this study will require 206 rats (i.e., $df_{err} = 203$) to achieve power of .80. If you make the conservative assumption that in the population *PV* = .01 (i.e., assume that there is a small effect), you will need 936 rats to achieve this level of power.

Retrieving Effect Size Information From *F* Ratios

Unfortunately, many studies report the outcomes of significance tests without presenting the more important information about effect sizes. In the one-way ANOVA, it is quite easy to translate information about significance to information about effect size. In Chapter 2, we presented a formula (Equation 2.7) that bears repeating:

$$PV = (df_{hyp} \cdot F)/[(df_{hyp} \cdot F) + df_{err}]$$

As we noted in Chapter 2, this formula cannot be used for complex ANOVAs, but it is perfect for the one-way analysis of variance. Suppose two studies report nonsignificant results, the first reporting $F(1, 500) = 3.52$, and the second reporting $F(1, 32) = 3.70$. Would you regard the results in these two studies as similar?

If you compute *PV*, you will find that differences between groups explained 6/10 of 1 percent of the variance in the first study, but 10.3% of the variance in the second. You might still pay attention to the fact that neither study produced significant results, but the most reasonable interpretation of these data is that the first study is dealing with a truly miniscule effect (with over 500 cases, there would be plenty of power to detect nontrivial effects), whereas the second study simply lacks the power needed to detect even moderately strong effects. These do not look like similar findings once effect size information is taken into account.

Which Means Differ?

A significant *F* in the one-way analysis of variance indicates that the null hypothesis that all means are identical can be rejected, but it does not necessarily tell you which means are and which are not reliably different. A variety of procedures has been developed to provide a more detailed follow-up in studies that report significant differences between treatment means.

The least significant difference (LSD) procedure. Suppose an investigator performs an ANOVA for an experiment in which there are three different treatments and obtains a statistically significant *F*. Knowing that ANOVA asks the global question of whether there are any differences between treatments, the investigator decides to use *t*-tests to compare all possible pairs of treatments, provided the *F* in ANOVA is statistically significant, and decides to use the same alpha level (e.g., .05) for all comparisons. This can easily be done using the LSD procedure, which involves computing the smallest difference in treatment group means that will be judged to be statistically significant, using the formula:

$$\text{LSD} = t_{\alpha/2[\text{df}_{\text{error}}]}\sqrt{\frac{2\text{MSE}}{k}} \qquad (6.3)$$

where

t = Square root of the value of *F* needed to achieve significance for 1 and df_{err} degrees of freedom at the $\alpha/2$ level

MSE = Mean square error

k = Number of groups

The *t*-value used in this formula is simply the square root of the *F* needed to achieve statistical significance with the degrees of freedom of 1 and df_{err} for an alpha level twice as high as the desired alpha for each comparison. The One-Stop *F* Calculator can be used to find the value of *F* needed to reach statistical significance at the .10 level for df 1 and 57. This *F* (obtained using the Significance Testing option) is 2.79, so the equivalent *t* is 1.67 (the square root of 2.79).

Power for the LSD Procedure. When power is calculated for the LSD procedure, the Calculate Power for a Completed Study with a Selected Alpha option of the One-Stop *F* Calculator can be used. Simply enter 0.0 for the ES (traditional null hypothesis), .05 for alpha, the *F* ratio that is equivalent of *t* in Equation 6.3 (in the example above, *F* = 2.79), and the values of df_{hyp} and df_{err} (here, 1 and 57). In this study, power is disappointingly low (power = .358), suggesting that if the investigator is seriously interested in comparing individuals means, a good deal more data are needed.

Ryan's procedure. There are a number of alternatives to the LSD, many of which were designed to address the potential inflation of Type I error that results from conducting many different tests. As we have noted in several earlier chapters, the likelihood of Type I errors is much lower than most people think, especially when tests of the traditional null hypothesis are conducted. Nevertheless, it is useful to describe at least one of the methods that attempts to deal with uncertainty about error rates.

An investigator who wants to make the entire experiment the conceptual unit for all statistical tests can use Ryan's (1962) procedure. Ryan's procedure is a stairstep procedure in which potential *t*-tests are performed until the procedure indicates no further *t*-tests need to be calculated. Each individual test is conducted using an alpha level that provides an overall alpha level of .05 for the experiment as a whole.

Consider the experiment with four groups. Assume that a traditional null hypothesis with an alpha level of .05 is used. Further assume that df_{err} is 300 and means for the four groups are M1 = 55, M2 = 23, M3 = 91, M4 = 12. The *F* ratio ANOVA must be statistically significant before any means can be compared using Ryan's procedure. Suppose here that $F(3, 300) = 10.0$, which is easily significant.

Once a significant *F* is established, groups are ordered from the group with the lowest mean to the group with the highest mean: M4, M2, M1, M3. The first *t*-test compares group 4 (lowest mean) and group 3 (highest mean). Figure 6.1 shows the four means ordered from lowest to highest mean. Figure 6.1 also shows the four steps between the lowest mean (M4) and the highest mean (M3).

The first *t*-test compares the means that are farthest away from one another, here M4 and M3, which are four steps apart. In order to preserve an overall alpha level of .05, the alpha levels for specific tests need to be adjusted. The "corrected" alpha level (alpha') for this test is

Order Means Used in Ryans Procedure

Steps	1	2	3	4
	M4	M2	M1	M3
	12	23	55	91

Figure 6.1   Order means used in Ryans procedure.

$$\text{alpha}' = \frac{2\alpha}{J(R-1)} \qquad (6.4)$$

where

J = Number of groups
R = Number of steps between the two means
Alpha' in this example is $[(2 \cdot .05)/(4 \cdot (4-1))] = .0083$.

The Significance Testing option of the One-Stop F Calculator can be used to determine the critical value of F for the t-test. Enter 0.0 for ES, .008 for alpha, and 1 and 300 for df_{hyp} and df_{err}, and you will find that the critical value of F for significance testing is $F = 7.12$. The F from ANOVA was greater than 7.12 (the reported F value was 10.0), which means you can reject the null hypothesis that M4 does not differ from M3. Note that you should report that M4 differs from M3 at the .05 level, not the .0083 level.

If the first t-test (M4 versus M3) was not statistically significant, no further t-tests would be performed. If the first t-test is statistically significant, two more t-tests are justified. In Figure 6.1, there are two sets of means that are three steps removed from each other, M4 and M1 and M2 and M3. The corrected alpha' for both of these t-tests is once again given by equation 6.4 (i.e., alpha' = $[(2 \cdot .05)/(4 \cdot (3-1))] = .0125$).

The Significance Testing option is once again used to determine the critical value of F for the two t-tests, by entering 0.0 for ES, .012 for alpha, and 1 and 300 for df_{hyp} and df_{err}. This critical value is $F = 6.38$, which allows you to reject the null hypotheses that M4 does not differ from M1 and that M2 does not differ from M3.

If means that are three steps apart are significantly different, t-tests are justified for means that are two steps apart (e.g., M3 versus M1, M4 versus M2, and M2 versus M1), and finally, significant results at two steps justify comparisons of adjacent means. Note that the critical value for F becomes less stringent as the investigator tests means that are closer together in terms of number of steps. Also note that it is harder to find statistical significance for all t-tests with Ryan's procedure as opposed to the LSD procedure.

Power can be calculated for each of the *t*-tests performed with Ryan's procedure, using the "Calculate Power for a Completed Study With a Selected Alpha Level option, by entering 0.0 for ES, the alpha' value, the *F* equivalent of *t* for the *t*-test, 1 and 300 degrees of freedom. Of course Ryan's procedure can be adapted for use with minimum-effect hypotheses, by simply entering the appropriate ES when using the One-Stop *F* Calculator.

Summary

Many studies in the behavioral and social sciences revolve around comparisons between the average scores received in treatment and control groups. The independent-groups *t*-test is widely used and, unfortunately, often applied in studies with too little power. Another common comparison made in social science research is between different measurements (e.g., pre-tests versus post-tests) obtained from the same individuals. The dependent *t*-test offers more power but also more complexity than the more common independent-groups test; both complexity and power are a direct result of the fact that the measures being compared are likely to be correlated.

The analysis of variance represents a more flexible and general version of the statistical procedures that underlie the *t*-test. The *t*-test compares two scores, whereas ANOVA allow you to compare scores from any number of groups or treatments (including two). ANOVA is particularly well suited for the models presented in this book because it is built around the *F* test and around effect size measures that indicate the percentage of variance explained by treatments—in particular, eta-squared. Several applications of power analysis in the analysis of variance were presented and discussed. Finally, it is common in ANOVA to plan and conduct detailed follow-up tests. ANOVA tells you whether all means are the same or whether some differ from others, but does not tell you which treatments produce reliably different outcomes. Power analyses for procedures used to examine comparisons of specific sets of treatments or conditions have been presented and discussed.

7

Multifactor ANOVA Designs

▼ ▼ ▼ ▼ ▼

Experiments and quasi-experimental studies in the behavioral and social sciences often involve several independent variables that are manipulated or studied jointly. For example, an educational psychologist might be interested in the effects of both the amount of instruction (e.g., 2, 3, or 4 days a week) and the method of instruction (e.g., traditional lecture versus hands-on learning) on the achievement of students. A factorial experiment is one in which the individual and joint effects of both of these independent variables can be studied. So, for example, an investigator might randomly assign each of 240 students to one of the conditions illustrated in Figure 7.1.

If students are randomly assigned to these six conditions, there should be 40 students in each cell of Figure 7.1. (In this sort of study, it is common to use lowercase n to designate the number of people in each condition and uppercase N to designate the total number of participants.)

Sometimes, it is not possible to assign students at random. For example, it might be administratively impossible to move students around at random, but you might be able to assign classes or groups of students to each cell, creating a quasi-experimental study. The distinction between a true experiment and a quasi-experimental study is that experiments involve random assignment of each individual to conditions, whereas quasi-experimental studies do not allow every subject to be randomly assigned to conditions. The methods used to analyze data from experiments and quasi-experiments are identical, but true experiments permit stronger inferences about causation.

The Factorial Analysis of Variance

The analysis of variance (ANOVA) is a statistical technique that involves asking the question, "Why do some people get high scores and others get low scores on the dependent variable?" (Or, "Why do scores vary?") In its most general form, in a study where subjects are assigned to different treatments and their scores on some common dependent variable are obtained, ANOVA answers this question by breaking down the variability of scores into two components, as illustrated in Equation 7.1.

$$\text{Variability in scores} = \text{Variability due to differences in treatment means}$$
$$+ \text{Variability } \textbf{within} \text{ each of the treatments} \quad (7.1)$$

In a study where there is only one independent variable (e.g., the number of days of instruction), Equation 7.1 corresponds to:

$$\text{Variability in scores} = \text{Variability due to treatments}$$
$$+ \text{Variability due to error} \quad (7.2)$$

In this sort of study, the mean square between (MS_B) provides an estimate of the variability associated with treatments; the mean square within (MS_W) provides an estimate of the variability in scores among subjects who receive the same treatment (i.e., variability that is not due to the treatments). Thus, MS_W represents variability due to error, i.e., the variability that you would expect if all the differences among scores were merely random, chance fluctuations. The statistic $F = MS_B/MS_W$ tells you whether the variability due to treatments is large relative to the variability in scores due to error, i.e., whether the variability due to treatments is larger than what you would expect if everything was due to chance. If the variability due to treatments represents more than chance fluctuations, you can conclude that your treatments had some effect. In a one-way ANOVA, all of the variability in scores is broken down into these two components (between versus within), and as a result, it is easy to use the F statistic to estimate the effect size, PV.

As we noted in Chapters 2 and 6, in a one-way ANOVA, $PV = \text{df}_{\text{hyp}} \cdot F/[(\text{df}_{\text{hyp}} \cdot F) + \text{df}_{\text{err}})]$. In factorial ANOVA, the questions asked and the breakdown of the variability in scores becomes more complex, and as a result, the estimation of PV and of statistical power also becomes more complex. In this chapter, we generalize the formula used for estimating PV from the F values obtained in a factorial ANOVA study.

Factorial experiments allow you to ask several questions simultaneously. For example, the factorial study illustrated in Figure 7.1 allows you to ask three questions: (1) What is the effect of the number of days of instruction?

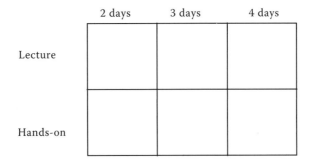

Figure 7.1   A factorial experiment.

(2) What is the effect of the style of teaching? and (3) Do these two variables interact? (i.e., does the effect of the amount of instruction depend on the method of instruction used?). Different research designs might allow researchers to ask a wider range of questions (e.g., in a later section of this chapter, we discuss repeated-measures designs, which allow you to examine systematic subject effects and subject by treatment interactions), or might provide a more narrowly focused examination of the data (e.g., designs with nested factors can be more efficient but may not provide an opportunity to ask all of the questions that are possible in a fully crossed factorial design). In multifactor ANOVA studies, it is common to have different levels of power for each of hypotheses tested.

Different questions imply different levels of power. In the design illustrated in Figure 7.1, there are three distinct hypotheses that can be tested via ANOVA, two main effect hypotheses (i.e., the hypothesis that the type of instruction and the amount of instruction influence learning), and one interaction hypothesis (i.e., the hypothesis that the effects of the type of instruction depends on the amount of instruction). All other things being equal, you will have more power for testing the hypothesis that the type of instruction matters than for testing the hypothesis that the amount of instruction matters. You will have more power for testing either of these main-effect hypotheses than for testing the hypothesis that the amount and type of instruction interact. To understand why this is true, it is necessary to think concretely about the type of question ANOVA is designed to answer.

As we noted in Chapter 6, in some ways, the term *analysis of variance* is an unfortunate one because it can lead people to forget what ANOVA was designed to do. The analysis itself focuses on identifying sources of variability or variance (hence, the acronym ANOVA), but the reason for doing the analysis is often to compare means. For example, when I ask whether the main effect for type of instruction is large, what I am really asking is whether the mean score of people who received lecture training is substantially different from the mean score of people who received hands-on instruction. Similarly, when I ask whether the main effect for amount of instruction is large, what I really want to know is whether the scores of people who received more instruction are substantially different from the scores of people who received less instruction. Interaction hypotheses in the design illustrated in Figure 7.1 involve comparisons of individual cell means.

A general principle running through all of the power analyses discussed in Chapters 1 and 2 is that there is more power when hypotheses are tested in large samples than when similar hypotheses are tested in smaller samples. That is, power increases with N. In ANOVA, the level of power for comparing means (i.e., for testing hypotheses about main effects and interactions) depends largely on the number of observations that go into calculating each mean. Suppose, for example, that 240 subjects show up for the study illustrated in Figure 7.1. Tests of the main effect for type of instruction will compare the mean score of the 120 people who receive lectures with the mean score of the 120 people who receive hands-on instruction. Tests of the main effect of amount of instruction will compare three means, each based on 80 subjects (i.e., 80 people received 2 days of instruction, 80 received 3 days, and 80 received 4 days). Tests of the interaction effect will involve comparing cell means, each of which is based on 40 people (e.g., 40 subjects received 2 days of lecture, another 40 received 3 days of hands-on instruction, and so on). All other things being equal, power is higher for statistical tests that involve comparing means from samples of 120 people (here, tests of the main effect of instruction type) than for tests that involve comparisons samples of 80 people (here, tests of the main effect of amount of instruction). Statistical tests that involve comparisons among means obtained from samples of 40 people (here, tests of the interaction) will often have even lower levels of power.

In ANOVA, it is common to distinguish between the number of observations in each cell of a design (designated by the lowercase n) and the total number of observations in a study (designated by the uppercase N). In the study described above, the interaction means are based on $n = 40$ subjects, and the main effect means for the type of instruction and amount of instruction main effects are based on samples of $3n$ and $2n$ subjects (i.e., 120 and 80), respectively. If all other things were equal, you would expect more power in the larger sample. Unfortunately, all things are rarely if ever equal, and it is difficult to state as a general principle that tests of main effects will always be more powerful than tests of interactions, or that main effect tests that involve comparing fewer means (and therefore fewer df_{hyp}) will be more powerful than main effect tests that involve comparing more means (and therefore more df_{hyp}). The reason for this is that the effect sizes for each of the separate questions pursued in ANOVA can vary. For example, suppose that there is a very large interaction effect, a moderately large main effect for the amount of instruction, and a very small main effect for the type of instruction. This might lead to the highest level of power for tests of the interaction and to the lowest level of power for tests of the type of instruction main effect.

Estimating power in multifactor ANOVA. The process of estimating the power of tests of main effects and interactions in ANOVA is a straightforward extension of the processes described in Chapters 1 and 2. In particular, power depends on sample size, effect size, and the decision criteria. For example, assume that you expected a small main effect ($PV = .01$) for the type of instruction, a moderately large main effect ($PV = .10$) for the amount of instruction, and an equally large effect ($PV = .10$) for the interaction. If $N = 240$ (i.e., there are 240 subjects randomly assigned to the six cells in this design), you would expect power to equal approximately .30 for the type of instruction main effect (assuming $\alpha = .05$). You would expect power levels of approximately .99 for the amount of instruction main effect and the type by amount interaction. In other words, power levels would be quite low for testing some effects and quite high for others in this study.

Estimating PV from F in a multifactor ANOVA. In a one-way ANOVA, all of the variability in scores is broken down into two components, variability due to treatments and variability due to error. Once you know the value of F in a one-way ANOVA, it is easy to determine the value of PV, which reflects the proportion of variance due to differences between treatments. In a multifactor ANOVA, F does not, by itself, give enough information to allow you to calculate PV. For example, in the study illustrated in Figure 7.1, the F for the type of instruction main effect tells you how large this effect is relative to MS_{err}, but it does not tell you how much of the total variance is accounted for by differences in types of instruction. In a multifactor ANOVA, the PV for one main effect depends in part on the size of the other main effects and interactions.

If you have the values of each of the F statistics (and their degrees of freedom) computed in a multifactor ANOVA, it is often possible to solve for the percentage of variance explained by each of the effects (we describe exceptions below). Returning to our example, suppose you found the following:

Type of instruction: $F(1, 234) = 3.64$
Amount of instruction: $F(2, 234) = 15.19$
Type X amount interaction: $F(2, 234) = 16.41$

These three sets of F values and degrees of freedom provide all of the information needed to determine the PV for each of these three effects, as well as the PV for the error term.

To see how this information can be used to calculate PV, we start by noting that

$$F = \text{MS}_{\text{hyp}}/\text{MS}_{\text{err}} \tag{7.3}$$

and

$$F \cdot \text{df}_{\text{hyp}} = \text{SS}_{\text{hyp}}/\text{MS}_{\text{err}} \tag{7.4}$$

In a design where there are two main effects (label these A and B) and one interaction (labeled AB), it is easy to show that:

$$PV_{\text{err}} = \text{df}_{\text{err}}/[\text{df}_{\text{err}} + (F_A \cdot \text{df}_A) + (F_B \cdot \text{df}_B) + (F_{AB} \cdot \text{df}_{AB})] \tag{7.5}$$

If you know the percentage of variance explained by error, it follows that the rest of the variance is explained by the model as a whole (i.e., by the combined effects of the A effect, the B effect, and the AB interaction). That is,

$$PV_{\text{model}} = 1 - PV_{\text{err}} \tag{7.6}$$

Finally, once you know the combined effects of A, B, and AB, all that remains is to determine the percentage of variance explained by each. These values are given by

$$PV \text{ for } A = PV_{\text{model}} \cdot [(F_A \cdot \text{df}_A)/((F_A \cdot \text{df}_A) + (F_B \cdot \text{df}_B) + (F_{AB} \cdot \text{df}_{AB}))] \tag{7.7}$$

$$PV \text{ for } B = PV_{\text{model}} \cdot [(F_B \cdot \text{df}_B)/((F_A \cdot \text{df}_A) + (F_B \cdot \text{df}_B) + (F_{AB} \cdot \text{df}_{AB}))] \tag{7.8}$$

$$PF \text{ for } AB = PV_{\text{model}} \cdot [(F_{AB} \cdot \text{df}_{AB})/((F_A \cdot \text{df}_A) + (F_B \cdot \text{df}_B) + (F_{AB} \cdot \text{df}_{AB}))] \tag{7.9}$$

Worked Example: Calculating *PV* From *F* and df in Multifactor ANOVA

Suppose an article provides information about statistical significance but not about effect size. It is often possible, and if possible, worthwhile, to calculate effect size estimates. Earlier in the chapter, we presented the following data:

Type of instruction: $F(1, 234) = 3.64$
Amount of instruction: $F(2, 234) = 15.19$
Type X amount interaction: $F(2, 234) = 16.41$

Applying Equation 7.5, you find:

$$PV_{err} = df_{err}/[df_{err} + (F_A \cdot df_A) + (F_B \cdot df_B) + (F_{AB} \cdot df_{AB})]$$

$$= 234/[234 + (3.46 \cdot 1) + (15.19 \cdot 2) + (16.41 \cdot 2)]$$

$$PV_{err} = 234/300.66 = .78$$

Applying Equation 7.6, you find

$$PV_{model} = 1 - PV_{err}$$

$$PV_{model} = 1 - .78 = .22$$

Applying Equations 7.7–7.9, you find

$$PV \text{ for } A = PV_{model} \cdot [(F_A \cdot df_A)/((F_A \cdot df_A) + (F_B \cdot df_B) + (F_{AB} \cdot df_{AB}))]$$

$$= .22 \cdot [(3.64 \cdot 1)/((3.64 \cdot 1) + (15.19 \cdot 2) + (16.41 \cdot 2)]$$

$$= .22 \cdot .054 = .012$$

$$PV \text{ for } B = PV_{model} \cdot [(F_B \cdot df_B)/((F_A \cdot df_A) + (F_B \cdot df_B) + (F_{AB} \cdot df_{AB}))]$$

$$= .22 \cdot [(15.19 \cdot 2)/((3.64 \cdot 1) + (15.19 \cdot 2) + (16.41 \cdot 2)]$$

$$= .22 \cdot .46 = .10$$

$$PV \text{ for } AB = PV_{model} \cdot [(F_{AB} \cdot df_{AB})/((F_A \cdot df_A) + (F_B \cdot df_B) + (F_{AB} \cdot df_{AB}))]$$

$$= .22 \cdot [(16.14 \cdot 2)/((3.64 \cdot 1) + (15.19 \cdot 2) + (16.41 \cdot 2)]$$

$$= .22 \cdot .48 = .10$$

In other words, the proportion of variance explained by each of the factors in this ANOVA model is:

Factor	PV
A	.012
B	.10
AB	.10
Error	.78

It is easy to extend Equations 7.5 through 7.9 to designs with three, four, or more factors. There are only two real limitations to these equations. First, they can only be used with fully crossed factorial designs, where an equal number of subjects is assigned to every possible combination of levels of A, B, etc. Thus, equations of this sort will not allow you to easily compute PV from F in nested designs or incomplete designs. Corresponding calculations are possible but laborious. Second, and more importantly, these equations apply only to fixed-effect models, in which all significance tests involve comparing the MS for each effect in the model to MS_{err}. Models that include random effects require more complex significance tests, and it is not possible to develop a simple set of formulas that cover all possible combinations of fixed and random effects. Luckily, fixed-effect models are much more common in the behavioral and social sciences than random-effect or mixed models (e.g., the default method for virtually all statistical analysis packages is to use fixed-effect models for structuring significance tests), especially in designs that do not include repeated measures.

Factorial ANOVA Example

In a meticulously designed study, Martin, Mackenzie, Lovegrove, and McNicol (1993) examined the effect of tinted lenses on the reading performance of children with specific reading disabilities (SRDs). This treatment was first suggested by Irlen (1983) who distinguished a condition called "scotopic sensitivity syndrome" which could be ameliorated to some degree by prescription lenses with certain tints. Controversy surrounds this treatment because it seems highly unlikely to many psychologists that filtering a few wavelengths from the perceptual array could have any impact on the higher cognitive processes associated with reading (Evans & Drasdo, 1991). Irlen proposed a mechanism involving perceptual distortions at certain wavelengths on the retina, but other authors have attributed any improvement in reading to placebo effects (Cotton & Evans, 1990; Winter, 1987).

From an original sample of 300, Martin et al. (1993) selected 60 subjects for further study. Twenty children were normal readers, 20 children had SRDs that could be treated by tinted lenses, and 20 children had SRDs deemed unsuitable for the treatment. The sample selection process controlled for such variables as native language, eyesight, intelligence, behavioral disorders, organic problems, and exposure to previous therapies. The three groups were compared on three occasions (pre-test, post-test, and follow-up) using the Neale Analysis of Reading Ability (Neale, 1973) which provided measures of reading accuracy and comprehension. A post-test occurred 1 year after the pre-test and follow-up occurred 6 months after that. Although the sample in this study was small, the authors were able to achieve substantial sensitivity because of their careful procedures and because they used a repeated-measures design, in which multiple observations were obtained from each subject.

The data in this study were analyzed using a 3 x 3 analysis of variance. Martin et al. (1993) reported a significant main effect for groups on accuracy [$F(2, 57) = 65.57$] and comprehension [$F(2, 57) = 7.72$]. The main effect for occasion was also significant in each case [$F(2, 114) = 24.99$ for accuracy and $F(2, 114) = 36.43$ for comprehension]. The One-Stop *F* Table contains a range of useful information that helps put these results in perspective.

Power estimation: Main effects. There are good reasons to believe that the main effects in this study are large, and if this is true, the power of all main effect tests was extremely high. For the groups' main effect the critical *F* value for achieving power of .80 to reject the traditional null ($\alpha = .05$) is 5.06. The *F* equivalent for a large effect in this study is 9.50, suggesting power well in excess of .80. Power is also greater than .80 for rejecting (at the .05 level) the minimum-effect null hypothesis that main effects account for 1% or less of the variance in treatments. Here, the critical *F* value was 6.19. However, in tests of the groups' main effect, there is not power in excess of .80 for tests of the minimum-effect null for a small to medium effect (i.e., that treatments account for less than 5% of the variance in the population; the critical $F = 9.76$).

The same conclusions can be drawn about the occasions' main effect. In this case the critical *F* value for achieving power of .80 to reject the 1% minimum-effect null hypothesis at the .05 level is 6.96; for tests of the 5% minimum-effect null, the critical value is 12.72. With $df_{hyp} = 2$ and $df_{err} = 114$, a large effect (i.e., $F = .25$) yields an *F* equivalent value of 19.00, which is well in excess of the critical *F* needed to attain power of .80 for tests of the minimum-effect null hypotheses described above.

Testing interaction hypotheses. Examination of the main effects does not really address the principal research question, i.e., the effects of tinted lenses on reading performance of children with SRDs. If tinted lenses work, we should observe performance of the treated SRDs to be more similar to the untreated SRDs in the pre-test condition but more similar to the subjects without reading disorders during post-test, hopefully persisting until follow-up. This is an interaction hypothesis. The interaction of groups by occasion was significant in the traditional sense for accuracy [$F(4, 114) = 2.98$] and comprehension [$F(4, 114) = 3.13$]. In both cases the critical $F(\alpha = .05)$ value was 2.45 for tests of the traditional null. A minimum-effect null (i.e., that the interaction effect accounts for 1% or less of the variance: critical $F = 3.10$) can also be rejected for comprehension measures.

The power of tests of these interactions can be determined from the One-Stop *F* Table. Suppose, for example, that the interaction effect is moderately large. If the population $PV = .10$, the *F* equivalent for $df_{hyp} = 4$, $df_{err} = 114$ is

3.16. The corresponding critical value for a power of .80 is 3.07. Power to reject the 1% minimum-effect null is somewhat lower. In this case, critical *F* values are 2.27 and 3.90 for power levels of .5 and .8, respectively. The *F* equivalent for a moderate effect (i.e., *PV* = .10) falls between these critical values, so we can use Equation 2.7 (Chapter 2) to obtain a more accurate estimate. The power to reject the 1% minimum-effect null is approximately .5 + .3 (3.16 − 2.27)/(3.90 − 2.27) = .66. Thus, although acceptable for testing the traditional null hypothesis, this study is not quite adequate for addressing minimum-effect null hypotheses.

There is a reasonable level of power for detecting moderately strong interactions. Suppose, however, that the interaction effect is small (e.g., *PV* = .01). With df_{hyp} = 4 and df_{err} = 114, the equivalent *F* value is now .287, which is obviously too small to yield even marginal levels of power. In other words, the sample in this study is large enough to give adequate power if and only if the true interaction is at least moderately strong.

In a complex experiment, each statistical test may show a different level of power. First, the predicted and/or actual effect sizes may differ for main effects, simple interactions, and higher-order interactions. Second, the degrees of freedom for different tests in a model may vary, sometimes substantially. In general, it is most likely to have higher power for testing main effects and lower power for testing complex interactions. First, main effects usually have more degrees of freedom. Second, main effects are usually (but not always) stronger than complex interactions. When the focus of your study is a complex three- or four-way interaction, very large samples might be needed to provide adequate power.

Martin et al. (1993) conclude that tinted lenses have no effect on reading ability, but the significant interactions just discussed do not warrant such a conclusion. The comprehension interaction, in particular, shows that treated children with SRDs performed like untreated children with SRDs in the pretest but improved to almost the same level as normal children in the posttest and follow-up, after the lenses were applied.

Fixed, Mixed, and Random Models

Earlier in this chapter, we mentioned the concept of fixed versus random factors. The distinction between the two is not always clear, but it can have important implications for analysis of variance and power analysis. To illustrate the difference between fixed and random factors, consider an experiment in which subjects are randomly assigned to perform a simple motor task (e.g., keeping a cursor on a moving target) under various types of distractions. Two factors are varied, noise level (three different levels: 70, 90, 110 db) and room temperature (four different levels: 60, 67, 80, 90 degrees).

The data suggest that both noise and temperature, as well as the combination of the two, are likely to influence performance. The question is whether noise and temperature are fixed or random factors.

The best way to determine whether a factor is fixed or random is to read the discussion section of an article. A factor is fixed if the inferences that are made are restricted to the levels actually included in the study. So, if the inference is about the difference between 70, 90, and 110 db of noise, noise is a fixed factor. On the other hand, if the discussion says "the more noise, the worse the performance," the inference goes beyond the levels of noise actually included in the experiment and uses these as a sample from a broader population of values that might have been included. If the researcher draws inferences about levels of noise not included in the experiment, noise is a random factor.

As this example implies, it is not necessarily the variable itself or even the design of an experiment that causes factors to be classified as fixed or random. Sometimes, a variable will necessarily be fixed because all possible levels have already been included in the experiment (e.g., if gender is a factor in a design); but in most cases, it is the inferences drawn by the researcher and not the variables or the design that matter most.

The analysis of variance is simplest when all factors are fixed, and virtually all analyses in the social and behavioral sciences are conducted on this basis (fixed effects are the default assumption of virtually every piece of ANOVA software). Calculations for SSs, dfs, and MSs are the same for fixed, mixed, and random models (mixed models include both fixed and random factors), but there are important differences in the way significance tests are conducted. In particular, the use of random effects leads to questions about the meaning of error in the F ratio. In a fixed-effect study, F ratios are created by dividing the mean square of interest by the mean square for error. In studies that involve random factors, the choice of error terms for constructing F ratios depends on which factors are fixed and which are random.

If both factors in the study described above are treated as random factors, the denominator for the F ratio for the noise factor is given by $F = MS_{noise}/MS_{noise \cdot temperature}$ and the F ratio for the temperature factor is given by $F = MS_{temperature}/MS_{noise \cdot temperature}$. That is, the denominator for the F ratio for each of these random effects is the mean square for the noise × temperature interaction (the error term for testing this interaction is MS_{err}).

Table 7.1 shows what is used as a denominator for fixed, mixed, and random models in experiments that involve two factors (A and B).

Because it is difficult to determine the exact structure of the F test in research designs that might involve various mixes of fixed and random factors (the status of some factors as fixed or random might not even be determined until the data have been collected), it is difficult to develop power analyses for all variations of ANOVA designs. The power analyses developed

Table 7.1 Denominators for Fixed, Mixed, and Random Models

	Fixed	Mixed		Random
		Factor A Fixed **Factor B Random**	**Factor A Random** **Factor B Fixed**	
Factor A MS_{err}	MS_{AB}	MS_{err}	MS_{AB}	
Factor B	MS_{err}	MS_{err}	MS_{AB}	MS_{AB}
AB Interaction MS_{err}	MS_{err}	MS_{err}	MS_{err}	

Note that all three models use MS_{err} for denominator of the AB interaction.

here, and in other texts that discuss power analysis for ANOVA, are based on the assumption that all factors are fixed.

Randomized Block ANOVA: An Introduction to Repeated-Measures Designs

Several years ago, a colleague interviewed for a job at a university where animal learning researchers decided to break the mold. Instead of the usual laboratory with rats, pigeons, and other small animals, researchers had a laboratory where alligators tried to solve a flooded maze. It is a good bet that the researchers did not get more alligators every time a power analysis told them *N* was too small.

There are many research areas where it is virtually impossible to use large numbers of subjects. Sleep research often involves multiple nights in a large sleep laboratory, with a large number of observations each night. Vision research often involves hundreds of trials per subject. Although the advice that researchers should aim for large *N* applies even in these areas so they can generalize their conclusions to the wider population, a research design that involves large *N* is often beyond the resources of an investigator. Repeated-measures designs allow researchers to obtain a large amount of information from a relatively small number of subjects, by obtaining several scores from each subject.

In Chapter 5 we discussed a one-way ANOVA study in which rats received a small, medium, or large reward for every trial in a straight alley runway. Each rat contributed one score for only one level of the independent variable. Suppose the design for the study is changed so that each of 50 rats experiences all three conditions. That is, a rat might receive small rewards for 30 days; on day 30, this rat is tested. Next, the rat might receive medium rewards for 30 days; on day 30, the rat is tested. Finally, that rat might receive large rewards for 30 days, and finally take one last test run. Each rat

Table 7.2 Sources of Variance in a Randomized Block Study

Source	df	Comment
Rats	49	Differences in the average performance across rats
Reward	2	Differences in the average performance across conditions
Error	98	Variability in scores not explained by rat or reward main effects

Note: With 50 rats and 3 data points per rat, the total number of observations is 150.

provides three scores for analysis, time to run through the straight alley on day 30 for each level of reward. In a good design, the order in which each rat experiences the three reward conditions would be randomized or counterbalanced from rat to rat.

Many books refer to subjects in a repeated-measures study as blocks; the design of this experiment is often referred to as a randomized block design. This design allows the measurement of individual differences and the removal of variability from block to block (i.e., from rat to rat) from the error term, increasing statistical power. In particular, a randomized block design breaks down the variability of scores into variability that can be explained by differences between treatments, variability that can be explained by differences between blocks, and error variance. In this study, the three sources of variance and their degrees of freedom are shown in Table 7.2.

The statistic $F = MS_{rat}/MS_{err}$ is used to determine if variability among rats is large relative to variability caused by error. The statistic $F = MS_{reward}/MS_{err}$ is used to determine if variability caused by treatments is large relative to variability for error. From the perspective of power analysis, there are at least two advantages to this randomized block design. First, it increases the total number of observations (i.e., there are only 50 rats, but 150 data points in the study). Second, it removes variability associated with systematic differences among the rats from the error term. If some rats are just faster than others, irrespective of reward levels, this variability in speed would represent another source of error in a simple one-way ANOVA.

Independent Groups Versus Repeated Measures

Most discussions of statistical power start with the assumptions that subjects are randomly assigned to treatments and one score on the dependent variable is obtained from each subject. One hallmark of independent groups or between-subjects design is that observations are statistically independent. That is, the score obtained from subject 2 in a study is assumed to be independent of the score obtained from subject 1. The independent groups design has many attractive features, but it is not always the best design for a study.

The randomized block design provides an introduction to the use of repeated measures to help improve the power of studies. Chapter 8 examines complex repeated-measures designs, but before moving on to those designs, it is useful to understand some of the complexities repeated-measures designs entail. First, power analysis suggests that the larger the N, the more power there is for a statistical test. In a between-subjects study, there is no ambiguity because N refers to number of subjects. In a study involving repeated measures, N usually refers to the number of observations with several observations coming from each subject, and different ways of producing the same number of observations will have different implications for statistical power. For example, suppose a study involves 10 subjects, each of whom provides five observations. Although there are 50 observations, the study is not statistically equivalent to a study in which there are 50 subjects, each of whom provides a single observation. Similarly, doubling the number of observations has different effects, depending on the way observations are doubled. Ten subjects, each providing 10 observations, provide a different level of power than will be obtained if there are 20 subjects, each providing 5 observations, or 100 subjects, each providing 1 observation.

Table 7.3 shows a key difference between a repeated-measures study and a study that uses between-subject designs in which each subject provides one observation. Suppose studies to be compared use a .05 alpha level and a small to moderate treatment effect is expected (e.g., the maximum differences between treatment means is $d = .50$). Further assume there are relatively small correlations between repeated measures (i.e., r values of .20 or less). Table 7.3 shows the number of subjects that would be needed for a between-subjects study versus a repeated-measures study to achieve power of .80 (Maxwell & Delaney, 1990).

A comparison of these two designs provides interesting information. First, if the total number of observations is held constant, researchers obtain more

Table 7.3 Number of Subjects Required to Achieve Power = .80 (Maximum $d = .50$, $r = .20$)

Between-Subject		Repeated Measures		
Number of Treatments	Number of Subjects	Number of Treatments	Number of Subjects	Number of Observations
2	128	2	53	106
3	237	3	65	195
4	356	4	74	296
5	485	5	82	410
6	624	6	88	528

power from the repeated measures than from a between-groups design. With two treatments, only 53 subjects with two observations per subject are required to provide power of .80. A between-groups design requires 128 subjects to achieve power of .80. If there are four treatments, power of .80 is obtained with 74 subjects in repeated-measures and 356 subjects in between-subjects designs.

Suppose the correlation between observations is higher (e.g., the average correlation between observations is .40 rather than .20). As Table 7.4 shows, the higher the correlation between observations, the larger the statistical advantage repeated-measures designs provide. In Chapter 6, we noted that the correlation between observations was part of the formula for the standard error term in the dependent t-test and that large correlations meant smaller standard errors. This principle carries over to repeated-measures designs. For example, with three treatments, 50 subjects are required to achieve power in a repeated-measures design when the average correlation among measures is $r = .40$, whereas 65 subjects would be required when $r = .20$. There are several ways to explain why repeated-measures studies are more powerful than similar between-subjects studies. First, as a comparison of Tables 7.3 and 7.4 suggests, correlation among pairs of repeated measures makes a big difference. The analysis of variance involves breaking down variability in scores into variance caused by treatments and variance caused by error. If observations for a given subject are consistently high or consistently low, there is a high correlation for each pair of treatments and less error variance. Usually there is less random variability in data from a repeated-measures design than in comparable independent groups design.

The decreased variability in repeated-measures or correlated-measures designs is analogous to the central idea in traditional psychometric theory. By grouping together several intercorrelated observations, it is possible to get a highly reliable measure of where a subject stands on the dependent variable. Repeated-measures designs allow researchers to take advantage of

Table 7.4 Number of Subjects Required to Achieve Power = .80 (Maximum $d = .50$, $r = .40$)

Between-Subject		Repeated Measures		
Number of Treatments	Number of Subjects	Number of Treatments	Number of Subjects	Number of Observations
2	128	2	40	80
3	237	3	50	150
4	356	4	57	228
5	485	5	63	315
6	624	6	68	408

the fact that several correlated observations from a subject are more reliable as compared with a single observation from a subject.

In addition, repeated-measures designs allow for identification and removal of sources of variance in scores that are treated as error in a between-subject design. In particular, repeated-measures designs allow for estimation and removal of systematic subject effects that cannot be estimated or controlled in between-subject designs.

Going back to an earlier example of a study in which subjects are asked to complete a complex psychomotor task under different sorts of distraction, noise (70, 90, 110 db) and room temperature (60, 67, 80, 90 degrees Fahrenheit), suppose you have enough time and money to collect 120 observations. Table 7.5 shows the effects that can be estimated (along with their degrees of freedom) in a between-subjects study (using 120 subjects) and in a within-subjects study in which 10 subjects participate in all 12 conditions.

The repeated-measures design allows you to find out whether there are systematic subject effects (some subjects might be better at this sort of task than others), subject by noise interactions (some subjects may be more distracted by noise than others), and subject by temperature interactions (some subjects may be more distracted by hot or cold than others). These subject effects can all be estimated and removed from the residual error term. In contrast, between-subject designs lump all of these effects into "error." If there are meaningful subject effects and subject by treatment interactions, repeated-measures designs will allow you to remove them from error, while between-subjects designs will treat these systematic effects as part of the overall error term. Anything you can do to reduce error is likely to increase statistical power, and one reason for the power of repeated measure designs is that they allow you to isolate these subject effects.

Finally, there is a more general statistical explanation for the power of repeated-measures designs. In Chapter 2, we discussed the noncentral F distribution, and noted that as the noncentrality parameter gets larger, the mean

Table 7.5 Sources of Variance in Between-Versus Within-Subjects Designs

Between	df	Within	df
Noise (N)	2	Noise	2
Temperature (T)	3	Temperature (T)	3
N · T	6	N · T	6
Error	108	Subjects (S)	9
		N · S	18
		T · S	27
		Error	54

of the F distribution increases and the variance grows larger as well. One thing that affects the noncentrality parameter is the effect size; it is this relationship that allowed us to create F tables for minimum-effect F tests. Thus, the larger the effect of your interventions and treatments, the stronger the upward shift in the distribution of F values you expect to find in your study.

Vonseh and Schork (1986) note that in repeated-measure studies the value of the noncentrality parameter depends on both the effect size and the correlations among repeated measures. The precise effects of the correlations among repeated measures on the distribution of F are complex and nonlinear, but in general, the higher the correlation among your measures, the more noncentral the distribution of F becomes. Repeated-measures studies tend to yield larger values of F and, therefore, more power.

Why doesn't everyone use repeated-measures designs? Repeated-measures designs are more powerful, more efficient, and easier to implement than between-subjects designs. For example, suppose a power analysis tells you that 400 subjects are needed to obtain a reasonable level of power. You might go out and recruit 400 individuals, getting a single score from each one (a between-subjects design). Alternately, you might need to recruit only 10 subjects, and get 40 observations from each (in fact, this will yield more power than a between-subjects design with $N = 400$). Given the practical and statistical advantages of repeated-measured designs, you might wonder why anyone uses between-subjects designs.

Although repeated-measures designs are attractive in many ways, they often turn out to be inappropriate for many research topics. Consider, for example, a study examining the effectiveness of five different methods of instruction for teaching second-grade students basic mathematics. A repeated-measures design that exposes all students to all five methods will run into a serious problem, often labeled a "carry-over effect." That is, whatever the students learn with the first method they are exposed to will affect their learning and performance on subsequent methods. By about the fourth time students have gone over the material (using each of four methods), they probably will have learned it, and will certainly be getting pretty sick of it. The first four trials will almost certainly affect outcomes on trial number five.

In general, many research questions make a repeated-measures design difficult to implement. Studies of learning or interventions designed to change attitudes, beliefs, or the physical or mental state of subjects might all be difficult to carry out in a repeated-measures framework. If the interventions you are studying change subjects, it might be difficult to interpret data when several different interventions are implemented, one after the other. The fact that human beings have good memories probably compromises most repeated-measures designs using human participants to some extent. Similarly, some research paradigms involve tasks that are complex or time consuming, and even if it is theoretically feasible to repeat the task under a variety of conditions, there may be serious practical barriers to obtaining multiple observations from each subject. Some studies allow for mixed designs, in which some of the factors studied represent repeated measures and others represent between-subject factors, and these designs often represent the best compromise between the power and efficiency of repeated-measures designs and the independence of observations that characterizes between-subject designs.

One of the apparent strengths of repeated-measures designs is also a potential weakness (i.e., the ability to obtain a large number of observations from a small number of subjects). For example, in some areas of physiological psychology, it might be common to obtain several hundred observations from each subject, and it is not unusual to see studies where the number of subjects is 10 to 20, and sometimes samples are even smaller. These are not small-sample studies in the traditional sense because the number of observations is potentially huge (e.g., in some areas of vision research, studies in which 10 subjects each provide 400 trials are common). However, the small number of subjects does raise important concerns about the generalizability of your results. Even if true random sampling procedures are used, you have to be concerned about the possibility that the results obtained from one group of 10 subjects might be quite different from those obtained from another group of 10. In between-subject studies, you might not have the same set of worries. A random sample of 400 subjects is almost certain to provide results that generalize to the parent population, and a second random sample of 400 is almost certain to provide converging findings. In some cases where it is feasible to obtain hundreds of observations from each of a few subjects, you might conclude that it is better to obtain a handful of observations from a larger set of subjects.

Complexities in Estimating Power in Repeated-Measures Designs

The application of ANOVA (and of power analysis) in repeated-measures designs can be complicated because these designs lead to violations of important statistical assumptions that underlie the analysis of variance. In particular, research designs that involve obtaining multiple measures from each respondent can lead to violations of assumptions of independence of sphericity (i.e., the assumption that the variances of the differences between all possible pairs of repeated measures are equal). To obtain accurate results in such designs, both the degrees of freedom and the estimate of the noncentrality parameter must be adjusted by the factor epsilon, which reflects the severity of violations of the assumption of sphericity, e.g., the best estimate of λ in repeated-measures designs is given by [epsilon $\cdot$ df$_{err}$ $\cdot$ $PV/(1 - PV)$; see Algina

& Keselman, 1997, for discussions of sphericity and power]. However, this correction factor is not always reported and cannot often be calculated on the basis of results that are likely to be reported in a journal article.

A conservative approach to this problem is to make a worst-case correction (Greenhouse & Geisser, 1959). The factor epsilon ranges in value from a maximum of 1 (indicating no violation) to a minimum of $1/(k - 1)$, where k represents the number of levels of the repeated-measures factor. When the degrees of freedom for factors involving repeated measures are multiplied by epsilon, it is possible to obtain a conservative test of significance by comparing the obtained F with the critical value of F using the epsilon-adjusted degrees of freedom.

For example, in this study, data are collected from each subject on three occasions, meaning that "occasion" is a repeated-measures factor, and the "occasion X group" factor has a repeated-measures component. The worst-case estimate of epsilon is that epsilon = .5; i.e., epsilon = $1/(3 - 1)$. To use this worst-case estimate of epsilon here, you would multiply the degrees of freedom for the occasion effect and the occasion X group effects by .5 (i.e., you would use degrees of freedom of $df_{hyp} = 1$, $df_{err} = 57$ and $df_{hyp} = 2$, $df_{err} = 114$, respectively, to test the occasion and occasion X group effects rather than the actual degrees of freedom of $df_{hyp} = 2$, $df_{err} = 57$ and $df_{hyp} = 4$, $df_{err} = 114$). Similarly, you would need to adjust the estimate of λ, also multiplying your estimate of λ by .5.

In practice, a good estimate of power can be obtained by simply multiplying both the degrees of freedom and PV by this worst-case estimate of epsilon (rather than directly adjusting your estimate of λ). If you compare the power estimate you obtain without any epsilon correction (the power estimates in this example did not include any correction for violations of the sphericity assumption) with the power estimate obtained making a worst-case assumption about violations, you will have a pretty good idea of the range of power values you could reasonably expect.

Summary

The analysis of variance can be used to ask a wide range of questions, and experiments can often be structured to allow researchers to examine both the individual and the joint effects of several variables. Power analyses for multifactor designs are more complicated than for one-way ANOVA because the same study often yields quite different levels of power for the different questions it asks. Usually, studies yield more power for questions about main effects than for questions about interactions (because the means that define main effects are based on larger samples than those that define interactions), but this is not always the case. As we noted in Chapter 1, power is a complex function of sample size, effect size, and decision criteria, and it is difficult to make any clear *a priori* statements about the power of different parts of a multifactor analysis.

The randomized block factorial design is an interesting and important variation on the more common independent-groups design, and it provides an introduction to the complexities of repeated-measures analyses. Research designs that involve multiple measures from each participant have the potential to yield very high levels of power but also present a number of analytic challenges, particularly in cases where violations of statistical assumptions are severe. The chapter that follows examines more complex repeated-measures designs.

8

Split-Plot Factorial and Multivariate Analyses

▼ ▼ ▼ ▼ ▼

A number of research designs include repeated measures, sometimes in combination with between-subjects factors. This chapter discusses variations on the multifactor designs discussed in Chapter 7 that include repeated measures and ends with a discussion of the multivariate analysis of variance.

Split-Plot Factorial ANOVA

A good deal of the early development of analysis of variance occurred in areas related to agricultural research, and this is sometimes the best explanation for the terminology still used in ANOVA. The split-plot factorial design was originally developed to help analyze data obtained when plots of agricultural land were divided for various uses.

Suppose a researcher randomly assigns each of 120 students to one of three methods of instruction (lecture, hands-on, or programmed instruction) and assesses their performance after 2, 3, 4, and 5 days of training, as shown in Figure 8.1. Methods of instruction represent a between-subjects factor; 40 different students are assigned to each level of this factor. Training time, on the other hand, is a repeated-measures factor. That is, each student is tested 4 times. In a split-plot design, each participant is exposed to one level of the between-subjects factor and to all levels of the within-subjects factor.

One of the distinguishing features of the split-plot factorial design is that it allows the estimation of variability due to systematic subject differences. However, because each subject receives only one method of instruction, subject differences are partially confounded with group differences. In

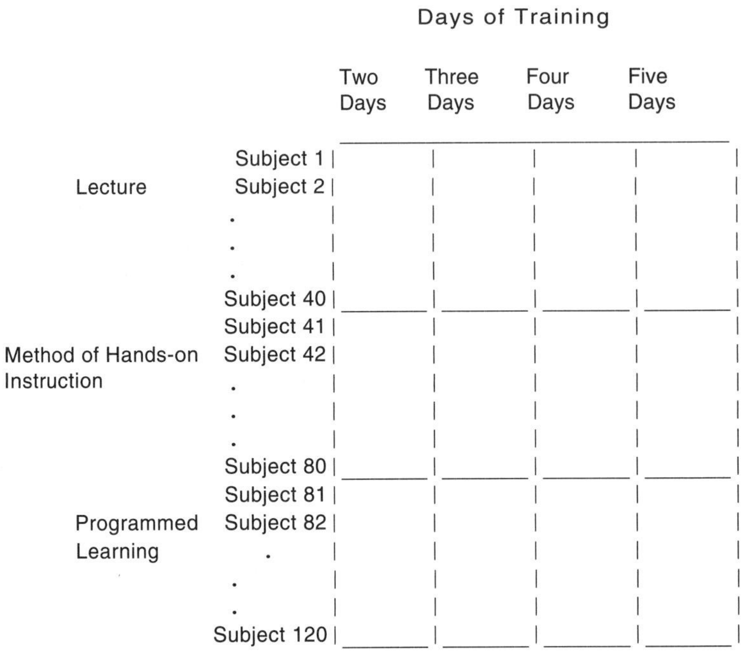

Days of Training

		Two Days	Three Days	Four Days	Five Days

Figure 8.1   A split-plot factorial design.

analyzing data from this design, we use the concept of nesting and analyze variability attributable to systematic subject differences *within groups*. The analytic layout and degrees of freedom for this design are shown in Table 8.1. Note that there are 480 total observations (i.e., 120 subjects, 4 observations per subject), and that no specific term is labeled "error." Rather, different terms in this model are used in constructing specific *F*-statistics.

Table 8.1   Sources of Variance, df, and Error Terms for Split-Plot Design

Source	df	Error Term for *F* Statistic
Methods of Instruction (M)	2	$MS_{S/M}$
Subjects within Methods (S/M)	117	
Training Time (T)	3	$MS_{S/M \cdot T}$
M · T	6	$MS_{S/M \cdot T}$
S/M · T	351	
Total	479	

In the split-plot factorial design, tests of the significance of the between-subjects factor use variability attributable to subjects, nested within levels of that factor, as a basis for constructing the F-statistic. In particular, the significance test for the Methods of Instruction factor compares the mean square for Methods with the mean square for Subjects nested within Methods (i.e., $F = MS_M/MS_{S/M}$). The rationale here is that all of the subjects within each training method received the same treatment. Therefore, variability within these treatment groups cannot be due to treatments, but rather must be due to nontreatment factors, which are treated as sources of error.

Significance tests for repeated-subjects factors (or for interactions that include repeated subjects factors) use the interaction between subjects and treatments as a basis for forming the F test. For example, the significance test for the Training Time factor compared variability attributable to training time with variability that is explained by the interaction between subject differences and training time (i.e., $F = MS_T/MS_{S/M \cdot T}$). Similarly, the F test for the Methods of Instruction by Training Time interaction involves computing $F = MS_{M \cdot T}/MS_{S/M \cdot T}$.

You might notice in Table 8.1 that the number of degrees of freedom for Subjects nested within Methods of Instruction has a value that does not seem intuitively obvious (i.e., df = 117). Because subjects are nested within three different methods of instruction, the best way to determine degrees of freedom is to calculate the df within each of the three training methods (there are 40 subjects who receive each training method, so there are 39 degrees of freedom within each method), then multiplying by the number of methods yields df = 3 · 39 = 117. The degrees of freedom for the interaction between training time and subjects nested within methods of instruction in given by multiplying 117 by the number of methods (i.e., df = 3 · 117 = 351).

In other ANOVA designs, power has been affected by the degrees of freedom for both the hypothesis and the error term, and the same is true for split-plot factorial designs. That is, in evaluating power, the first step is to compute df_{hyp} and df_{err}.

Estimating Power for a Split-Plot Factorial ANOVA

As in other ANOVA designs, power depends on ES, alpha, df_{hyp} and df_{error}, and *PV* for each main effect and interaction. Suppose, for example, that you decide to test minimum-effect hypotheses, testing the null hypothesis that the main effects and interactions account for 1% or less of the variance in responses. On the basis of prior experience and existing research, you believe that Methods of Instruction will have a relatively small effect (e.g., $PV = .05$) and that Training Time and the M · T interaction will have a moderately large effect (e.g., $PV = .10$) on responses. To assess the power of the test of the Methods of Instruction main effect, choose the Power Analysis option of the One-Stop F Calculator and enter ES = .01, alpha = .05, df_{hyp} = 2, and df_{err} = 117. Make an initial guess about power (e.g., that power = .50) and hit the Calculate command button. Continue to adjust your guesses about power until the program shows $PV = .01$. In this study, power for the Methods of Instruction main effect is equal to .35.

To assess power for the Time of Training effect, enter ES = .01, alpha = .05, df_{hyp} = 3, and df_{err} = 351, then enter an initial guess about power. Continue to adjust your guesses about power until the program shows $PV = .01$. In this study, power for the Time of Training main effect is equal to .996.

Finally, to assess power for the M · T interaction effect, enter ES = .01, alpha = .05, df_{hyp} = 3, and df_{err} = 351, then enter an initial guess about power. Continue to adjust your guesses about power until the program shows $PV = .01$. In this study, power for the Time of Training main effect is equal to .989.

You might note that there is tremendous power for testing Time of Training and M · T effects, in large part because each of these tests combined relatively strong effects with relatively large df_{err}.

Power for Within-Subject Versus Between-Subject Factors

Studies that use repeated measures usually have more power than comparable between-subjects studies, but there are a number of factors that influence this generalization, and an exact description of the effects of including repeated measures on power can be complex. First, as Bradley and Russell's (1998) analysis of split-plot designs shows, the use of repeated measures tends to increase power for some statistical tests and decrease power for others. In general, tests of repeated-measures factors have higher power and tests of between-subjects factors have lower power than they would in comparable studies that rely exclusively on between-subjects designs. The increase in power for repeated-measures factors is proportional to the square root of $(1 + \rho)$, where ρ represents the average correlation between repeated measures, whereas the decrease in power for between-subjects factors in split-plot designs is proportional to the square root of $(1 - \rho)$. If the correlation between measures is small the effects of using repeated measures on the power of either type of test are small.

Second, the effects of adding additional repetitions of measures to a study can often be smaller than you might think (Overall, 1996). In particular, adding a new set of measures does not always add new information, and as the redundancy of new information increases, the contribution of additional measurements to the power of a study decreases. This effect is comparable to one seen in psychometrics, where adding a few new items to a short scale can dramatically increase reliability, whereas adding the same number of new items to a longer scale may have no discernable effect.

One result of the effects of correlations among observations on power analysis is that the tables and software provided with this book will tend to produce conservative estimates of power and of sample-size requirements for repeated-measures factors. On the whole, we think it is best to err on the side of designing studies with more rather than with less power, so the relatively small bias that can be produced as a result of failing to take the correlations among observations into account when calculating power does not strike us as a bad thing.

Split-Plot Designs With Multiple Repeated-Measures Factors

Suppose 120 subjects are randomly assigned to one of three exercise programs (e.g., strength-oriented, cardiovascular, combined). Forty subjects in each program follow two different diet regimens (high protein, high fiber), and three different cycles of exercise and rest (massed exercise, frequent short breaks, fewer but longer breaks). This design is shown in Figure 8.2; the source table for this study is shown in Table 8.2.

As with the simpler split-plot design in Table 8.1, this design includes both a between-subjects factor (exercise) and within-subjects factors (diet, break cycle).

In general, power analysis for this design proceeds very much in the same way as power analyses for the split-plot design shown in Table 8.1. Estimates of effect sizes are still needed, and once the effect size and degrees of freedom are established, power estimation proceeds in the same way as in the other designs described in Chapters 7 and 8. That is, power always depends on the effect size, the decision criteria, and the degrees of freedom.

The Multivariate Analysis of Variance

Throughout this book, we have concentrated on a family of statistical methods that all have one feature in common—i.e., that there is some specific

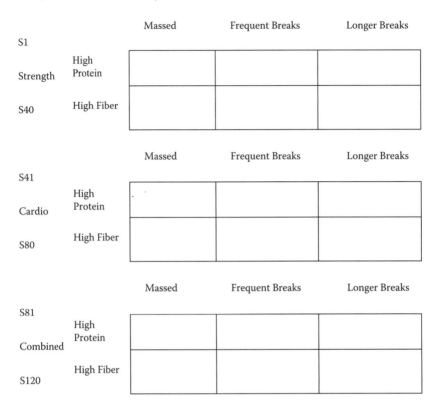

Figure 8.2   Design with multiple repeated-measures factors.

variable that represents the focus of the analysis, the dependent variable. In many studies, researchers are likely to collect data on several dependent variables and to conduct multivariate rather than univariate analyses. For example, suppose you are interested in determining whether there are differences in the outcomes of four specific training programs that have been proposed for teaching pilots to use a new global positioning technology. You might evaluate their performance in terms of the number of errors made in applying this technology, in terms of the amount of time needed to learn the technology, or in terms of increased efficiency in planning and sticking to flight routes. Rather than conducting three separate analyses of variance (i.e., one for errors, one for time spent, and one for flight planning), you are likely to use multivariate methods that combine these three dependent variables into a single analysis. Specifically, you are likely to carry out a multivariate analysis of variance (MANOVA).

There is a substantial literature dealing with power analysis in MANOVA (e.g., Maxwell & Delaney, 1990; Stevens, 1980, 1988, 2002; Vonesh & Schork,

Table 8.2 Split-Plot Design With Two
Repeated-Measures Factors

Source	df	*F* Test
Exercise	2	$MS_E/MS_{S/E}$
Subjects/Exercise	117	
Diet	1	$MS_D/MS_{S/E \cdot D}$
Break cycle	2	$MS_B/MS_{S/E \cdot B}$
D · B	2	$MS_{D \cdot B}/MS_{S/E \cdot D \cdot B}$
E · D	2	$MS_{E \cdot D}/MS_{S/E \cdot D \cdot B}$
E · B	4	$MS_{E \cdot B}/MS_{S/E \cdot D \cdot B}$
D · E · B	4	$MS_{D \cdot E \cdot B}/MS_{S/E \cdot D \cdot B}$
S/E · D	117	
S/E · B	234	
S/E · D · B	234	

1986). In a very general sense, the issues in determining the power of MANOVA are quite similar to those that affect the power of univariate ANOVAs. First, the power of MANOVA depends on *N*, the effect size, and the alpha level, just as in univariate ANOVA. Large samples, strong effects, and lenient alpha levels lead to high levels of power, whereas small samples, small effects, and stringent alpha levels lead to lower levels of power. Second, a principle already noted for repeated-measures ANOVA also applies to MANOVA. In general, power is higher when the variables being examined (here, the multiple dependent variables that are combined to carry out MANOVA) are more highly correlated than when they are uncorrelated. Finally, the power of MANOVA depends on the number of dependent variables. A study that uses four or five dependent measures will tend to have more power than a study that uses only one (leading to a univariate ANOVA) or two. Stevens (1988, 2002) presents useful tables for estimating power in MANOVA.

A simple, if somewhat conservative, approach to power analysis in MANOVA is to conduct a power analysis for the dependent variable that is expected to produce the smallest effect. If you have power of .80, for example, in a univariate ANOVA for this particular dependent variable, you can be sure that you will have power in excess of .80 for a MANOVA that combines this variable with other dependent variables for which stronger effects are expected.

Finally, it is useful to note that MANOVA can be used as a substitute for many repeated-measures analyses, ranging from dependent *t*-tests (when there are only two measures) to factorial repeated-measures designs. If there are several dependent variables, MANOVA presents a more powerful alternative to ANOVA or the *t*-test. In general, MANOVA will have slightly more power than would be obtained when analyzing the same data using a repeated-measures design (i.e., one that treats the dependent variables as a set of repeated measures).

Summary

Power analyses can be easily extended to research designs that include a mix of within- and between-subjects factors; this chapter discusses the widely used split-plot factorial design. One of the complexities of this design is that subjects are nested within treatments. Nevertheless, the application of the methods of power analysis described in this book is quite straightforward when working with this particular design.

We end this chapter with a discussion of the multivariate analysis of variance (MANOVA). It is simple to obtain conservative estimates of the power of multivariate analyses of these sorts, either by conducting a univariate analysis for the dependent variable that shows the weakest effects (a very conservative approach) or by analyzing power for the univariate repeated-measures design that corresponds with MANOVA (less conservative). As with all of the other analyses described in this book, power depends on the effect size, the number of observations, and the criteria used to define statistical significance.

9

The Implications of Power Analyses

▼　▼　▼　▼　▼

The power of a statistical test is the probability that you will reject the null hypothesis being tested, given that this null hypothesis is in fact wrong. As we have noted throughout, the traditional null hypothesis that treatments have no effect whatsoever (or that the correlation between two variables is precisely zero, or any other hypothesis of "no effect") is very often wrong, and in this context the statistical power of a test is essentially the probability that the test will lead to the correct conclusion. When testing the traditional null hypothesis, it is obvious that power should always be as high as possible. When testing a minimum-effect hypothesis (e.g., that the effect of treatments is negligibly small, but not necessarily precisely zero), the implications of varying levels of statistical power are potentially more complex, and a wider range of issues needs to be considered in determining how to use and interpret statistical power analysis.

This chapter begins with a discussion of the implications of statistical power analysis for tests of both traditional and minimum-effect null hypotheses. Next, we discuss the benefits of taking statistical power seriously. Some of these are direct and obvious (e.g., if you do a power analysis, you are less likely to conduct a study in which the odds of failure substantially outweigh the odds of success), but there are also a number of indirect benefits to doing power analyses that may, in the long run, be even more important than the direct benefits. Finally, we consider the question of whether power analysis renders the whole exercise of testing the traditional null hypothesis moot. If power is very high (or very low), the outcome of most statistical tests is not really in doubt, and the information from these tests might be severely limited as power reaches either extreme.

Tests of the Traditional Null Hypothesis

In Chapter 1, we noted that two types of errors might be possible in testing a statistical hypothesis. First, you might reject the null hypothesis when it is in fact true (a Type I error). Second, you might fail to reject the null hypothesis when it is in fact wrong (a Type II error). Textbooks invariably stress the need to balance one type of error against the other (e.g., procedures that minimize Type I errors also lead to low levels of power), but when the null hypothesis is almost certain to be wrong there is little to be gained and much to be lost by attempting to maintain such a "balance" (Murphy, 1990).

The fact that the traditional null hypothesis is so often wrong leads to three conclusions about statistical power: (1) you cannot have too much power, (2) you should take the simplest and most painless route to maximizing power, and (3) tests with insufficient power should never be done.

You cannot have too much power. If the null hypothesis is very likely to be wrong, it is very unlikely you will ever make a Type I error, and the only way you are likely make an error in statistical hypothesis testing is by failing to reject H_0. Our reason for repeating this point so many times is that it flies in the face of convention, where substantial attention is often devoted to the unlikely possibility that a Type I error might occur. In tests of the traditional null, power is essentially the probability that the test will reach the right conclusion (because the traditional null is usually wrong), and there is little coherent statistical rationale for arguing that power should *not* be high. There are many practical problems with attaining high levels of power, as we note below. However, it is always to your advantage to maximize power in tests of the traditional null hypothesis.

Maximizing power: The hard way and the easy way. There are two practical and eminently sensible ways to attain high levels of power. The easy way is to change the alpha level. As we showed in Chapter 2, power is higher when a relatively lenient alpha level is used. Traditionally, the choice of criteria for defining statistical significance has been between alpha levels of .05 and .01. When testing the traditional null, there is little scientific or statistical advantage to using a stringent test, and you should generally set the alpha level for your tests as high as possible. Unfortunately, you are likely to meet resistance if you use alpha levels of .10, .20, or anything other than .05 or some other conventional figure, but this resistance is misplaced. Higher alpha rates yield more power, often with no meaningful increase in the likelihood of a Type I error.

The second strategy for maximizing power is to increase the sensitivity of your study, which generally implies using larger samples. Even though this strategy is more demanding than simply changing the alpha level, we strongly recommend it. Large, carefully constructed samples increase the generalizability and stability of your findings, and they decrease the possibility that sampling error will lead to meaningless or misleading results. We say more about this in sections that follow.

While it is clearly harder to increase power by increasing N than by increasing α, this strategy has the immense benefit of improving your study. Simply changing the alpha level does nothing to enhance the meaningfulness or interpretability of your research, but the use of large samples helps to minimize one of the recurring problems in social science research—the overreliance on the unstable results obtained in small samples (Schmidt, 1992).

Tests with insufficient power should never be done. Suppose you were diagnosed with an ulcer and your doctor told you about a new treatment. This treatment is more likely to make things worse than to make things better, and alternative treatments are available that do not have this problem. Would you try the new treatment? Our answer is "no," and we believe this analogy applies exactly to statistical tests of the traditional null hypothesis. If power is low, you should not carry out a test of the traditional null hypothesis.

When power is less than .50 and you are virtually certain that H_0 is wrong, the test is more likely to yield a wrong answer than a right one. More to the point, the test is unlikely to produce new and useful knowledge; it is more likely to mislead you. If you are virtually certain before the test that H_0 is false, a test that rejects H_0 doesn't tell you much that you didn't already know. A test that fails to reject H_0 shouldn't change your mind either (if H_0 is wrong virtually by definition, the results of your test shouldn't change this), but people will sometimes be misled by their data. Low-power tests are unlikely to have any effect except to mislead and confuse researchers and readers.

Tests of Minimum-Effect Hypotheses

The alternative to testing the traditional null hypothesis that treatments have no effect is to test the minimum-effect null hypothesis that the effect of treatments is so small that it could be safely ignored. Different disciplines or research areas might require substantially different operational definitions of a "negligibly small" effect, and the standards suggested in previous chapters and in our One-Stop F Table (i.e., treatments accounting for less that 1%, or in some cases less than 5%, of the variance in outcomes have negligibly small effects) will not always apply. Nevertheless, we believe that tests of minimum-effect null hypotheses are necessary if the whole enterprise of statistical hypothesis testing is to prove useful.

Statistical power analysis can be used to its fullest advantage in tests of minimum-effect null hypotheses. Because the hypothesis being tested may very well be true (i.e., although treatments are very unlikely to have absolutely no effect, the hypothesis that they have trivial effects is often a realistic one), it becomes important to develop specific procedures and criteria for "accepting the null" or determining when the evidence is consistent or inconsistent with the proposition that the effects of a particular treatment *are* indeed negligible; power analysis is extremely useful for this purpose. It also becomes important to give serious consideration to an issue that is usually (and incorrectly) presented in the context of traditional null hypothesis tests (i.e., the appropriate balance between Type I and Type II errors).

Accepting the null. In traditional null hypothesis testing, the idea of accepting the null hypothesis is sometimes treated as a sort of heresy. Rather than allowing one to accept the hypothesis that treatments have no effect, the traditional framework usually leaves you with two options: (1) deciding that there is sufficient evidence to reject the null (i.e., a significant outcome), and (2) deciding that there is not yet enough evidence to reject the null (i.e., a nonsignificant result). Because you already *know* that the traditional null is almost certain to be false, the fact that you have not yet accumulated enough evidence to confirm this fact tells you more about your study than about the substantive phenomenon you are studying.

As we have noted throughout, power is substantially affected by the size of the sample. If N is very small, you will not reject the null, no matter what research question you are pursuing. If N is large enough, you will reject the traditional null, again, no matter what research question you are pursuing. It is hard to resist the conclusion that tests of the traditional null hypothesis are little more than indirect measures of your sample size! In tests of the traditional null, the most logical interpretation of a nonsignificant result is that your sample is too small.

Occasionally, the door is left open for treating nonsignificant results as meaningful. For example, some journals allow for the possibility of publishing nonsignificant results, at least under some conditions (e.g., the inaugural issue of the journal *Human Performance* included an editorial suggesting that nonsignificant results would be treated as meaningful if specific research design criteria, including a demonstration of adequate statistical power, were met). The argument that is sometimes offered is that if well-designed studies fail to detect an effect, this might provide some evidence that that effect is likely to be a very small one, and that the null hypothesis might be very close to being true, even if the effect of treatments is not *precisely* zero. Bayesian approaches have been applied to the problem of statistically demonstrating that an effect is so small that it should be effectively ignored (Rouanet, 1996). Nevertheless, the bias against "accepting the null" runs so strong in tests of the traditional null hypothesis that this framework simply doesn't leave any appealing alternative when the effect of treatments *is* negligibly small. You will either collect a very large sample and reject the null (which may mislead you into thinking that the effect of treatments is something other than trivial) or you will fail to reject it and perhaps collect more data about an essentially meaningless question.

In tests of minimum-effect hypotheses, there is a realistic possibility that the hypothesis being tested (i.e., that the effect of treatments is at best negligible) is indeed true, and there is a real need to develop procedures or conventions for deciding when to "accept the null." We believe that power analysis plays a critical role in determining and defining those procedures or conventions.

Suppose the hypothesis being tested is that the effect of treatments is at best negligible (e.g., treatments account for 1% or less of the variance in outcomes). A powerful study could provide strong evidence that this hypothesis is in fact true. For example, if power is .80, this translates into odds of 4 to 1 that a statistical test will reject this hypothesis *if it is in fact false*. Failure to reject the null under these conditions can mean only one of two things: (1) the null really is true, or (2) the null is false, and this is that one test in five that yields the wrong result. The most logical conclusion to reach in this study is that the effects *are* negligibly small.

As we noted in Chapter 3, a complete evaluation of the meaning of the outcomes of statistical tests requires some knowledge about the probability that the null hypothesis being tested actually is true (i.e., the prior probability of H_0). The central weakness of traditional null hypothesis testing is that this prior probability is thought to be vanishingly small, and perhaps zero (Murphy, 1990). If this prior probability is zero, tests of the null hypothesis cannot provide much useful information.

The central weakness of the alternative approach described in this book, in which minimum-effect hypotheses are framed and tested, is that this prior probability is generally unknown. In Chapter 3, we noted that the prior probability of the traditional null hypothesis would necessarily be very low, and by most definitions is zero. It is likely that the prior probability of a minimum-effect null will also be somewhat low, especially if you are testing the hypothesis that the effect of treatments is at best negligible. Our rationale for believing that this prior will be small is that most treatments in the social and behavioral sciences do indeed have an effect. In Chapter 1, we noted Lipsey and Wilson's (1993) review of over 300 meta-analyses of research studying the efficacy of psychological, educational, and behavioral treatments. These meta-analyses, in turn, summarize the results of thousands of studies in areas ranging from smoking cessation success rates to the effectiveness of computer-aided instruction. Over 85% of the meta-analyses they summarized reported effects that exceeded conventional criteria for "small effects" (i.e., $d = .20$ or $PV = .01$ or less). It is clear from the massive body of research summarized in that paper that a broad range of treatments and applications in the social and behavioral sciences have at least some

effect, and the likelihood that a new treatment will have an absolutely negligible effect strikes us as small, especially if the new treatment is solidly
based in theory and research.

Balancing errors in testing minimum-effect hypotheses. In tests of the traditional null hypothesis, Type I errors are practically impossible and there
is virtually nothing to be lost by setting alpha as high as possible. In tests
of the minimum-effect hypothesis, the strategy of setting alpha as high as
possible is no longer appropriate. The whole distinction between traditional
and minimum-effect null hypotheses is that there is some realistic possibility that a minimum-effect null is true, and it is therefore possible to make
a Type I error.

Although Type I errors are a real possibility in tests of minimum-effect
null hypotheses, this does not mean that power should be ignored in carrying out these tests. The *possibility* of Type I errors should not blind you to
the substantial likelihood that you will make Type II errors if you choose
an unduly stringent alpha level. Choose any cell of the One-Stop *F* Table in
Appendix B, and you will see that (1) a larger *F* value is needed to reject the
minimum-effect null than to reject the traditional null, given the same alpha
level, and (2) a larger *F* value is needed to reject the hypothesis that effects
are small to moderate (i.e., they account for 5% or less of the variance) than
to reject the hypothesis that these effects are negligibly small (i.e., they
account for 1% or less of the variance). That is, all other things being equal,
it is harder to reject a minimum-effect hypothesis than to reject the hypothesis that treatments have no effect whatsoever. The more demanding the
hypothesis (e.g., 5% versus 1% as the upper bound to be tested), the harder
it is to reject H_0. In our view, there is usually no good reason to make things
even more difficult than they already are by choosing an unrealistically
stringent alpha level. Earlier, we suggested that when testing the traditional
null hypothesis, the .01 alpha level should usually be avoided. We believe
the same advice holds for tests of minimum-effect hypothesis; the .01 alpha
level should still be avoided in most cases.

We suggest a two-part test for determining whether you should use an
alpha level of .01 rather than .05. First, .01 makes sense only if the consequences of a Type I error are relatively serious. In Chapter 4, we discussed
concrete ways of comparing the perceived seriousness of Type I and Type II
errors and noted that researchers often act as if falsely rejecting the null is
much more serious than failing to reject the null when you should. This may
well be true in some settings, but before deciding to set a stringent alpha
level (thus markedly decreasing your power), we believe you should explicitly consider the relative costs of the two errors. Choose .01 only if there is
a good reason to believe that a Type I error is substantially more serious
than a Type II error.

Second, .01 makes sense only if the prior probability that the null hypothesis is true is reasonably high. That is, if the hypothesis to be tested is that a treatment has at most a negligible effect (e.g., it accounts for 1% or less of the variance in outcomes), you should be concerned with Type I errors *only* if there is some realistic possibility that the effects of treatments are indeed trivial. Finally, keep in mind that this is a two-part test. Use the .01 level rather than the .05 level only if the consequences of a Type I error are large *and* the possibility that one might actually occur is substantial. In all other cases, we think you should use .05 as an alpha level and that you should use an even more lenient alpha level whenever possible.

Power Analysis: Benefits, Costs, and Implications for Hypothesis Testing

If power analysis is taken seriously, there will be fundamental changes in the design, execution, and interpretation of research in the social and behavioral sciences. We believe that most of these changes will be beneficial and are enthusiastic advocates of power analysis. As we note below, the indirect benefits of power analysis may prove, in the long run, even more important than the direct benefits of adopting this approach. There are, of course, some costs associated with incorporating power analysis in the design and interpretation of research; however, we believe the benefits still substantially outweigh the costs. Finally, it is useful to consider the implications of having extreme levels of power (either extremely high or extremely low) when conducting statistical hypothesis tests.

Direct Benefits of Power Analysis

As we noted in Chapter 1, power analysis can be used as both a planning tool (e.g., determining how many subjects should be included in a study) and a diagnostic tool (e.g., making sense out of previous studies that have either reported or failed to report "significant" results). Individuals who incorporate statistical power analysis into their research repertoire are better equipped to both plan and diagnose research studies, and they directly benefit from the information provided by power analyses.

Planning research. Statistical power analysis provides a rational framework for making important decisions about the design and scope of one's study. To be sure, there are many subjective decisions that must be made in applying power analysis (e.g., what effect size is anticipated, what alpha level is best), and the techniques described in this book do not represent a foolproof formula for making decisions about research design (e.g., choosing between repeated-measures or between-subjects designs) or sample size. The advantage of power analysis over other methods of making these important decisions, which are often made on the basis of force of habit or by following the lead of other researchers, is that it makes explicit the consequences of these design choices for your study. If you are seriously interested in rejecting the null hypothesis, we think a power analysis is absolutely necessary in making good choices about study design and sample size.

Power analysis also highlights the importance of a decision that is usually ignored or made solely on the basis of conventions in one's field (e.g., the alpha level that defines "statistical significance.") The choice of stringent criteria (e.g., $\alpha = .01$) is sometimes interpreted as scientifically rigorous, whereas the choice of less rigorous criteria (e.g., $\alpha = .10$) is sometimes derided as "soft science." Nothing could be further from the truth. In fact, any decision about alpha levels implies some wish to balance Type I and Type II errors, and power analysis is absolutely necessary if you wish to make any kind of sense of that balance. Once you appreciate the implications of choosing different alpha levels for the statistical power of your studies, you are more likely to make sensible choices about this critical parameter.

If power analysis is taken seriously, it is likely that fewer studies with small samples or insufficient sensitivity will be done. In our view, researchers benefit substantially by knowing whether the study they have in mind has any real likelihood of detecting treatment effects. As we note below, the indirect benefits to the field as a whole that might come with a decline in small-sample research are even greater than the benefits to the individual researcher.

Interpreting research. One criticism of tests of the traditional null hypothesis is that they can routinely mislead researchers and readers. Researchers who uncover a "significant" result are likely to confuse that with an important or meaningful result. This is hardly surprising; most dictionary definitions of *significant* include "important," "weighty," or "noteworthy" as synonyms. Similarly, *nonsignificant* is easily confused with "not important" or "nonmeaningful." As power analysis clearly shows, very meaningful and important treatment effects are likely to be "nonsignificant" if the study lacks power, whereas completely trivial effects are likely to be "significant" if enough data are collected. It is impossible to sensibly interpret "significant" or "nonsignificant" results without considering the level of statistical power in the study that produced those results.

To give a concrete illustration, suppose you reviewed a dozen studies, all of which reported a "nonsignificant" correlation between attitudes toward drug use and subsequent drug consumption. What does this mean? If the studies are all based on small samples, it is entirely possible that there *is* a real and meaningful correlation between attitudes and subsequent behavior (e.g., if $N = 30$ and $\alpha = .05$, power for detecting a correlation as large as .30 is only .50), and that the studies simply did not have enough power to detect it. On the other hand, if all the studies included very large samples (e.g., $N = 2,500$), you could probably conclude that there is essentially no relationship between present attitudes and future behavior. Although the traditional null hypothesis might not be literally true in this instance, it would have to be very nearly true. With this much power, the studies you reviewed would have almost certainly detected any consistent relationships between attitudes and behavior.

Indirect Benefits of Power Analysis

The widespread use of power analysis is likely to confer many indirect benefits. Most notably, studies designed with statistical power in mind are likely to use large samples and sensitive procedures. Perhaps even more important, power analysis directs the researcher's attention toward the most important parameter of all—the effect size. The ultimate benefit of statistical power analysis may be that it forces researchers to think about the strength of the effects they study, rather than thinking only about whether a particular effect is "significant."

Large samples, sensitive procedures. Small samples are the bane of social science research (Hunter & Schmidt, 1990; Schmidt, 1992). These studies produce unstable results, which in turn produce attempts to develop theories to "explain" what may be little more than sampling error. If power analyses were routinely included in the process of designing and planning studies, large samples would be the norm and sampling error would not loom as so large a barrier to cumulative progress in research.

Proponents of meta-analysis (e.g., Schmidt, 1992) note that by combining the outcomes of multiple small-sample studies, it is possible to draw sensible conclusions about effect sizes, even if the individual study samples are too small to provide either sufficient power or stable results. There is merit to this position, but there are also two problems with this solution to the problem of small samples. First, it creates a two-tiered structure in which the primary researchers do all the work, with little possibility of rewards (i.e., they do studies that cannot be published because of insufficient power and sensitivity) and the meta-analyst gets all the credit for amassing this material into an interpretable whole. Second, it leaves the meta-analyst at the mercy of a pool of primary researchers. Unless there are many studies examining *exactly* the question the meta-analyst wants answered, the only alternatives are to change the question or to aggregate studies that in fact differ in important ways. Neither alternative seems attractive, and if power analysis becomes routine, neither will be strictly necessary. If future studies include large samples and sensitive procedures, the need for meta-analyses will become less pressing than it is today.

The decision to use large samples is itself likely to improve other aspects of the research. For example, if you know that you will have to devote considerable time and resources to data collection, you will probably take more care to pre-test, use reliable measures, follow well–laid out procedures, etc. In contrast, if running a study amounts to little more than rounding up 25 undergraduates and herding them to your lab, the need for careful planning, precise measurement, etc., might not be pressing. In large-sample research, you may have only one chance to get things right, and you are less likely to rely on shoddy measures, incomplete procedures, etc. The net result of all this is that studies carried out with careful attention to statistical power are likely to be better and more useful than studies carried out with little regard for power.

Focus on effect size. If you scan most social science journals, you will find that the outcomes of significance tests are routinely reported, but effect size information is sometimes nowhere to be found. Our statistical training tends to focus our attention on p values and significance levels and not on the substantive question of how well our treatments, interventions, tests, etc., work (see Cowles, 1989, for a historical analysis of why social scientists focus on significance tests). One of the most important advantages of statistical power analysis is that it makes it virtually impossible to ignore effect sizes.

The whole point of statistical analysis is to help you understand your data, and it has become increasingly clear over the years that an exclusive focus on significance testing is an impediment to understanding what the data mean (Cohen, 1994; Schmidt, 1992; Wilkinson et al., 1999). Statistical power analysis forces you to think about the sort of effect you expect, or at least about the sort of effect you want to be able to detect; once you start thinking along these lines, it is unlikely you will forget to think about the sort of effect you actually *did* find. If power analysis did nothing more than direct researchers' attention to the size of their effects, it would be well worth the effort.

Costs Associated With Power Analysis

Statistical power analysis brings a number of benefits, but there are also costs. Most notably, researchers who pay attention to statistical power will find it harder to carry out studies than researchers who do not think about power when planning or evaluating studies. Most researchers (the authors included) have done studies with small samples and insufficient power and have "gotten away with it," in the sense that they reported significant results. Even when power is low, there is always some chance that you will reject H_0, and a clever researcher can make a career out of "getting lucky." Power analysis will lead you to do fewer small-sample studies, which in the long run might mean fewer studies period. It is relatively easy to do a dozen small-sample studies, with the knowledge that some will work and some will not. It is not so easy to do a dozen large-sample studies, and one long-term result of applying power analysis is that the sheer number of studies performed in a field might go down. We don't see this as a bad thing, at least if many low-quality, small-sample studies are replaced with a few higher-quality, large-sample studies. Nevertheless, the prospects for building a lengthy *vita* by doing dozens of studies might be diminished if you pay serious attention to power analysis.

The most serious cost that might be associated with the widespread use of power analysis is an overemphasis on scientific conservatism. If studies are hard to carry out and require significant resources (time, money, energy), there may be less willingness to try new ideas and approaches or to test creative hypotheses. The long-term prospects for scientific progress are not good if researchers are unwilling or unable to take risks or try new ideas.

Implications of Power Analysis: Can Power Be Too High?

Throughout this book, we have advocated paying attention to the probability that you will be able to reject a null hypothesis you believe to be wrong (i.e., power). The pitfalls of low power are reasonably obvious, but it is worth considering whether power can be too high. Suppose you follow the advice laid out in this book and design a study with a very high level of power (e.g., power = .95). One implication is there is little real doubt about the outcomes of your statistical tests; with few exceptions, your tests will yield "significant" outcomes.

When power is extreme (either high or low), you are not likely to learn much by conducting a formal hypothesis test. This might imply that power can be too high. We don't think so. Even when the outcome of a formal statistical hypothesis test is virtually known in advance, statistical analysis still has clear and obvious value. First, the statistics used in hypothesis testing usually provide an effect size estimate or the information needed to make this estimate. Even if the statistical test itself provided little new information (with very high or very low power, you know how things will turn out), the *process* of carrying out a statistical test usually provides information that can be used to evaluate the stability and potential replicability of your results.

Consider, for example, the familiar *t*-test. The *t*-statistic is a ratio of the difference between sample means to the standard error of the difference.[1] If the level of power in your study is very high, tests of the significance of *t* might not be all that informative; high power means that it will exceed the threshold for "significance" in virtually all cases. However, the *value* of *t* is still informative because it gives you an easy way of determining the standard error term, which in turn can be used in forming confidence intervals. For example, if the $M_1 - M_2 = 10.0$ and $t = 2.50$, it follows that the standard error of the difference between the means is 4.0 (i.e., 10.0/2.5), and a 95% confidence interval for the difference between means would be 7.84 units wide (i.e., $1.96 \cdot 4.0$). This confidence interval gives a very concrete indication of how much variation one might expect from study to study when comparing M_1 with M_2.

In general, the standard error terms for test statistics tend to become smaller as samples get larger. This is a concrete illustration of the general principle that large samples provide stable and consistent statistical estimates, whereas small samples provide unstable estimates. Even in settings where the significance of a particular statistical test is not in doubt, confidence intervals provide very useful information. Obtaining a confidence interval allows you to determine just how much sampling error you might expect in your statistical estimates.

The paragraph above illustrates a distinction that is sometimes blurred by researchers—i.e., the distinction between statistical analysis and null hypothesis testing. Researchers in the behavioral and social sciences have tended to over-emphasize formal hypothesis tests and have paid too little attention to critical questions such as, "How large is the effect of the treatments studied here?" (Cohen, 1994; Cowles, 1989; Wilkinson et al., 1999). Ironically, serious attention to the topic of power analysis is likely to *reduce* researchers' dependence on significance testing. The more you know about power, the more likely you are to take steps to maximize statistical power, which means that rejecting the null should be nearly a foregone conclusion. Once you understand that the null hypothesis test is *not* the most important facet of your statistical analysis, you are likely to turn your attention to the aspects of your analysis that are more important, such as estimating effect sizes.

Does all this mean that null hypothesis tests should be abandoned? Probably not. First, as we have noted throughout this book, many of the outstanding criticisms of the null hypothesis can be easily addressed by shifting from tests of point hypotheses (e.g., that treatments have no effect

---

[1] The formula for t is $t = \dfrac{M_1 - M_2}{SE_{M_1 - M_2}}$ or $t = \dfrac{M_1 - M_2}{\sqrt{\dfrac{\sigma_1^2}{n_1} + \dfrac{\sigma_2^2}{n_2}}}$.

whatsoever) to tests of range or interval hypotheses (e.g., that the effects of treatments fall within some range of values denoting small effects). Second, the prospects for fundamental changes in research strategies seem poor, judging from the historical record (Cowles, 1989). Statisticians have been arguing for decades that the use of confidence intervals is preferable to the use of null hypothesis tests, with little apparent effect on actual research practice. Critics of null hypothesis tests have not suggested an alternative that is both viable *and* likely to be widely adopted. There is every indication that null hypothesis tests are here to stay and that careful attention should be given to methods of making the process of hypothesis testing as useful and informative as possible. Careful attention to the principles of power analysis is likely to lead to better research and better statistical analyses.

Summary

Power analysis has profound implications for statistical hypothesis testing, regardless of whether you test the traditional null hypothesis (i.e., that treatments had no effect whatsoever) or a minimum-effect null hypothesis (e.g., that the effects of treatments are at best small). In tests of the traditional null, Type I errors are very unlikely (because the traditional null is essentially false by definition), and your only real concern in structuring significance tests should be for maximizing power. This can be done by collecting huge samples or by using extremely sensitive procedures. But there is an easier way to accomplish this goal: When testing the traditional null hypothesis, you should always set your alpha level as high as you dare. Unfortunately, the weight of tradition rarely allows you to choose an alpha level higher than .05 (alpha of .10 is seen in some social science research, but even there, it is barely tolerated). You should never choose a more stringent level, unless there is some very unusual and compelling reason to do so.

Tests of minimum-effect null hypotheses are less familiar, but in fact, virtually everything you know about hypothesis testing applies to tests of this sort. In fact, much of what you already know about hypothesis testing applies better to tests of minimum-effect null hypotheses than to tests of the traditional null.

When testing minimum-effect null hypotheses, you must seriously consider the possibility that the null hypothesis will be true. This opens the door for what is sometimes considered statistical heresy (i.e., accepting the null). It also opens the door to the possibility that Type I errors will be made, which means that alpha levels, statistical tests, balancing Type I and Type II errors, etc., have some real meaning in this context.

Power analysis has many benefits. It helps you make informed decisions about the design of your own research (especially about the number of cases needed and the choice of alpha levels), and it also helps you make sense out of other researchers' "significant" or "nonsignificant" results. However, the indirect benefits of power analysis may be the most important. Power analysis is likely to lead you to use larger samples, which in turn will often encourage you to use better measures, more pre-tests, more carefully designed procedures, etc. Power analysis also helps to focus your attention on effect sizes, rather than focusing exclusively on the p value associated with some statistical test. All of this is likely to improve the quality and consistency of social science research.

There are some costs associated with using power analysis. In particular, you will often find it hard to obtain samples large enough to provide sufficient power. This is especially true in studies where the central hypothesis involves some complex higher-order interaction between multiple independent variables. It can be prohibitively difficult to obtain enough power to sensibly test such hypotheses. Reliance on power analysis may also indirectly discourage researchers from trying out new concepts, hypotheses, or procedures.

Throughout this book, we have advocated careful attention to statistical power. As the level of power increases, you should have less and less doubt about the outcomes of null hypothesis tests. Ironically, careful attention to power is likely to *decrease* the relative importance of null hypothesis tests and increase the attention you pay to other aspects of your statistical analysis, notably effect sizes and confidence intervals. We see this as a good thing. Null hypothesis testing is valuable (especially when testing minimum-effect null hypotheses), but it should not be the primary focus of your statistical analysis. Rather, well-conducted null hypothesis tests should be only a part of the analytic arsenal bought to bear when attempting to determine what your data really mean. Power analysis is the first step in carrying out sensible tests of both traditional and minimum-effect null hypotheses.

References

Algina, J., & Keselman, H. J. (1997). Detecting repeated measures effects with univariate and multivariate statistics. *Psychological Methods, 2,* 208–218.

Beaty, J. C., Cleveland, J. N., & Murphy, K. R. (2001). The relationship between personality and contextual performance in "strong" versus "weak" situations. *Human Performance, 14,* 125–148.

Bradley, D. R., & Russell, R. R. (1998). Some cautions regarding statistical power in split-plot designs. *Behavioral Research Methods: Instruments and Computers, 30,* 462–477.

Bunce, D., & West. M. A. (1995). Self perceptions and perceptions of group climate as predictors of individual innovation at work. *Applied Psychology: An International Review, 44,* 199–215.

Carroll, J. B. (1993). *Human cognitive abilities: A survey of factor-analytic studies.* Cambridge, England: Cambridge University Press.

Cascio, W. F., & Zedeck, S. (1983). Open a new window in rational research planning: Adjust alpha to maximize statistical power. *Personnel Psychology, 36,* 517–526.

Chow, S.L. (1988). Significance test or effect size? *Psychological Bulletin, 103,* 105–110.

Clapp, J. F., & Rizk, K. H. (1992). Effect of recreational exercise on midtrimester placental growth. *American Journal of Obstetrics and Gynecology, 167,* 1518–1521.

Cohen, J. (1962). The statistical power of abnormal-social psychological research. *Journal of Abnormal and Social Psychology, 65,* 145–153.

Cohen, J. (1988). *Statistical power analysis for the behavioral sciences* (2nd ed.). Hillsdale, NJ: Lawrence Erlbaum Associates.

Cohen, J. (1994). The earth is round (p < .05). *American Psychologist, 49,* 997–1003.

Cohen, J., & Cohen, P. (1983). *Applied multiple regression/correlation analysis for the behavioral sciences.* Hillsdale, NJ: Lawrence Erlbaum Associates.

Cortina, J. M., & Dunlap, W. P. (1997). On the logic and purpose of significance testing. *Psychological Methods, 2,* 161–173.

Cotton, M.M., & Evans, K.M. (1990). An evaluation of the Irlen lenses as a treatment for specific reading disorders, *Australian Journal of Psychology, 42,* 1–12.

Cowles, M. (1989). *Statistics in psychology: An historical perspective.* Hillsdale, NJ: Lawrence Erlbaum Associates.

Cowles, M., & Davis, C. (1982). On the origins of the .05 level of statistical significance. *American Psychologist, 37,* 553–558.

Evans, B.J., & Drasdo, N. (1991). Tinted lenses and related therapies for learning disabilities: A review. *Ophthalmic and Physiological Optics, 11,* 206–217.

Fick, P. L. (1995). Accepting the null hypothesis. *Memory and Cognition, 23,* 132–138.

Greenhouse, S. W., & Geisser, S. (1959). On method in the analysis of profile data. *Psychometrika, 24,* 95–112.

Greenwald, A. G. (1993). Consequences of prejudice against the null hypothcsis. In G. Keren & C. Lewis (Eds.), *A handbook for data analysis in the behavioral sciences: Methodological issues* (pp. 419–448). Hillsdale, NJ: Lawrence Erlbaum Associates.

Grissom, R. J. (1994). Probability of the superior outcome of one treatment over another. *Journal of Applied Psychology, 79,* 314–316.

Guilford, J. P., & Fruchter, B. (1978). *Fundamental statistics in psychology and education* (6th ed.). New York: McGraw-Hill.

Gutenberg, R. L., Arvey, R. D., Osburn, H. G., & Jenneret, P. R. (1983). Moderating effects of decision-making/information processing job dimensions on test validities. *Journal of Applied Psychology, 68,* 602–608.

Haase, R. R., Waechter, D. M., & Solomon, G. S. (1982). How significant is a significant difference? Average effect size of research in counseling psychology. *Journal of Counseling Psychology, 29,* 58–65.

Hagen, R. L. (1997). In praise of the null hypothesis statistical test. *American Psychologist, 52,* 15–24.

Hedges, L. V. (1987). How hard is hard science, how soft is soft science? *American Psychologist, 42,* 443–455.

Himel, H. N., Liberati, A., Laird, R. D., & Chalmers, T. C. (1986). Adjuvant chemotherapy for breast cancer: A pooled estimate based on published randomized control trials. *Journal of the American Medical Association, 256,* 1148–1159.

Horton, R. L. (1978). *The general linear model: Data analysis in the social and behavioral sciences.* New York: McGraw-Hill.

Hunter, J. E., & Hirsh, H. R. (1987). Applications of meta-analysis. In C. L. Cooper & I. T. Robertson (Eds.), *International review of industrial and organizational psychology* (pp. 321–357). Chichester, England: Wiley.

Hunter, J. E., & Hunter, R. F. (1984). Validity and utility of alternative predictors of job performance. *Psychological Bulletin, 96,* 72–98.

Hunter, J. E., & Schmidt, F. L. (1990). *Methods of meta-analysis: Correcting error and bias in research findings.* Newbury Park, CA: Sage.

Irlen, H. (1993). Scotopic Sensitivity and Reading disability. Paper presented at the 91st Annual Convention of the American Psychological Association, Anaheim, California.

Kraemer, H. C., & Thiemann, S. (1987). *How many subjects?* Newbury Park, CA: Sage.

Labovitz, S. (1968). Criteria for selecting a significance level: A note on the sacredness of .05. *American Sociologist, 3,* 220–222.

Landy, F. J., Farr. J. L., & Jacobs, R. R. (1982). Utility concepts in performance measurement. *Organizational Behavior and Human Performance, 30,* 15–40.

Lipsey, M. W. (1990). *Design sensitivity.* Newbury Park, CA: Sage.

Lipsey, M. W., & Wilson, D. B. (1993). The efficacy of psychological, educational, and behavioral treatment. *American Psychologist, 48,* 1181–1209.

Martin, F., Mackenzie, B., Lovegrove, W., & McNicol, D. (1993). Irlen lenses in the treatment of specific reading disability: An evaluation of outcomes and processes. *Australian Journal of Psychology, 45,* 141–150.

Maxwell, S. E., & Delaney, H. D. (1990). *Designing experiments and analysing data.* Belmont, CA: Wadsworth.

McDaniel, M. A. (1988). Does pre-employment drug use predict on-the-job suitability? *Personnel Psychology, 41,* 717–729.

Meehl, P. (1978). Theoretical risks and tabular asterisks: Sir Karl, Sir Ronald, and the slow progress of psychology. *Journal of Consulting and Clinical Psychology, 46,* 806–834.

Mone, M. A., Mueller, G. C., & Mauland, W. (1996). The perceptions and usage of statistical power in applied psychology and management research. *Personnel Psychology, 49,* 103–120.

Morrison, D. E., & Henkel, R. E. (1970). *The significance test controversy: A reader.* Chicago: Aldine.

Murphy, K. (1990). If the null hypothesis is impossible, why test it? *American Psychologist, 45,* 403–404.

Murphy, K., & Myors, B. (1999). Testing the hypothesis that treatments have negligible effects: Minimum-effect tests in the general linear model. *Journal of Applied Psychology, 84,* 234–248.

Nagel, S. S., & Neff, M. (1977). Determining an optimal level of statistical significance. *Evaluation Studies Review Annual, 2,* 146–158.

Neale, M.B. (1973). *The Neale Analysis of Reading Ability,* London, Macmillan.

Osburn, H. G., Callender, J. C., Greener, J. M., & Ashworth, S. (1983). Statistical power of tests of the situational specificity hypothesis in validity generalization studies: A cautionary note. *Journal of Applied Psychology, 68,* 115–122.

Overall, J. E. (1996). How many repeated measurements are useful? *Journal of Clinical Psychology, 52,* 243–252.

Patnaik, P. B. (1949). The non-central t- and F-distributions and their applications. *Biometrika, 36,* 202–232.

Pearson, E. S., & Hartley, H. O. (1951). Charts of a power-function for analysis of variance tests, derived from the non-central F-distribution. *Biometrika, 38,* 112–130.

Reeve, C. P. (1986a). Accurate computation of the log of the gamma function. Statistical Engineering Division Note 86-1. Gaithersburg, MD: National Bureau of Standards.

Reeve, C. P. (1986b). An algorithm for computing the beta C. D. F. to a specified accuracy. Statistical Engineering Division Note 86-3. Gaithersburg, MD: National Bureau of Standards.

Reeve, C. P. (1986c). An algorithm for computing the doubly noncentral F. C. D. F. to a specified accuracy. Statistical Engineering Division Note 86-4. Gaithersburg, MD: National Bureau of Standards.

Rosenthal, R. (1991). *Meta-analytic procedures for social research.* Newbury Park. CA: Sage.

Rosenthal, R. (1993). Cumulating evidence. In G. Keren & C. Lewis (Eds.), *A handbook for data analysis in the behavioral sciences: Methodological issues* (pp. 519–559). Hillsdale, NJ: Lawrence Erlbaum Associates.

Rouanet, H. (1996). Bayesian methods for assessing the importance of effects. *Psychological Bulletin, 119,* 149–158.

Ryan, T. A. (1962). The experiment as the unit for computing rates of error. *Psychological Bulletin, 59,* 301–305.

Sackett, P. R., Harris, M. M., & Orr, J. M. (1986). On seeking moderator variables in the meta-analysis of correlational data: A Monte Carlo investigation of statistical power and resistance to Type I error. *Journal of Applied Psychology, 71,* 302–310.

Schmidt, F. L. (1992). What do the data really mean? Research findings, meta-analysis and cumulative knowledge in psychology. *American Psychologist, 47,* 1173–1181.

Schmidt, F L. (1996). Statistical significance testing and cumulative knowledge in psychology: Implications for training of researchers. *Psychological Methods, 1,* 115–129.

Schmidt, F. L., Hunter, J. E., McKenzie, R. C., & Muldrow. T. W. (1979). Impact of valid selection procedures on work-force productivity. *Journal of Applied Psychology, 71,* 432–439.

Schmidt, F. L., Mack, M. J., & Hunter, J. E. (1984). Selection utility in the occupation of U.S. park ranger for three modes of test use. *Journal of Applied Psychology, 69,* 490–497.

Schmitt, N., Gooding, R.Z., Noe, R.D. & Kirsch, M. (1984). Metaanalyses of validity studies published between 1964 and 1982 and the investigation of study characteristics. *Personnel Psychology, 37,* 407–422.

Sedlmeier, P., & Gigerenzer, G. (1989). Do studies of statistical power have an effect on the power of studies? *Psychological Bulletin, 105,* 309–316.

Serlin, R. A., & Lapsley, D. K. (1985). Rationality in psychological research: The good-enough principle. *American Psychologist, 40,* 73–83.

Serlin, R. A., & Lapsley, D. K. (1993). Rational appraisal of psychological research and the good-enough principle. In G. Keren & C. Lewis (Eds.), *A handbook for data analysis in the behavioral sciences: Methodological issues* (pp. 199–228). Hillsdale, NJ: Lawrence Erlbaum Associates.

Siegel, S. (1956). *Nonparametric statistics for the behavioral sciences.* New York: McGraw-Hill.

Stevens, J. P. (1980). Power of multivariate analysis of variance tests. *Psychological Bulletin, 86,* 728–737.

Stevens, J. (1988). *Applied multivariate statistics for the social sciences.* Hillsdale, NJ: Lawrence Erlbaum Associates.

Stevens, J. P. (2002). *Applied multivariate statistics for the social sciences* (4th ed.). Hillsdale, NJ: Lawrence Erlbaum Associates.

Tatsuoka, M. (1993a). Effect size. In G. Keren & C. Lewis (Eds.), *A handbook for data analysis in the behavioral sciences: Methodological issues* (pp. 461–479). Hillsdale. NJ: Lawrence Erlbaum Associates.

Tatsuoka, M. (1993b). Elements of the general linear model. In G. Keren & C. Lewis (Eds.), *A handbook for data analysis in the behavioral sciences: Statistical issues* (pp. 3–42). Hillsdale, NJ: Lawrence Erlbaum Associates.

Tiku, M.L., & Yip, D.Y.N. (1978). A four-moment approximation based on the F distribution. *Australian Journal of Statistics, 20*(3), 257–261.

Vonesh, E. F., & Schork, M. A. (1986). Sample sizes in the multivariate analysis of repeated measurements. *Biometrics, 42,* 601–610.

Wilcox, R. R. (1992). Why can methods for comparing means have relatively low power, and what can you do to correct the problem? *Current Directions in Psychological Science, 1,* 101–105.

Wilkinson, L., & Task Force on Statistical Inference. (1999). Statistical methods in psychology journals: Guidelines and explanations. *American Psychologist, 54,* 594–604.

Winter, S. (1987). Irlen lenses: An appraisal. *The Australian Educational and Developmental Psychologist, 4,* 1–5.

Yuen, K. K. (1974). The two-sample trimmed t for unequal population variances. *Biometrika, 61,* 165–170.

Zimmerman, D. W., & Zumbo, B. D. (1993). The relative power of parametric and nonparametric statistical methods. In G. Keren & C. Lewis (Eds.), *A handbook for data analysis in the behavioral sciences: Methodological issues* (pp. 481–518). Hillsdale, NJ: Lawrence Erlbaum Associates.

Zwick, R., & Marascuilo, L. A. (1984). Selection of pairwise comparison procedures for parametric and nonparametric analysis of variance models. *Psychological Bulletin, 95,* 148–155.

Appendix A

Working With the Noncentral *F* Distribution

There are several analytic approaches for estimating the noncentral *F* distribution for the purpose of power analysis. First, of course, it is possible to calculate the distribution of *F* for any combination of df_{hyp}, df_{err}, and λ. Programs for estimating this distribution can be found on a variety of websites (e.g., http://www.danielsoper.com/statcalc/calc06.aspx).

Second, you might use tables of the familiar *F* distribution that are included in most statistics texts to estimate values in a noncentral *F* distribution, using reasonably simple approximation based on the central *F* distribution (Horton, 1978; Patnaik, 1949; see also Tiku & Yip, 1978). The distribution of the noncentral *F*, with the degrees of freedom df_{hyp} and df_{err}, is strongly related to the central *F* distribution with the degrees of freedom g and df_{err}, where

$$g = (df_{hyp} + \lambda)^2/(df_{hyp} + 2\lambda) \tag{A.1}$$

For example, suppose a researcher randomly assigns 123 subjects to one of three treatments and reports the following results:

	Sum of Squares	df	Mean Square	F	PV
Treatments	10.00	2	5.00	2.50	.04
Error	240.00	120	2.00		
Total	250.00				

This table gives you enough information to estimate the noncentrality parameter ($\lambda = SS_{treatments}/MS_{err} = 10/2 = 5.0$), and this in turn allows you to estimate the noncentral *F* distribution that corresponds to this study. First, calculate the value of *g*:

$$g = (2 + 5.0)^2/(2 + 10) = 49/12 = 4.08$$

Because *g* will be used to estimate the degrees of freedom of the central *F* distribution that is most closely linked to the noncentral *F* distribution with 2 and 120 degrees of freedom and a noncentrality parameter of $\lambda = 5.0$, this value is rounded downwards to 4.0. That is, the noncentral *F* distribution we are interested in will be closely related to the central F distribution with degrees of freedom of 4 and 120.

To calculate power, first calculate the quantity $F*$:

$$F* = F_{(critical)}/[(df_{hyp} + \lambda)/df_{hyp}] \qquad (A.2)$$

where $F_{(critical)}$ is the critical F value ($\alpha = .05$) for the familiar central F with degrees of freedom g and df_{err}. If you go to an F table, you will find that the critical value for testing the null hypothesis is 3.07. Therefore, $F*$ is given by

$$F* = 3.07/[(2 + 5.0)/2] = 3.07/3.50 = .877$$

Once you have determined the value of $F*$, any reasonably detailed table of the familiar central F distribution will allow you to determine the proportion of the F distribution that has a value greater than or equal to $F*$. In the central F distribution with 4 and 120 degrees of freedom (remember, $g = 4$ and $df_{err} = 120$), approximately 50% of the F values are .877 or greater. Therefore, in a population in which treatments are expected to account for 4% of the variance in outcomes (i.e., $PV = .04$), a study that is based on $N = 123$ will have power of .50.

A third method is to use a computer program specifically designed for computing probabilities in the noncentral F distribution. For example, it is possible to obtain estimates of the appropriate noncentral F using simple functions that are built into a number of widely used programs (e.g., SPSS, Excel). In SPSS, the statement is

COMPUTE p = NCDF.F($F_{observed}$, df_{hyp}, df_{err}, df_{err} PV/(1 − PV))

Using the data from our previous example, this statement would become

COMPUTE p = NCDF.F(2.50, 2, 120, 5.00)

This statement will return a value of approximately .50, which is the power of this test given df_{hyp}, df_{err}, and λ values of 2, 120, and 5.00, respectively.

Appendix B

One-Stop *F* Table

df_{err}			1	2	3	4	5	6	7	8	9	10	12	15	20	30	40	60	120
3	nil	.05	10.13	9.55	9.28	9.12	9.01	8.94	8.89	8.85	8.81	8.79	8.74	8.70	8.66	8.62	8.59	8.57	8.55
	nil	.01	34.12	30.82	29.46	28.71	28.24	27.91	27.67	27.49	27.35	27.23	27.05	26.87	26.69	26.50	26.41	26.32	26.22
	pow	.50	8.26	7.21	6.78	6.54	6.39	6.29	6.22	6.16	6.12	6.08	6.02	5.97	5.91	5.86	5.82	5.80	5.76
	pow	.80	18.17	15.70	14.83	14.42	14.19	13.93	13.85	13.69	13.66	13.64	13.55	13.48	13.42	13.30	13.26	13.17	12.66
	1%	.05	10.43	9.70	9.37	9.19	9.07	8.99	8.93	8.88	8.84	8.81	8.77	8.72	8.67	8.63	8.60	8.58	8.55
	1%	.01	35.15	31.28	29.75	28.93	28.41	28.05	27.79	27.59	27.44	27.31	27.12	26.93	26.73	26.53	26.43	26.33	26.23
	pow	.50	8.53	7.33	6.85	6.60	6.44	6.33	6.25	6.19	6.14	6.10	6.04	5.98	5.92	5.86	5.83	5.81	5.79
	pow	.80	18.72	16.04	14.96	14.50	14.25	13.98	13.89	13.82	13.69	13.66	13.56	13.48	13.42	13.34	13.31	13.25	13.07
	5%	.05	11.72	10.30	9.76	9.48	9.30	9.18	9.09	9.02	8.97	8.92	8.86	8.79	8.73	8.66	8.63	8.59	8.56
	5%	.01	39.41	33.23	31.00	29.84	29.13	28.64	28.30	28.03	27.82	27.66	27.41	27.15	26.90	26.64	26.52	26.39	26.26
	pow	.50	9.57	7.82	7.17	6.83	6.62	6.48	6.38	6.30	6.24	6.19	6.12	6.04	5.97	5.89	5.86	5.82	5.8O
	pow	.80	20.77	17.02	15.60	14.98	14.63	14.30	14.16	14.07	13.90	13.86	13.72	13.62	13.51	13.40	13.38	13.33	13.18
4	nil	.05	7.71	6.94	6.59	6.39	6.26	6.16	6.09	6.04	6.00	5.96	5.91	5.86	5.80	5.75	5.72	5.69	5.66
	nil	.01	21.20	18.00	16.69	15.98	15.52	15.21	14.98	14.80	14.66	14.55	14.37	14.20	14.02	13.84	13.75	13.65	13.56
	pow	.50	6.68	5.48	5.00	4.73	4.55	4.43	4.34	4.27	4.22	4.17	4.10	4.03	3.96	3.89	3.86	3.82	3.78
	pow	.80	14.17	11.30	10.22	9.66	9.24	9.02	8.86	8.75	8.60	8.53	8.44	8.30	8.19	8.04	7.95	7.87	7.80
	1%	.05	8.02	7.08	6.68	6.45	6.31	6.20	6.13	6.07	6.03	5.99	5.93	5.87	5.81	5.75	5.72	5.69	5.66
	1%	.01	22.05	18.36	16.92	16.14	15.65	15.31	15.06	14_87	14.72	14.60	14.42	14.24	14.05	13.86	13.76	13.66	13.56
	pow	.50	6.94	5.60	5.07	4.78	4.60	4.46	4.37	4.30	4.24	4.19	4.12	4.05	3.97	3.90	3.86	3.82	3.79
	pow	.80	14.64	11.50	10.34	9.75	9.39	9.07	8.91	8.78	8.69	8.56	8.46	6.32	8.20	8.O8	7.96	7.88	7.88
	5%	.05	9.31	7.67	7.05	6.72	6.52	6.38	6.28	6.20	6.14	6.09	6.02	5.94	5.86	5.79	5.75	5.71	5.67
	5%	.01	25.49	19.86	17.85	16.81	16.17	15.74	15.42	15.19	15.00	14.85	14.63	14.40	14.17	13.93	13.82	13.70	13.58

df_{hyp}

pow	.50	8.05	6.10	5.39	5.01	4.77	4.61	4.50	4.40	4.33	4.28	4.19	4.10	4.02	3.93	3.88	3.84	3.80
pow	.80	16.63	12.42	10.93	10.18	9.65	9.36	9.15	9.00	8.82	8.73	8.61	8.43	8.25	8.12	8.00	7.91	7.78
5 nil	.05	6.61	5.79	5.41	5.19	5.05	4.95	4.88	4.82	4.77	4.73	4.68	4.62	4.56	4.50	4.46	4.43	4.40
nil	.01	16.26	13.27	12.06	11.39	10.97	10.67	10.46	10.29	10.16	10.08	9.89	9.72	9.55	9.38	9.29	9.20	9.11
pow	.50	5.91	4.66	4.14	3.87	3.70	3.57	3.48	3.41	3.35	3.31	3.23	3.15	3.08	3.00	2.96	2.91	2.87
pow	.80	12.35	9.38	8.19	7.60	7.24	6.94	6.77	6.59	6.50	6.43	6.28	6.11	5.97	5.83	5.74	5.65	5.51
1%	.05	6.94	5.93	5.50	5.26	5.10	4.99	4.91	4.85	4.80	4.76	4.70	4.63	4.57	4.50	4.47	4.44	4.40
1%	.01	17.07	13.61	12.26	11.54	11.08	10.76	10.53	10.35	10.21	10.10	9.93	9.75	9.58	9.39	9.30	9.21	9.12
pow	.50	6.20	4.78	4.24	3.93	3.75	3.61	3.51	3.44	3.37	3.33	3.25	3.17	3.09	3.00	2.96	2.92	2.88
pow	.80	12.85	9.50	8.38	7.68	7.30	6.99	6.81	6.68	6.53	6.46	6.30	6.17	5.98	5.84	5.76	5.66	5.54
5%	.05	8.31	6.54	5.88	5.53	5.32	5.17	5.06	4.98	4.91	4.86	4.78	4.70	4.62	4.54	4.49	4.45	4.41
5%	.01	20.28	14.97	13.10	12.13	11.54	11.14	10.85	10.63	10.45	10.31	10.10	9.89	9.68	9.46	9.35	9.24	9.13
pow	.50	7.42	5.33	4.56	4.18	3.94	3.77	3.65	3.55	3.48	3.42	3.32	3.23	3.13	3.03	2.98	2.93	2.88
pow	.80	14.92	10.5	8.90	8.11	7.64	7.27	7.05	6.84	6.72	6.62	6.44	6.24	6.07	5.89	5.78	5.67	5.55
6 nil	.05	5.99	5.14	4.76	4.53	4.39	4.28	4.21	4.15	4.10	4.06	4.00	3.94	3.87	3.81	3.77	3.74	3.70
nil	.01	13.74	10.92	9.78	9.15	8.75	8.47	8.26	8.10	7.98	7.87	7.72	7.56	7.40	7.23	7.14	7.06	6.96
pow	.50	5.45	4.15	3.67	3.39	3.21	3.08	2.99	2.92	2.86	2.82	2.74	2.66	2.58	2.49	2.45	2.40	2.31
pow	.80	11.33	8.29	7.15	6.51	6.12	5.84	5.65	5.50	5.38	5.28	5.10	4.95	4.80	4.65	4.56	4.46	4.31
1%	.05	6.35	5.30	4.85	4.60	4.44	4.33	4.24	4.18	4.13	4.08	4.02	3.95	3.89	3.82	3.78	3.74	3.70
1%	.01	14.56	11.25	9.93	9.29	8.85	8.55	8.33	8.16	8.03	7.92	7.76	7.59	7.42	7.24	7.15	7.06	6.97
pow	.50	5.77	4.32	3.75	3.45	3.25	3.12	3.02	2.95	2.89	2.84	2.76	2.68	2.59	2.50	2.45	2.41	2.31
pow	.80	11.86	8.54	7.28	6.60	6.19	5.90	5.69	5.53	5.41	5.31	5.16	5.00	4.82	4.66	4.56	4.46	4.32
5%	.05	7.82	5.94	5.25	4.89	4.66	4.51	4.40	4.31	4.24	4.19	4.11	4.02	3.94	3.85	3.80	3.76	3.71
5%	.01	17.73	12.58	10.78	9.86	9.29	8.91	8.63	8.42	8.25	8.12	7.92	7.72	7.51	7.30	7.20	7.09	6.98
pow	.50	7.11	4.88	4.13	3.72	3.47	3.29	3.17	3.06	2.98	2.93	2.83	2.74	2.64	2.53	2.48	2.42	2.32
pow	.80	14.05	9.45	7.88	7.04	6.53	6.18	5.93	5.70	5.55	5.43	5.26	5.08	4.90	4.69	4.60	4.49	4.33
8 nil	.05	5.32	4.46	4.07	3.84	3.69	3.58	3.50	3.44	3.39	3.35	3.28	3.22	3.15	3.08	3.04	3.00	2.96

(continued on next page)

One-Stop *F* Table (continued)

df_err		1	2	3	4	5	6	7	8	9	10	12	15	20	30	40	60	120
									df_hyp									
nil	.01	11.26	8.65	7.59	7.01	6.63	6.37	6.18	6.03	5.91	5.81	5.67	5.52	5.36	5.20	5.12	5.03	4.94
pow	.50	4.94	3.63	3.12	2.82	2.66	2.52	2.41	2.36	2.30	2.24	2.18	2.11	2.04	1.95	1.91	1.86	1.73
pow	.80	10.22	7.17	5.99	5.33	4.95	4.65	4.44	4.30	4.16	4.05	3.91	3.75	3.59	3.41	3.33	3.23	3.12
1%	.05	5.74	4.64	4.18	3.92	3.75	3.63	3.54	3.47	3.42	3.37	3.31	3.24	3.16	3.09	3.05	3.01	2.96
1%	.01	12.14	8.99	7.79	7.15	6.74	6.46	6.25	6.09	5.96	5.86	5.70	5.54	5.38	5.21	5.13	5.04	4.94
pow	.50	5.36	3.79	3.22	2.88	2.71	2.56	2.45	2.39	2.32	2.29	2.20	2.13	2.05	1.96	1.91	1.86	1.73
pow	.80	10.86	7.42	6.14	5.44	5.03	4.72	4.49	4.34	4.20	4.12	3.93	3.77	3.60	3.42	3.34	3.23	3.13
5%	.05	7.44	5.37	4.62	4.24	3.99	3.93	3.71	3.62	3.55	3.49	3.40	3.31	3.22	3.12	3.07	3.03	2.97
5%	.01	15.41	10.35	8.61	7.72	7.18	6.81	6.54	6.34	6.19	6.06	5.86	5.67	5.47	5.27	5.17	5.07	4.96
pow	.50	6.94	4.48	3.65	3.20	2.92	2.76	2.62	2.54	2.45	2.38	2.30	2.2O	2.10	2.00	1.94	1.88	1.74
pow	.80	13.34	8.47	6.79	5.90	5.35	5.01	4.74	4.56	4.39	4.25	4.07	3.88	3.69	3.48	3.37	3.26	3.14
10 nil	.05	4.96	4.10	3.71	3.48	3.33	3.22	3.14	3.07	3.02	2.98	2.91	2.84	2.77	2.70	2.66	2.62	2.58
nil	.01	10.04	7.56	6.55	5.99	5.64	5.39	5.20	5.06	4.94	4.85	4.71	4.56	4.11	4.25	4.17	4.08	3.99
pow	.50	4.68	3.33	2.83	2.53	2.34	2.21	2.11	2.04	1.98	1.93	1.86	1.81	1.74	1.66	1.62	1.58	1.41
pow	.80	9.65	6.58	5.40	4.75	4.34	4.05	3.84	3.68	3.55	3.44	3.28	3.14	2.97	2.75	2.69	2.59	2.50
1%	.05	5.46	4.31	3.83	3.57	3.39	3.27	3,18	3.11	3.05	3.01	2.94	2.86	2.79	2.71	2.67	2.63	2.58
1%	.01	11.02	7.93	6.77	6.14	5.75	5.48	5.28	5.12	5.00	4.90	4.75	4.59	4.43	4.26	4.18	4.09	3.99
pow	.50	5.14	3.56	2.94	2.60	2.40	2.25	2.15	2.07	2.01	1.99	1.91	1.83	1.75	1.67	1.63	1.58	1.42
pow	.80	10.37	6.89	5.57	4.87	4.42	4.12	3.90	3.73	3.59	3.51	3.34	3.16	2.98	2.79	2.71	2.60	2.50
5%	.05	7.39	5.13	4.34	3.93	3.67	3.50	3.37	3.27	3.20	3.13	3.04	2.94	2.85	2.75	2.70	2.64	2.59
5%	.01	14.48	9.38	7.64	6.75	6.21	5.85	5.58	5.38	5.23	5.10	4.91	4.72	4.52	4.32	4.22	4.12	4.01
pow	.50	6.94	4.35	3.43	2.96	2.67	2.48	2.34	2.23	2.15	2.09	1.99	1.89	1.81	1.71	1.65	1.60	1.42
pow	.80	13.14	8.06	6.28	5.37	4.81	4.44	4.16	3.95	3.79	3.66	3.46	3.26	3.07	2.85	2.74	2.63	2.52

12	nil	.05	4.74	3.89	3.49	3.26	3.11	3.00	2.91	2.85	2.80	2.75	2.69	2.62	2.54	2.47	2.43	2.38	2.34
	nil	.01	9.33	6.93	5.95	5.41	5.06	4.82	4.64	4.50	4.39	4.30	4.16	4.01	3.86	3.70	3.62	3.54	3.45
	pow	.50	4.52	3.17	2.63	2.33	2.15	2.02	1.93	1.86	1.80	1.76	1.66	1.61	1.53	1.47	1.43	1.39	1.35
	pow	.80	9.30	6.23	5.03	4.38	3.97	3.69	3.48	3.32	3.20	3.09	2.91	2.76	2.58	2.41	2.31	2.21	2.09
	1%	.05	5.31	4.12	3.63	3.36	3.18	3.06	2.96	2.89	2.83	2.79	2.71	2.64	2.56	2.48	2.43	2.39	2.34
	1%	.01	10.40	7.34	6.19	5.57	5.19	4.92	4.72	4.57	4.45	4.35	4.20	4.04	3.88	3.72	3.63	3.54	3.45
	pow	.50	5.05	3.38	2.75	2.42	2.21	2.07	1.97	1.89	1.83	1.79	1.68	1.62	1.54	1.47	1.43	1.40	1.36
	pow	.80	10.12	6.55	5.22	4.51	4.07	3.77	3.54	3.37	3.24	3.13	2.95	2.78	2.60	2.42	2.31	2.21	2.10
	5%	.05	7.47	5.0:	4.20	3.76	3.49	3.31	3.17	3.07	2.99	2.93	2.83	2.73	2.62	2.52	2.46	2.41	2.35
	5%	.01	14.07	8.88	7.12	6.23	5.68	5.31	5.05	4.85	4.69	4.56	4.37	4.18	3.98	3.78	3.68	3.57	3.47
	pow	.50	7.08	4.26	3.30	2.81	2.51	2.32	2.18	2.08	2.00	1.93	1.80	1.72	1.61	1.52	1.47	1.42	1.36
	pow	.80	13.18	7.84	6.00	5.07	4.49	4.11	3.83	3.62	3.46	3.33	3.10	2.91	2.69	2.48	2.36	2.24	2.11
14	nil	.05	4.60	3.74	3.34	3.11	2.96	2.85	2.76	2.70	2.65	2.60	2.53	2.46	2.39	2.31	2.27	2.22	2.18
	nil	.01	8.86	6.51	5.56	5.04	4.69	4.46	4.28	4.14	4.03	3.94	3.80	3.66	3.50	3.35	3.27	3.18	3.09
	pow	.50	4.41	3.06	2.52	2.23	2.00	1.88	1.79	1.72	1.67	1.59	1.54	1.46	1.39	1.32	1.28	1.26	1.23
	pow	.80	9.06	5.99	4.80	4.16	3.72	3.44	3.23	3.07	2.95	2.82	2.67	2.50	2.33	2.14	2.04	1.95	1.83
	1%	.05	5.24	4.00	3.50	3.22	3.04	2.91	2.82	2.75	2.69	2.64	2.56	2.49	2.40	2.32	2.27	2.23	2.18
	1%	.01	10.04	6.96	5.82	5.21	4.83	4.56	4.36	4.21	4.09	3.99	3.84	3.69	3.53	3.36	3.28	3.19	3.10
	pow	.50	5.01	3.30	2.66	2.32	2.12	1.93	1.83	1.76	1.70	1.66	1.56	1.47	1.41	1.32	1.28	1.26	1.23
	pow	.80	9.98	6.35	5.01	4.30	3.85	3.52	3.30	3.13	3.00	2.89	2.71	2.53	2.35	2.15	2.05	1.95	1.84
	5%	.05	7.62	5.02	4.13	3.66	3.38	3.19	3.05	2.94	2.86	2.79	2.69	2.58	2.47	2.36	2.31	2.25	2.19
	5%	.01	13.93	8.61	6.82	5.91	5.36	4.98	4.72	4.51	4.35	4.22	4.03	3.83	3.63	3.43	3.33	3.22	3.11
	pow	.50	7.25	4.27	3.26	2.76	2.45	2.20	2.06	1.96	1.88	1.78	1.69	1.58	1.48	1.37	1.32	1.29	1.25
	pow	.80	13.32	7.76	5.86	4.90	4.32	3.89	3.61	3.40	3.23	3.08	2.88	2.66	2.45	2.22	2.10	1.98	1.85
16	nil	.05	4.49	3.63	3.24	3.01	2.85	2.74	2.66	2.59	2.54	2.49	2.42	2.35	2.27	2.19	2.15	2.10	2.06
	nil	.01	8.53	6.23	5.29	4.77	4.44	4.20	4.03	3.89	3.78	3.69	3.55	3.41	3.26	3.10	3.02	2.93	2.84
	pow	.50	4.33	2.98	2.39	2.10	1.92	1.80	1.67	1.61	1.56	1.53	1_44	1.36	1.28	1.22	1.18	1.15	1.12

(continued on next page)

One-Stop *F* Table (continued)

			\multicolumn{17}{c}{df_{hyp}}

df_{err}			1	2	3	4	5	6	7	8	9	10	12	15	20	30	40	60	120
	pow	.80	8.88	5.83	4.61	3.97	3.56	3.28	3.05	2.89	2.77	2.67	2.49	2.32	2.14	1.96	1.86	1.76	1.64
	1%	.05	5.20	3.92	3.41	3.13	2.94	2.81	2.72	2.64	2.58	2.53	2.46	2.38	2.29	2.20	2.16	2.11	2.06
	1%	.01	9.81	6.71	5.57	4.96	4.58	4.31	4.12	3.97	3.85	3.75	3.60	3.45	3.29	3.12	3.03	2.94	2.85
	pow	.50	5.00	3.25	2.60	2.26	2.00	1.86	1.77	1.65	1.60	1.56	1.46	1.38	1.29	1.23	1.18	1.15	1.13
	pow	.80	9.90	6.22	4.87	4.15	3.68	3.37	3.15	2.95	2.82	2.71	2.53	2.35	2.16	1.98	1.87	1.76	1.65
	5%	.05	7.81	5.04	4.10	3.61	3.32	3.12	2.97	2.86	2.77	2.70	2.59	2.48	2.37	2.25	2.19	2.13	2.07
	5%	.01	13.91	8.47	6.63	5.71	5.15	4.77	4.49	4.29	4.13	4.00	3.80	3.60	3.39	3.19	3.08	2.97	2.86
	pow	.50	7.45	4.31	3.26	2.73	2.36	2.16	2.02	1.86	1.79	1.73	1.60	1.49	1.37	1.28	1.22	1.18	1.14
	pow	.80	13.52	7.75	5.79	4.80	4.17	3.77	3.48	3.24	3.07	2.94	2.71	2.49	2.26	2.04	1.92	1.80	1.66
18	nil	.05	4.41	3.55	3.16	2.93	2.77	2.66	2.58	2.51	2.46	2.41	2.34	2.27	2.19	2.11	2.06	2.02	1.97
	nil	.01	8.28	6.01	5.09	4.58	4.25	4.01	3.84	3.71	3.60	3.51	3.37	3.23	3.08	2.92	2.84	2.75	2.66
	pow	.50	4.21	2.87	2.34	2.05	1.87	1.70	1.62	1.56	1.47	1.44	1.35	1.28	1.21	1.13	1.08	1.06	1.04
	pow	.80	8.73	5.68	4.49	3.84	3.44	3.13	2.93	2.77	2.62	2.52	2.35	2.19	2.01	1.82	1.71	1.61	1.50
	1%	.05	5.19	3.87	3.35	3.06	2.87	2.74	2.64	2.57	2.50	2.45	2.38	2.30	2.21	2.12	2.07	2.02	1.97
	1%	.01	9.67	6.54	5.39	4.78	4.40	4.13	3.94	3.79	3.67	3.57	3.42	3.27	3.11	2.94	2.85	2.76	2.66
	pow	.50	5.01	3.21	2.56	2.16	1.95	1.82	1.67	1.60	1.55	1.47	1.38	1.30	1.22	1.14	1.11	1.06	1.04
	pow	.80	9.87	6.13	4.76	4.01	3.56	3.26	3.01	2.84	2.71	2.58	2.39	2.22	2.03	1.84	1.73	1.62	1.50
	5%	.05	8.02	5.09	4.09	3.59	3.28	3.07	2.92	2.80	2.71	2.64	2.52	2.41	2.29	2.17	2.11	2.05	1.98
	5%	.01	13.99	8.40	6.52	5.58	5.00	4.62	4.34	4.13	3.97	3.83	3.63	3.43	3.22	3.01	2.90	2.79	2.68
	pow	.50	7.65	4.37	3.27	2.66	2.34	2.14	1.94	1.83	1.76	1.65	1.52	1.42	1.31	1.20	1.13	1.09	1.06
	pow	.80	13.75	7.77	5.76	4.71	4.10	3.69	3.37	3.14	2.98	2.81	2.59	2.37	2.14	1.91	1.77	1.65	1.52
20	nil	.05	4.34	3.49	3.10	2.87	2.71	2.60	2.51	2.45	2.39	2.35	2.28	2.20	2.12	2.04	1.99	1.95	1.90
	nil	.01	8.09	5.85	4.94	4.43	4.10	3.87	3.70	3.56	3.46	3.37	3.23	3.09	2.94	2.78	2.69	2.61	2.52

	pow	.50	4.17	2.82	2.29	2.00	1.77	1.66	1.58	1.47	1.43	1.35	1.32	1.21	1.14	1.05	1.01	0.99	0.97
	pow	.80	8.63	5.58	4.39	3.75	3.32	3.04	2.83	2.65	2.53	2.41	2.26	2.07	1.90	1.70	1.60	1.50	1.18
	1%	.05	5.20	3.84	3.30	3.01	2.82	2.69	2.59	2.51	2.45	2.39	2.32	2.23	2.14	2.05	2.00	1.95	1.90
	1%	.01	9.58	6.41	5.26	4.65	4.27	4.00	3.80	3.65	3.53	3.44	3.29	3.13	2.97	2.80	2.71	2.62	2.52
	pow	.50	5.03	3.19	2.47	2.13	1.92	1.73	1.63	1.57	1.47	1.43	1.34	1.23	1.15	1.06	1.04	0.99	0.97
	pow	.80	9.87	6.07	4.66	3.93	3.48	3.14	2.92	2.75	2.59	2.49	2.31	2.11	1.92	1.72	1.62	1.51	1.39
	5%	.05	8.20	5.15	4.11	3.58	3.26	3.04	2.88	2.76	2.67	2.59	2.47	2.36	2.23	2.11	2.05	1.98	1.91
	5%	.01	14.11	8.38	6.46	5.49	4.91	4.51	4.23	4.02	3.85	3.71	3.51	3.30	3.09	2.88	2.77	2.65	2.54
	pow	.50	7.95	4.43	3.30	2.67	2.34	2.12	1.92	1.81	1.68	1.63	1.50	1.35	1.24	1.12	1.06	1.02	0.98
	pow	.80	14.02	7.82	5.75	4.68	4.05	3.63	3.30	3.08	2.88	2.74	2.51	2.27	2.04	1.79	1.66	1.54	1.40
22	nil	.05	4.29	3.44	3.05	2.82	2.66	2.55	2.46	2.40	2.34	2.30	2.22	2.15	2.07	1.98	1.94	1.89	1.84
	nil	.01	7.94	5.72	4.82	4.31	3.99	3.76	3.59	3.45	3.35	3.26	3.12	2.98	2.83	2.67	2.58	2.49	2.40
	pow	.50	4.13	2.79	2.25	1.97	1.74	1.62	1.49	1.44	1.35	1.32	1.24	1.18	1.08	1.00	0.97	0.92	0.90
	pow	.80	8.55	5.50	4.32	3.67	3.24	2.96	2.73	2.58	2.43	2.33	2.16	2.00	1.81	1.62	1.52	1.40	1.29
	1%	.05	5.23	3.82	3.27	2.97	2.78	2.64	2.54	2.46	2.40	2.35	2.27	2.18	2.09	2.00	1.95	1.90	1.84
	1%	.01	9.53	6.32	5.16	4.55	4.16	3.90	3.70	3.55	3.43	3.33	3.18	3.02	2.86	2.69	2.60	2.50	2.41
	pow	.50	5.06	3.18	2.45	2.10	1.89	1.70	1.61	1.49	1.44	1.36	1.27	1.20	1.09	1.01	0.97	0.94	0.90
	pow	.80	9.88	6.03	4.60	3.87	3.41	3.08	2.85	2.66	2.52	2.39	2.21	2.04	1.83	1.63	1.53	1.42	1.29
	5%	.05	8.41	5.22	4.13	3.58	3.25	3.02	2.86	2.73	2.63	2.56	2.44	2.31	2.19	2.06	1.99	1.92	1.85
	5%	.01	14.26	8.40	6.43	5.44	4.84	4.44	4.15	3.93	3.76	3.62	3.41	3.20	2.99	2.77	2.66	2.54	2.43
	pow	.50	8.17	4.51	3.33	2.68	2.34	2.06	1.91	1.75	1.67	1.56	1.43	1.33	1.19	1.07	1.02	0.95	0.92
	pow	.80	14.27	7.89	5.77	4.66	4.02	3.56	3.26	3.00	2.82	2.66	2.43	2.20	1.95	1.71	1.58	1.45	1.31
24	nil	.05	4.25	3.40	3.01	2.78	2.62	2.51	2.42	2.35	2.30	2.25	2.18	2.11	2.03	1.94	1.89	1.84	1.79
	nil	.01	7.82	5.61	4.72	4.22	3.90	3.67	3.50	3.36	3.26	3.17	3.03	2.89	2.74	2.58	2.49	2.40	2.31
	pow	.50	4.10	2.76	2.22	1.94	1.71	1.60	1.47	1.41	1.32	1.30	1.22	1.12	1.02	0.96	0.90	0.87	0.85
	pow	.80	8.48	5.44	4.25	3.61	3.18	2.90	2.67	2.52	2.37	2.27	2.10	1.92	1.73	1.54	1.44	1.33	1.21
	1%	.05	5.26	3.80	3.25	2.94	2.75	2.61	2.50	2.42	2.36	2.31	2.23	2.14	2.05	1.95	1.90	1.85	1.79

(continued on next page)

One-Stop *F* Table (continued)

df_{err}			1	2	3	4	5	6	7	8	9	10	12	15	20	30	40	60	120
	1%	.01	9.51	6.25	5.08	4.47	4.08	3.81	3.62	3.46	3.34	3.24	3.09	2.93	2.77	2.60	2.51	2.41	2.31
	pow	.50	5.10	3.18	2.43	2.08	1.81	1.68	1.53	1.47	1.42	1.34	1.25	1.14	1.08	0.96	0.93	0.89	0.85
	pow	.80	9.91	6.00	4.56	3.82	3.33	3.02	2.77	2.60	2.47	2.34	2.15	1.96	1.78	1.56	1.46	1.34	1.22
	5%	.05	8.63	5.30	4.16	3.59	3.25	3.01	2.84	2.71	2.61	2.53	2.41	2.28	2.15	2.02	1.95	1.88	1.81
	5%	.01	14.43	8.43	6.42	5.41	4.80	4.39	4.09	3.87	3.69	3.55	3.34	3.13	2.91	2.68	2.57	2.45	2.33
	pow	.50	8.38	4.58	3.37	2.G9	2.35	2.06	1.91	1.74	1.66	1.55	1.42	1.32	1.17	1.03	0.98	0.92	0.87
	pow	.80	14.52	7.97	5.79	4.66	4.01	3.54	3.23	2.96	2.79	2.62	2.38	2.16	1.90	1.64	1.52	1.38	1.24
26	nil	.05	4.22	3.37	2.98	2.74	2.59	2.47	2.39	2.32	2.26	2.22	2.15	2.07	1.99	1.90	1.85	1.80	1.75
	nil	.01	7.72	5.53	4.64	4.14	3.82	3.59	3.42	3.29	3.18	3.09	2.96	2.81	2.66	2.50	2.42	2.33	2.23
	pow	.50	4.07	2.73	2.20	1.85	1.69	1.52	1.44	1.34	1.30	1.22	1.15	1.10	1.01	0.91	0.86	0.84	0.80
	pow	.80	8.42	5.38	4.20	3.53	3.13	2.82	2.62	2.44	2.32	2.20	2.03	1.87	1.68	1.48	1.37	1.27	1.15
	1%	.05	5.29	3.80	3.23	2.92	2.72	2.58	2.48	2.40	2.33	2.28	2.19	2.11	2.01	1.92	1.86	1.81	1.75
	1%	.01	9.51	6.21	5.03	4.40	4.01	3.75	3.55	3.39	3.27	3.17	3.02	2.86	2.70	2.52	2.43	2.34	2.24
	pow	.50	5.14	3.18	2.42	2.07	1.80	1.66	1.51	1.45	1.35	1.32	1.23	1.12	1.02	0.92	0.90	0.84	0.81
	pow	.80	9.95	5.98	4.53	3.78	3.29	2.98	2.73	2.55	2.40	2.29	2.11	1.91	1.71	1.50	1.40	1.28	1.15
	5%	.05	8.85	5.38	4.20	3.61	3.25	3.01	2.84	2.70	2.60	2.51	2.39	2.26	2.12	1.99	1.92	1.84	1.77
	5%	.01	14.63	9.48	6.43	5.39	4.77	4.35	4.05	3.82	3.G4	3.50	3.29	3.07	2.84	2.62	2.50	2.38	2.26
	pow	.50	8.59	4.66	3.41	2.71	2.36	2.06	1.91	1.74	1.66	1.54	1.41	1.26	1.12	1.02	0.95	0.88	0.83
	pow	.80	14.78	8.06	5.83	4.67	4.00	3.52	3.21	2.94	2.76	2.58	2.35	2.09	1.84	1.60	1.46	1.32	1.17
28	nil	.05	4.19	3.34	2.95	2.71	2.56	2.44	2.36	2.29	2.23	2.19	2.12	2.04	1.96	1.87	1.82	1.77	1.71
	nil	.01	7.63	5.45	4.57	4.07	3.75	3.53	3.36	3.23	3.12	3.03	2.90	2.75	2.60	2.44	2.35	2.26	2.17
	pow	.50	4.05	2.71	2.18	1.83	1.67	1.50	1.42	1.32	1.28	1.21	1.13	1.04	0.95	0.90	0.83	0.79	0.77
	pow	.80	8.38	5.34	4.15	3.49	3.08	2.78	2.58	2.40	2.28	2.16	1.99	1.81	1.62	1.44	1.32	1.21	1.09

df_{hyp}

	1%	.05	5.33	3.80	3.22	2.90	2.70	2.56	2.45	2.37	2.30	2.25	2.17	2.08	1.98	1.89	1.83	1.78	1.72
	1%	.01	9.52	6.17	4.98	4.35	3.96	3.69	3.49	3.34	3.22	3.12	2.96	2.80	2.64	2.46	2.37	2.27	2.17
	pow	.50	5.19	3.19	2.42	2.06	1.78	1.65	1.50	1.43	1.33	1.30	1.17	1.11	1.01	0.91	0.86	0.82	0.77
	pow	.80	10.00	5.97	4.50	3.75	3.26	2.94	2.69	2.52	2.36	2.25	2.04	1.87	1.67	1.46	1.34	1.23	1.10
	5%	.05	9.07	5.47	4.25	3.64	3.26	3.01	2.83	2.70	2.59	2.50	2.37	2.24	2.10	1.96	1.89	1.81	1.73
	5%	.01	14.83	8.55	6.45	5.39	4.75	4.33	4.02	3.79	3.61	3.46	3.24	3.02	2.79	2.56	2.44	2.32	2.19
	pow	.50	8.80	4.74	3.45	2.74	2.37	2.07	1.91	1.74	1.59	1.54	1.41	1.25	1.11	0.98	0.91	0.85	0.78
	pow	.80	15.04	8.16	5.87	4.69	4.00	3.52	3.19	2.92	2.71	2.56	2.32	2.00	1.81	1.54	1.41	1.27	1.12
30	nil	.05	4.16	3.32	2.92	2.69	2.53	2.42	2.33	2.27	2.21	2.16	2.09	2.01	1.93	1.84	1.79	1.74	1.68
	nil	.01	7.56	5.39	4.51	4.02	3.70	3.47	3.30	3.17	3.07	2.98	2.84	2.70	2.55	2.39	2.30	2.21	2.11
	pow	.50	4.03	2.69	2.16	1.82	1.65	1.48	1.41	1.30	1.27	1.19	1.12	1.02	0.94	0.86	0.82	0.76	0.73
	pow	.80	8.33	5.30	4.12	3.45	3.05	2.74	2.54	2.36	2.24	2.12	1.95	1.77	1.58	1.39	1.28	1.17	1.04
	1%	.05	5.38	3.80	3.21	2.89	2.68	2.54	2.43	2.35	2.28	2.23	2.14	2.05	1.96	1.86	1.80	1.75	1.69
	1%	.01	9.54	6.15	4.94	4.31	3.92	3.64	3.44	3.29	3.17	3.07	2.91	2.75	2.59	2.41	2.32	2.22	2.12
	pow	.50	5.23	3.19	2.41	2.05	1.77	1.64	1.49	1.42	1.32	1.24	1.15	1.05	0.96	0.87	0.82	0.77	0.73
	pow	.80	10.06	5.97	4.49	3.73	3.23	2.91	2.66	2.49	2.32	2.19	2.01	1.81	1.61	1.41	1.30	1.17	1.05
	5%	.05	9.29	5.57	4.29	3.66	3.28	3.02	2.83	2.69	2.58	2.49	2.36	2.22	2.08	1.94	1.86	1.78	1.70
	5%	.01	15.04	8.62	6.47	5.40	4.75	4.31	4.00	3.76	3.58	3.43	3.20	2.98	2.75	2.51	2.39	2.27	2.14
	pow	.50	9.01	4.82	3.50	2.76	2.39	2.08	1.92	1.74	1.59	1.54	1.40	1.25	1.11	0.94	0.88	0.82	0.76
	pow	.80	15.31	8.26	5.91	4.71	4.01	3.51	3.19	2.91	2.69	2.54	2.30	2.04	1.78	1.50	1.36	1.23	1.07
40	nil	.05	4.08	3.23	2.84	2.61	2.45	2.34	2.25	2.18	2.12	2.08	2.00	1.92	1.84	1.74	1.69	1.64	1.58
	nil	.01	7.31	5.18	4.31	3.83	3.51	3.29	3.12	2.99	2.99	2.80	2.66	2.52	2.37	2.20	2.11	2.02	1.92
	pow	.50	3.97	2.63	2.02	1.76	1.52	1.42	1.29	1.25	1.16	1.08	1.02	0.93	0.86	0.76	0.70	0.65	0.61
	pow	.80	8.20	5.16	3.96	3.32	2.89	2.61	2.39	2.23	2.09	1.97	1.80	1.62	1.44	1.23	1.12	1.00	0.88
	1%	.05	5.64	3.85	3.21	2.86	2.64	2.49	2.38	2.29	2.22	2.16	2.07	1.97	1.87	1.77	1.71	1.65	1.58
	1%	.01	9.75	6.12	4.86	4.20	3.79	3.51	3.30	3.14	3.01	2.91	2.75	2.59	2.42	2.23	2.14	2.03	1.92
	pow	.50	5.49	3.26	2.42	2.04	1.75	1.54	1.45	1.33	1.22	1.20	1.12	1.01	0.88	0.77	0.71	0.66	0.61

(continued on next page)

One-Stop *F* Table (continued)

df_err			1	2	3	4	5	6	7	8	9	10	12	15	20	30	40	60	120
	pow	.80	10.38	6.01	4.46	3.67	3.15	2.80	2.56	2.36	2.19	2.08	1.90	1.70	1.43	1.25	1.14	1.01	0.88
	5%	.05	10.44	6.01	4.56	3.83	3.39	3.09	2.88	2.72	2.59	2.49	2.34	2.19	2.03	1.86	1.7b	1.69	1.60
	5%	.01	16.14	9.06	6.70	5.51	4.80	4.32	3.98	3.72	3.52	3.35	3.11	2.86	2.61	2.36	2.22	2.09	1.95
	pow	.50	10.00	5.35	3.73	3.00	2.49	2.15	1.97	1.77	1.61	1.55	1.35	1.19	1.05	0.88	0.80	0.72	0.63
	pow	.80	16.64	8.82	6.19	4.91	4.10	3.56	3.20	2.90	2.67	2.51	2.22	1.94	1.67	1.38	1.23	1.07	0.91
50	nil	.05	4.03	3.18	2.79	2.56	2.40	2.29	2.20	2.13	2.07	2.02	1.95	1.87	1.78	1.68	1.63	1.57	1.51
	nil	.01	7.17	5.06	4.20	3.72	3.41	3.19	3.02	2.89	2.78	2.70	2.56	2.42	2.26	2.10	2.01	1.91	1.80
	pow	.50	3.93	2.59	1.99	1.72	1.49	1.39	1.26	1.15	1.13	1.06	0.99	0.91	0.79	0.70	0.63	0.60	0.54
	pow	.80	8.11	5.09	3.88	3.25	2.82	2.54	2.31	2.13	2.01	1.89	1.73	1.55	1.35	1.14	1.02	0.91	0.78
	1%	.05	5.93	3.94	3.24	2.87	2.63	2.47	2.35	2.26	2.19	2.12	2.03	1.93	1.83	1.71	1.65	1.59	1.52
	1%	.01	10.04	6.18	4.85	4.16	3.74	3.44	3.23	3.07	2.94	2.83	2.67	2.50	2.32	2.13	2.03	1.92	1.81
	pow	.50	5.76	3.35	2.46	1.97	1.75	1.54	1.44	1.32	1.21	1.18	1.04	0.94	0.81	0.71	0.67	0.60	0.54
	pow	.80	10.74	6.11	4.48	3.63	3.13	2.76	2.52	2.31	2.14	2.03	1.82	1.61	1.39	1.17	1.05	0.92	0.78
	5%	.05	11.39	6.50	4.84	4.02	3.53	3.20	2.96	2.78	2.64	2.53	2.36	2.19	2.01	1.83	1.74	1.64	1.54
	5%	.01	17.26	9.56	6.98	5.69	4.92	4.40	4.03	3.75	3.53	3.35	3.09	2.82	2.55	2.28	2.14	1.99	1.84
	pow	.50	11.09	5.76	4.08	3.16	2.61	2.23	2.03	1.82	1.65	1.58	1.37	1.20	1.00	0.84	0.76	0.66	0.57
	pow	.80	17.86	9.36	6.55	5.11	4.24	3.66	3.27	2.95	2.70	2.53	2.22	1.92	1.61	1.31	1.16	0.99	0.81
60	nil	.05	3.99	3.15	2.76	2.53	2.37	2.25	2.17	2.10	2.04	1.99	1.92	1.83	1.75	1.65	1.59	1.53	1.47
	nil	.01	7.07	4.98	4.13	3.65	3.34	3.12	2.95	2.82	2.72	2.63	2.50	2.35	2.20	2.03	1.94	1.84	1.73
	pow	.50	3.90	2.57	1.97	1.70	1.47	1.30	1.24	1.13	1.04	1.04	0.91	0.84	0.78	0.65	0.58	0.54	0.48
	pow	.80	8.06	5.04	3.83	3.20	2.77	2.46	2.26	2.08	1.94	1.85	1.66	1.48	1.30	1.08	0.96	0.84	0.70
	1%	.05	6.24	4.04	3.29	2.90	2.64	2.47	2.35	2.25	2.17	2.11	2.01	1.91	1.80	1.68	1.62	1.55	1.47
	1%	.01	10.35	6.28	4.88	4.16	3.72	3.42	3.20	3.03	2.90	2.79	2.62	2.45	2.26	2.07	1.96	1.85	1.73

df_hyp

pow	.50	0.50	0.55	0.63	0.70	0.80	0.93	1.03	1.11	1.20	1.31	1.37	1.54	1.76	1.99	2.50	3.44	6.04
pow	.80	0.72	0.86	0.99	1.13	1.35	1.58	1.78	1.97	2.11	2.29	2.47	2.75	3.13	3.65	4.53	6.22	11.13
5%	.05	1.50	1.61	1.72	1.82	2.01	2.20	2.39	2.58	2.70	2.86	3.05	3.31	3.68	4.23	5.14	6.94	12.49
5%	.01	1.77	1.93	2.09	2.24	2.53	2.82	3.11	3.39	3.58	3.81	4.11	4.51	5.07	5.90	7.29	10.06	18.38
pow	.50	0.53	0.61	0.72	0.84	1.01	1.21	1.39	1.62	1.77	1.88	2.11	2.41	2.82	3.33	4.33	6.30	11.97
pow	.80	0.75	0.93	1.11	1.29	1.60	1.93	2.24	2.57	2.78	3.02	3.36	3.81	4.44	5.33	6.86	9.93	19.10
70 nil	.05	1.43	1.50	1.56	1.62	1.72	1.81	1.89	1.97	2.01	2.07	2.14	2.23	2.35	2.50	2.74	3.13	3.97
nil	.01	1.67	1.78	1.89	1.98	2.15	2.30	2.45	2.58	2.67	2.78	2.91	3.07	3.29	3.60	4.07	4.92	7.01
pow	.50	0.45	0.51	0.58	0.60	0.72	0.82	0.90	1.02	1.03	1.12	1.23	1.28	1.46	1.68	1.95	2.55	3.88
pow	.80	0.66	0.80	0.92	1.03	1.24	1.44	1.62	1.81	1.91	2.05	2.23	2.43	2.73	3.16	3.80	5.00	8.02
1%	.05	1.44	1.52	1.59	1.66	1.78	1.89	2.00	2.10	2.17	2.25	2.35	2.48	2.66	2.92	3.35	4.14	6.57
1%	.01	1.68	1.80	1.92	2.03	2.23	2.41	2.59	2.76	2.87	3.01	3.19	3.41	3.73	4.18	4.93	6.39	10.67
pow	.50	0.45	0.52	0.59	0.66	0.80	0.93	1.03	1.11	1.20	1.32	1.37	1.55	1.78	2.11	2.55	3.54	6.32
pow	.80	0.66	0.81	0.95	1.08	1.32	1.55	1.76	1.96	2.10	2.28	2.47	2.75	3.14	3.71	4.59	6.35	11.55
5%	.05	1.48	1.59	1.71	1.81	2.03	2.23	2.44	2.64	2.77	2.94	3.16	3.44	3.84	4.43	5.45	7.42	13.34
5%	.01	1.72	1.89	2.06	2.22	2.53	2.84	3.14	3.44	3.64	3.89	4.21	4.64	5.23	6.13	7.61	10.58	19.46
pow	.50	0.50	0.61	0.72	0.80	1.02	1.23	1.49	1.66	1.82	2.02	2.18	2.50	2.94	3.60	4.56	6.69	13.03
pow	.80	0.71	0.90	1.09	1.26	1.60	1.94	2.30	2.62	2.84	3.13	3.45	3.93	4.60	5.59	7.20	10.46	20.22
80 nil	.05	1.41	1.48	1.54	1.60	1.70	1.79	1.87	1.95	2.00	2.05	2.12	2.21	2.33	2.49	2.72	3.11	3.95
nil	.01	1.63	1.75	1.85	1.94	2.11	2.27	2.41	2.55	2.64	2.74	2.87	3.04	3.26	3.56	4.04	4.88	6.96
pow	.50	0.42	0.48	0.54	0.60	0.71	0.82	0.89	0.94	1.02	1.11	1.21	1.27	1.44	1.67	1.94	2.54	3.87
pow	.80	0.62	0.76	0.88	1.00	1.22	1.42	1.60	1.76	1.88	2.02	2.20	2.40	2.71	3.14	3.77	4.97	7.99
1%	.05	1.42	1.50	1.57	1.64	1.77	1.89	2.00	2.10	2.17	2.26	2.36	2.50	2.69	2.96	3.41	4.26	6.83
1%	.01	1.64	1.77	1.89	1.99	2.20	2.39	2.57	2.75	2.86	3.01	3.19	3.42	3.74	4.22	4.99	6.51	10.98
pow	.50	0.44	0.52	0.58	0.65	0.79	0.87	1.03	1.11	1.21	1.32	1.38	1.56	1.80	2.14	2.60	3.64	6.73
pow	.80	0.63	0.79	0.93	1.06	1.31	1.52	1.75	1.95	2.10	2.28	2.47	2.76	3.16	3.75	4.66	6.48	11.95
5%	.05	1.46	1.58	1.70	1.82	2.04	2.27	2.49	2.71	2.85	3.03	3.26	3.58	4.01	4.65	5.71	7.84	14.39

(continued on next page)

One-Stop F Table (continued)

df_{err}			1	2	3	4	5	6	7	8	9	10	12	15	20	30	40	60	120
90	5%	.01	20.52	11.08	7.93	6.35	5.41	4.77	4.32	3.98	3.72	3.50	3.18	2.86	2.54	2.21	2.04	1.87	1.69
	pow	.50	13.83	7.22	4.92	3.76	3.06	2.59	2.34	2.08	1.87	1.70	1.52	1.25	1.03	0.80	0.69	0.58	0.47
	pow	.80	21.36	11.02	7.55	5.81	4.76	4.06	3.59	3.21	2.91	2.67	2.34	1.97	1.61	1.25	1.06	0.88	0.67
	nil	.05	3.94	3.10	2.71	2.47	2.32	2.20	2.11	2.04	1.98	1.94	1.86	1.78	1.69	1.58	1.53	1.46	1.39
	nil	.01	6.92	4.85	4.01	3.53	3.23	3.01	2.84	2.72	2.61	2.52	2.39	2.24	2.09	1.91	1.82	1.72	1.60
	pow	.50	3.86	2.53	1.93	1.66	1.43	1.26	1.21	1.10	1.01	0.94	0.89	0.81	0.70	0.59	0.54	0.46	0.40
	pow	.80	7.97	4.95	3.75	3.12	2.69	2.38	2.18	2.00	1.86	1.74	1.58	1.40	1.20	0.98	0.86	0.73	0.59
	1%	.05	6.97	4.37	3.48	3.00	2.71	2.52	2.38	2.26	2.18	2.11	2.00	1.88	1.76	1.63	1.56	1.48	1.40
	1%	.01	11.29	6.64	5.06	4.26	3.77	3.43	3.19	3.01	2.86	2.74	2.56	2.38	2.18	1.97	1.86	1.74	1.61
	1%	.50	6.86	3.74	2.66	2.18	1.83	1.58	1.47	1.33	1.21	1.12	1.03	0.87	0.79	0.65	0.55	0.49	0.40
	pow	.80	12.12	6.62	4.74	3.19	3.19	2.78	2.52	2.28	2.10	1.95	1.75	1.51	1.29	1.04	0.89	0.76	0.60
	5%	.05	15.17	8.31	6.02	4.88	4.15	3.70	3.37	3.12	2.93	2.77	2.54	2.30	2.07	1.83	1.70	1.58	1.44
	5%	.01	21.57	11.59	8.25	6.59	5.58	4.92	4.44	4.08	3.80	3.57	3.24	2.90	2.55	2.21	2.03	1.85	1.66
	pow	.50	14.87	7.58	5.14	3.92	3.29	2.78	2.41	2.14	1.92	1.82	1.55	1.34	1.09	0.85	0.69	0.58	0.45
	pow	.80	22.43	11.51	7.87	6.04	4.97	4.23	3.70	3.30	2.99	2.77	2.39	2.03	1.65	1.27	1.06	0.87	0.65
100	nil	.05	3.93	3.09	2.70	2.46	2.30	2.19	2.10	2.03	1.97	1.92	1.85	1.77	1.67	1.57	1.51	1.45	1.37
	nil	.01	6.89	4.82	3.98	3.51	3.21	2.99	2.82	2.69	2.59	2.50	2.37	2.22	2.07	1.89	1.80	1.69	1.57
	pow	.50	3.85	2.52	1.92	1.66	1.43	1.26	1.20	1.10	1.01	0.93	0.88	0.80	0.70	0.59	0.50	0.46	0.39
	pow	.80	7.95	4.94	3.73	3.10	2.67	2.37	2.17	1.99	1.84	1.72	1.56	1.38	1.18	0.97	0.83	0.71	0.57
	1%	.05	7.24	4.49	3.55	3.04	2.74	2.54	2.39	2.28	2.19	2.11	2.00	1.88	1.76	1.62	1.55	1.47	1.38
	1%	.01	11.60	6.76	5.13	4.30	3.80	3.45	3.21	3.02	2.87	2.75	2.56	2.37	2.17	1.96	1.84	1.72	1.58
	pow	.50	7.11	3.84	2.71	2.22	1.85	1.59	1.49	1.34	1.22	1.12	1.04	0.87	0.74	0.61	0.55	0.49	0.39
	pow	.80	12.45	6.76	4.82	3.83	3.22	2.80	2.53	2.29	2.11	1.95	1.75	1.50	1.26	1.01	0.88	0.74	0.58

df_{hyp}

5%	.05	16.18	8.81	6.27	5.05	4.32	3.83	3.49	3.21	3.00	2.84	2.60	2.34	2.09	1.84	1.71	1.57	1.43
5%	.01	22.59	12.08	8.57	6.82	5.76	5.06	4.56	4.18	3.88	3.65	3.29	2.94	2.58	2.21	2.03	1.84	1.64
pow	.50	15.62	7.93	5.51	4.19	3.40	2.87	2.49	2.29	2.06	1.87	1.58	1.36	1.11	0.86	0.70	0.59	0.44
pow	.80	23.49	12.03	8.22	6.30	5.14	4.36	3.81	3.43	3.10	2.83	2.43	2.06	1.67	1.28	1.06	0.86	0.63
120 nil	.05	3.91	3.07	2.68	2.45	2.29	2.17	2.09	2.01	1.96	1.91	1.83	1.75	1.66	1.55	1.49	1.43	1.35
nil	.01	6.85	4.79	3.95	3.48	3.17	2.96	2.79	2.66	2.56	2.47	2.34	2.19	2.03	1.86	1.76	1.65	1.53
pow	.50	3.84	2.51	1.91	1.56	1.42	1.25	1.11	1.09	1.00	0.92	0.87	0.74	0.64	0.54	0.50	0.43	0.36
pow	.80	7.93	4.91	3.71	3.05	2.65	2.34	2.12	1.97	1.82	1.70	1.54	1.34	1.14	0.92	0.81	0.68	0.53
1%	.05	7.76	4.74	3.66	3.13	2.81	2.59	2.43	2.31	2.21	2.13	2.01	1.89	1.75	1.61	1.54	1.45	1.36
1%	.01	12.20	7.02	5.28	4.40	3.86	3.50	3.24	3.04	2.88	2.76	2.56	2.36	2.15	1.93	1.81	1.69	1.55
pow	.50	7.58	4.04	2.92	2.29	1.90	1.63	1.52	1.36	1.24	1.13	1.05	0.87	0.74	0.61	0.54	0.46	0.37
pow	.80	13.10	7.05	4.98	3.93	3.29	2.85	2.56	2.32	2.12	1.97	1.75	1.50	1.25	1.00	0.86	0.71	0.55
5%	.05	17.88	9.64	6.89	5.45	4.64	4.09	3.70	3.41	3.17	2.98	2.71	2.43	2.15	1.87	1.72	1.57	1.42
5%	.01	24.59	13.05	9.20	7.28	6.12	5.35	4.80	4.38	4.06	3.80	3.41	3.02	2.63	2.23	2.03	1.83	1.61
pow	.50	17.37	8.79	5.92	4.63	3.74	3.15	2.73	2.41	2.25	2.04	1.72	1.47	1.13	0.87	0.74	0.59	0.42
pow	.80	25.54	13.02	8.83	6.78	5.51	4.67	4.06	3.61	3.30	3.00	2.57	2.16	1.71	1.29	1.08	0.85	0.61
150 nil	.05	3.89	3.06	2.67	2.43	2.27	2.16	2.07	2.00	1.94	1.89	1.81	1.73	1.64	1.53	1.47	1.40	1.32
nil	.01	6.80	4.75	3.92	3.45	3.14	2.92	2.76	2.63	2.53	2.44	2.30	2.16	2.00	1.83	1.73	1.62	1.49
pow	.50	3.83	2.50	1.90	1.55	1.41	1.24	1.10	1.08	0.99	0.92	0.86	0.73	0.63	0.54	0.45	0.40	0.33
pow	.80	7.90	4.R9	3.09	3.02	2.63	2.32	2.09	1.94	1.80	1.68	1.52	1.31	1.11	0.90	0.77	0.64	0.49
1%	.05	8.61	5.01	3.86	3.28	2.92	2.66	2.49	2.36	2.25	2.17	2.03	1.90	1.76	1.61	1.53	1.44	1.34
1%	.01	13.04	7.40	5.51	4.56	3.98	3.59	3.31	3.09	2.93	2.79	2.58	2.37	2.15	1.92	1.79	1.66	1.51
pow	.50	8.26	4.42	3.09	2.40	1.98	1.78	1.56	1.40	1.27	1.15	1.06	0.88	0.74	0.61	0.51	0.43	0.34
pow	.80	14.11	7.43	5.21	4.09	3.40	2.96	2.62	2.37	2.16	2.00	1.77	1.51	1.25	0.98	0.83	0.68	0.51
5%	.05	20.52	10.86	7.64	6.06	5.11	4.48	4.03	3.69	3.41	3.20	2.88	2.57	2.24	1.92	1.75	1.59	1.41
5%	.01	27.47	14.46	10.12	7.95	6.65	5.78	S 10	4.69	4.33	4.04	3.60	3.17	2.73	2.28	2.06	1.83	1.59
pow	.50	19.73	10.24	6.86	5.19	4.19	3.52	3.04	2.67	2.48	2.25	1.90	1.61	1.23	0.93	0.75	0.59	0.41

(continued on next page)

One-Stop *F* Table (continued)

df_{err}			1	2	3	4	5	6	7	8	9	10	12	15	20	30	40	60	120
200	pow nil	.80	28.49	14.57	9.81	7.46	6.05	5.10	4,43	3.92	3.56	3.24	2.76	2.31	1.81	1.35	1.09	0.85	0.58
	nil	.05	3.88	3.04	2.65	2.42	2.26	2.14	2.05	1.98	1.93	1.88	1.80	1.71	1.62	1.51	1.45	1.38	1.30
	nil	.01	6.76	4.71	3.88	3.41	3.11	2.89	2.73	2.60	2.50	2.41	2.27	2.13	1.97	1.79	1.69	1.58	1.45
	pow	.50	3.82	2.48	1.89	1.54	1.40	1.23	1.09	1.07	0.98	0.91	0.79	0.72	0.63	0.49	0.45	0.37	0.30
	pow	.80	7.88	4.86	3.66	3.00	2.60	2.30	2.07	1.92	1.78	1.65	1.47	1.29	1.09	0.86	0.75	0.60	0.45
	1%	.05	9.58	5.57	4.22	3.49	3.08	2.81	2.61	2.46	2.33	2.23	2.09	1.93	1.78	1.61	1.52	1.43	1.32
	1%	.01	14.39	8.02	5.90	4.83	4.18	3.75	3.43	3.20	3.01	2.86	2.63	2.40	2.16	1.91	1.75	1.64	1.48
	pow	.50	9.37	4.88	3.36	2.68	2.20	1.88	1.64	1.46	1.40	1.28	1.09	0.96	0.75	0.61	0.51	0.43	0.33
	pow	.80	15.40	8.08	5.62	4.38	3.62	3.11	2.74	2.46	2.27	2.09	1.81	1.56	1.26	0.98	0_82	0.66	0.48
	5%	.05	24.55	12.87	8.94	7.02	5.88	5.11	4.56	4.15	3.84	3.56	3.18	2.79	2.40	2.01	1.82	1.62	1.41
	5%	.01	32.04	16.72	11.60	9.04	7.51	6.49	5.76	5.21	4.78	4.44	3.93	3.42	2.90	2.38	2.12	1.85	1.58
	pow	.50	23.65	11.85	8.17	6.17	4.96	4.16	3.58	3.15	2.81	2.53	2.21	1.79	1.42	1.01	0.81	0.63	0.41
	pow	.80	33.10	16.67	11.31	8.57	6.92	5.82	5.04	4.45	3.99	3.61	3.10	2.54	2.00	1.44	1.15	0.88	0.58
300	nil	.05	3.86	3.03	2.63	2.40	2.24	2.13	2.04	1.97	1.91	1.86	1.78	1.70	1.60	1.49	1.43	1.36	1.27
	nil	.01	6.72	4.68	3.85	3.38	3.08	2.86	2.70	2.57	2,47	2.38	2.24	2.10	1.94	1.76	1.66	1.55	1.41
	pow	.50	3.80	2.47	1.88	1.53	1.39	1.22	1.09	0.98	0.97	0.90	0.78	0.72	0.62	0.48	0.41	0.37	0.26
	pow	.80	7.85	4.84	3.64	2.98	2.58	2.28	2.05	1.87	1.75	1.63	1.44	1.27	1.07	0.83	0.71	0.58	0.41
	1%	.05	11.62	6.54	4.85	3.97	3.43	3.08	2.84	2.65	2.51	2.38	2.20	2.02	1.83	1.64	1.54	1.43	1.31
	1%	.01	16.85	9.18	6_63	5.36	4.59	4.07	3.70	3.42	3.20	3.03	2.76	2.49	2.22	1.93	1.78	1.62	1.45
	pow	.50	11.36	5.83	3.97	3.17	2.56	2.17	1.89	1.67	1.50	1.45	1.23	1.01	0.84	0.62	0.51	0.43	0.30
	pow	.80	17.91	9.26	6.37	4.96	4.04	3.44	3.02	2.69	2.44	2.27	1.95	1.63	1.33	1.00	0.82	0.66	0.45
	5%	.05	32.04	16.65	11.52	8.94	7.35	6.32	5.59	5.05	4.62	4.28	3.77	3.25	2.74	2.22	1.97	1.70	1.44
	5%	.01	40.62	20.94	14.40	11.13	9.16	7.86	6.92	6.21	5.67	5.23	4.58	3.92	3,26	2.60	2.27	1.94	1.59

(df_{hyp} across the top columns)

	pow	.50	31.22	15.66	10.47	7.87	6.49	5.42	4.66	4.09	3.64	3.29	2.75	2.29	1.73	1.22	0.96	0.70	0.43
	pow	.80	41.71	20.99	14.09	10.62	8.63	7.22	6.23	5.48	4.90	4.43	3.73	3.07	2.35	1.66	1.31	0.96	0.59
400	nil	.05	3.85	3.02	2.63	2.39	2.24	2.12	2.03	1.96	1.90	1.85	1.77	1.69	1.59	1.48	1.42	1.35	1.26
	nil	.01	6.70	4.66	3.83	3.37	3.06	2.85	2.68	2.56	2.45	2.36	2.23	2.08	1.92	1.74	1.64	1.53	1.39
	pow	.50	3.80	2.47	1.88	1.52	1.38	1.21	1.08	0.97	0.97	0.90	0.78	0.71	0.62	0.48	0.41	0.34	0.25
	pow	.80	7.84	4.83	3.63	2.96	2.57	2.26	2.04	1.86	1.74	1.62	1.43	1.25	1.06	0.82	0.69	0.55	0.39
	1%	.05	13.49	7.44	5.43	4.42	3.78	3.35	3.07	2.85	2.68	2.54	2.32	2.11	1.90	1.68	1.56	1.44	1.30
	1%	.01	19.02	10.26	7.33	5.87	4.98	4.39	3.97	3.65	3.40	3.20	2.90	2.60	2.29	1.97	1.80	1.63	1.44
	pow	.50	13.21	6.73	4.56	3.47	2.79	2.46	2.14	1.89	1.70	1.54	1.38	1.12	0.92	0.68	0.56	0.43	0.30
	pow	.80	20.18	10.35	7.07	5.42	4.40	3.77	3.29	2.93	2.65	2.42	2.10	1.75	1.41	1.04	0.86	0.66	0.44
	5%	.05	39.07	20.15	13.84	10.68	8.79	7.53	6.62	5.95	5.42	4.98	4.33	3.71	3.08	2.44	2.12	1.80	1.48
	5%	.01	48.68	24.94	17.05	13.11	10.74	9.16	8.04	7.19	6.53	6.00	5.21	4.42	3.63	2.84	2.44	2.04	1.63
	pow	.50	38.66	19.38	12.95	9.73	7.80	6.51	5.59	4.90	4.36	4.04	3.37	2.71	2.04	1.42	1.11	0.80	0.48
	pow	.80	49.91	25.07	16.78	12.64	10.16	8.50	7.32	6.43	5.73	5.24	4.39	3.55	2.71	1.88	1.47	1.06	0.63
500	nil	.05	3.85	3.01	2.62	2.39	2.23	2.12	2.03	1.95	1.90	1.85	1.77	1.68	1.59	1.48	1.41	1.34	1.25
	nil	.01	6.68	4.65	3.82	3.36	3.05	2.84	2.67	2.55	2.44	2.36	2.22	2.07	1.91	1.73	1.63	1.52	1.38
	pow	.50	3.79	2.46	1.87	1.52	1.38	1.21	1.08	0.97	0.97	0.89	0.77	0.71	0.56	0.48	0.41	0.34	0.25
	pow	.80	7.83	4.82	3.62	2.96	2.56	2.26	2.03	1.85	1.73	1.61	1.42	1.25	1.03	0.82	0.69	0.55	0.38
	1%	.05	15.23	8.29	5.98	4.82	4.13	3.65	3.29	3.04	2.84	2.69	2.45	2.21	1.97	1.72	1.59	1.45	1.30
	1%	.01	21.10	11.28	8.00	6.36	5.37	4.70	4.23	3.89	3.60	3.38	3.04	2.71	2.36	2.01	1.83	1.64	1.43
	pow	.50	14.99	7.61	5.14	3.90	3.15	2.64	2.38	2.10	1.89	1.71	1.44	1.24	0.95	0.69	0.56	0.44	0.30
	pow	.80	22.31	11.39	7.74	5.91	4.81	4.06	3.57	3.16	2.85	2.60	2.22	1.86	1.46	1.07	0.87	0.67	9.44
	5%	.05	46.31	23.76	16.24	12.45	10.16	8.63	7.57	6.77	6.15	5.65	4.91	4.16	3.40	2.66	2.28	1.90	1.52
	5%	.01	56.40	28.82	19.60	15.02	12.26	10.43	9.11	8.13	7.36	6.75	5.83	4.91	3.99	3.07	2.61	2.14	1.67
	pow	.50	45.18	22.62	15.10	11.32	9.05	7.54	6.65	5.82	5.13	4.67	3.90	3.13	2.42	1.62	1.26	0.90	0.52
	pow	.80	57.52	28.85	19.30	14.50	11.61	9.68	8.44	7.40	6.60	5.96	4.99	4.03	3.09	2.11	1.64	1.17	0.67
600	nil	.05	3.85	3.01	2.62	2.39	2.23	2.11	2.02	1.95	1.89	1.84	1.77	1.68	1.58	1.47	1.41	1.34	1.25

(continued on next page)

One-Stop *F* Table (continued)

df_err			1	2	3	4	5	6	7	8	9	10	12	15	20	30	40	60	120
	nil	.01	6.67	4.64	3.81	3.35	3.05	2.83	2.67	2.54	2.44	2.35	2.21	2.07	1.91	1.73	1.63	1.51	1.37
	pow	.50	3.79	2.46	1.87	1.52	1.38	1.21	1.08	0.97	0.96	0_89	0.77	0.71	0.56	0.48	0.41	0.34	0.25
	pow	.80	7.82	4.82	3.62	2.95	2.56	2.25	2.02	1.85	1.73	1.61	1.42	1.24	1.02	0.81	0.68	0.54	0.38
	1%	.05	16.94	9.11	6.51	5.21	4.43	3.91	3.54	3.24	3.01	2.84	2.57	2.31	2.03	1.76	1.62	1.47	1.31
	1%	.01	23.08	12.25	8.64	6.83	5.74	5.01	4.49	4.10	3.80	3.55	3.18	2.81	2.44	2.06	1.86	1.66	1.44
	pow	.50	16.14	8.46	5.71	4.32	3.49	2.93	2.52	2.32	2.07	1.88	1.59	1.28	1.04	0.75	0.61	0.47	0.30
	pow	.80	24.06	12.38	8.38	6.38	5.18	4.38	3.80	3.41	3.05	2.78	2.37	1.95	1.55	1.13	0.91	0.69	0.44
	5%	.05	52.82	26.98	18.38	14.08	11.50	9.78	8.55	7.63	6.91	6.34	5.48	4.59	3.73	2.86	2.44	2.00	1.56
	5%	.01	63.87	32.55	22.11	16.89	13.75	11.65	10.16	9.05	8.18	7.48	6.44	5.39	4.35	3.30	2.78	2.25	1.72
	pow	.50	52.51	26.28	17.54	13.17	10.55	8.80	7.55	6.61	5.88	5.30	4.42	3.63	2.73	1.88	1.41	1.00	0.57
	pow	.80	65.29	32.72	21.87	16.44	13.19	11.02	9.47	8.30	7.40	6.67	5.59	4.54	3.44	2.37	1.80	1.27	0.72
1,000	nil	.05	3.84	3.00	2.61	2.38	2.22	2.11	2.02	1.95	1.89	1.84	1.76	1.67	1.58	1.47	1.40	1.33	1.24
	nil	.01	6.66	4.63	3.80	3.34	3.04	2.82	2.66	2.53	2.42	2.34	2.20	2.06	1.90	1.71	1.61	1.49	1.35
	pow	.50	3.79	2.46	1.87	1.51	1.37	1.20	1.07	0.97	0.96	0.89	0.77	0.71	0.55	0.48	0.41	0.30	0.23
	1%	.80	7.81	4.81	3.61	2.94	2.55	2.24	2.02	1.84	1.72	1.60	1.41	1.23	1.01	0.80	0.67	0.52	0.36
	1%	.05	23.25	12.26	8.59	6.76	5.66	4.93	4.40	3.99	3.66	3.42	3.05	2.68	2.30	1.93	1.74	1.54	1.34
	1%	.01	30.44	15.89	11.01	8.59	7.13	6.16	5.47	4.95	4.54	4.22	3.73	3.24	2.75	2.25	2.00	1.74	1.46
	pow	.50	22.91	11.53	7.73	5.83	4.68	3.92	3.37	3.08	2.73	2.47	2.07	1.67	1.33	0.95	0.72	0.54	0.33
	pow	.80	31.72	16.01	10.78	8.16	6.58	5.53	4.78	4.27	3.81	3.45	2.91	2.38	1.86	1.33	1.04	0.76	0.47
	5%	.05	78.99	40.07	27.09	20.61	16.71	14.12	12.27	10.88	9.79	8.93	7.63	6.32	5.00	3.71	3.06	2.41	1.75
	5%	.01	92.43	46.81	31.60	23.96	19.41	16.37	14.20	12.57	11.30	10.29	8.77	7.25	5.73	4.21	3.45	2.68	1.92
	pow	.50	78.54	39.29	26.20	19.66	15.74	13.12	11.25	9.85	8.75	7.88	6.57	5.36	4.02	2.69	2.06	1.40	0.75

df_hyp

10,000		93.82	46.97	31.35	23.54	18.86	15.73	13.50	11.83	10.53	9.48	7.92	6.42	4.83	3.25	2.49	1.70	0.92
pow	.80	93.82	46.97	31.35	23.54	18.86	15.73	13.50	11.83	10.53	9.48	7.92	6.42	4.83	3.25	2.49	1.70	0.92
nil	.05	3.84	3.00	2.61	2.37	2.21	2.10	2.01	1.94	1.88	1.83	1.75	1.66	1.57	1.46	1.39	1.32	1.22
nil	.01	6.64	4.61	3.78	3.32	3.02	2.80	2.64	2.51	2.41	2.32	2.19	2.04	1.88	1.70	1.59	1.47	1.33
pow	.50	3.79	2.34	1.86	1.51	1.37	1.20	1.07	0.96	0.87	0.84	0.77	0.63	0.55	0.43	0.36	0.30	0.22
pow	.80	7.81	4.76	3.60	2.93	2.54	2.23	2.00	1.83	1.68	1_59	1.40	1.20	1.00	0.77	0.64	0.51	0.34
1%	.05	135.8	68.43	45.99	34.77	28.04	23.55	20.34	17.94	16.07	14.57	12.33	10.06	7.80	5.56	4.44	3.31	2.19
1%	.01	152.7	76.89	51.63	38.99	31.39	26.35	22.74	20.04	17.94	16.26	13.73	11.21	8.69	6.16	4.90	3.63	2.36
pow	.50	134.7	67.36	44.90	33.68	26.95	22.46	19.25	16.85	14.98	13.48	11.23	8.99	6.74	4.55	3.41	2.31	1.19
pow	.80	154.1	77.06	51.39	38.56	30.86	25.73	22.06	19.31	17.17	15.46	12.90	10.32	7.75	5.22	3.93	2.66	1.37
5%	.05	601.3	301.2	201.2	151.1	121.1	101.1	86.81	76.09	67.76	61.09	51.08	41.08	31.07	21.06	16.05	11.04	6.03
5%	.01	637.8	319.4	213.3	160.3	128.4	107.2	92.03	80.66	71.81	64.74	54.12	43.51	32.89	22.28	16.97	11.67	6.36
pow	.50	600.6	300.3	201.1	150.1	120.1	100.1	85.79	75.05	66.72	60.06	50.04	40.02	30.01	20.01	15.01	10.04	5.03
pow	.80	639.9	319.5	213.1	159.9	127.7	106.6	91.23	79.99	71.07	64.00	53.31	42.68	31.94	21.33	16.00	10.68	5.38

Appendix C

One-Stop *PV* Table

df_err			1	2	3	4	5	6	7	8	9	10	12	15	20	30	40
3	nil	.05	0.771	0.864	0.903	0.924	0.938	0.947	0.954	0.959	0.964	0.967	0.972	0.978	0.983	0.989	0.991
	nil	.01	0.919	0.954	0.967	0.975	0.979	0.982	0.985	0.987	0.988	0.989	0.991	0.993	0.994	0.996	0.997
	pow	.50	0.734	0.828	0.871	0.897	0.914	0.926	0.936	0.943	0.948	0.953	0.960	0.968	0.975	0.983	0.987
	pow	.80	0.858	0.913	0.937	0.951	0.959	0.965	0.970	0.973	0.976	0.978	0.982	0.985	0.989	0.993	0.994
	1%	.05	0.777	0.866	0.904	0.925	0.938	0.947	0.954	0.959	0.964	0.967	0.972	0.978	0.983	0.989	0.991
	1%	.01	0.921	0.954	0.967	0.975	0.979	0.982	0.985	0.987	0.988	0.989	0.991	0.993	0.994	0.996	0.997
	pow	.50	0.740	0.830	0.873	0.898	0.915	0.927	0.936	0.943	0.948	0.953	0.960	0.968	0.975	0.983	0.987
	pow	.80	0.862	0.914	0.937	0.951	0.960	0.965	0.970	0.974	0.976	0.979	0.982	0.985	0.989	0.993	0.994
	5%	.05	0.796	0.873	0.907	0.927	0.939	0.948	0.955	0.960	0.964	0.967	0.973	0.978	0.983	0.989	0.991
	5%	.01	0.929	0.957	0.969	0.975	0.980	0.983	0.985	0.987	0.988	0.989	0.991	0.993	0.994	0.996	0.997
	pow	.50	0.761	0.839	0.878	0.901	0.917	0.928	0.937	0.944	0.949	0.954	0.961	0.968	0.975	0.983	0.987
	pow	.80	0.874	0.919	0.940	0.952	0.961	0.966	0.971	0.974	0.977	0.979	0.982	0.986	0.989	0.993	0.994
4	nil	.05	0.658	0.776	0.832	0.865	0.887	0.902	0.914	0.924	0.931	0.937	0.947	0.956	0.967	0.977	0.983
	nil	.01	0.841	0.900	0.926	0.941	0.951	0.958	0.963	0.967	0.971	0.973	0.977	0.982	0.986	0.990	0.993
	pow	.50	0.625	0.733	0.789	0.825	0.850	0.869	0.884	0.895	0.905	0.912	0.925	0.938	0.952	0.967	0.975
	pow	.80	0.780	0.850	0.885	0.906	0.920	0.931	0.939	0.946	0.951	0.955	0.962	0.969	0.976	0.984	0.988
	1%	.05	0.667	0.780	0.834	0.866	0.887	0.903	0.915	0.924	0.931	0.937	0.947	0.957	0.967	0.977	0.983
	1%	.01	0.846	0.902	0.927	0.942	0.951	0.958	0.963	0.967	0.971	0.973	0.977	0.982	0.986	0.990	0.993
	pow	.50	0.634	0.737	0.792	0.827	0.852	0.870	0.884	0.896	0.905	0.913	0.925	0.938	0.952	0.967	0.975
	pow	.80	0.785	0.852	0.886	0.907	0.921	0.932	0.940	0.946	0.951	0.955	0.962	0.969	0.976	0.984	0.988
	5%	.05	0.699	0.793	0.841	0.871	0.891	0.905	0.917	0.925	0.932	0.938	0.947	0.957	0.967	0.977	0.983
	5%	.01	0.864	0.909	0.931	0.944	0.953	0.959	0.964	0.968	0.971	0.974	0.978	0.982	0.986	0.991	0.993
	pow	.50	0.668	0.753	0.802	0.834	0.856	0.874	0.887	0.898	0.907	0.914	0.926	0.939	0.953	0.967	0.975

df_hyp

		α															
5	pow	.80	0.806	0.861	0.891	0.911	0.923	0.933	0.941	0.947	0.952	0.956	0.963	0.969	0.976	0.984	0.988
	nil	.05	0.569	0.698	0.764	0.806	0.835	0.856	0.872	0.885	0.896	0.904	0.918	0.933	0.948	0.964	0.973
	nil	.01	0.765	0.842	0.879	0.901	0.916	0.928	0.936	0.943	0.948	0.953	0.960	0.967	0.974	0.983	0.987
	pow	.50	0.542	0.651	0.713	0.756	0.787	0.811	0.830	0.845	0.858	0.869	0.886	0.904	0.925	0.947	0.959
	pow	.80	0.712	0.790	0.831	0.859	0.879	0.893	0.905	0.913	0.921	0.928	0.938	0.948	0.960	0.972	0.979
	1%	.05	0.581	0.703	0.767	0.808	0.836	0.857	0.873	0.886	0.896	0.905	0.919	0.933	0.948	0.964	0.973
	1%	.01	0.773	0.845	0.880	0.902	0.917	0.928	0.936	0.943	0.948	0.953	0.960	0.967	0.975	0.983	0.987
	pow	.50	0.553	0.657	0.718	0.759	0.789	0.812	0.831	0.846	0.859	0.869	0.886	0.905	0.925	0.947	0.959
	pow	.80	0.720	0.793	0.834	0.860	0.880	0.894	0.905	0.914	0.922	0.928	0.938	0.949	0.960	0.972	0.979
	5%	.05	0.624	0.723	0.779	0.816	0.842	0.861	0.876	0.888	0.898	0.907	0.920	0.934	0.949	0.965	0.973
	5%	.01	0.802	0.857	0.887	0.907	0.920	0.930	0.938	0.944	0.950	0.954	0.960	0.967	0.975	0.983	0.987
	pow	.50	0.597	0.681	0.732	0.770	0.798	0.819	0.836	0.850	0.862	0.872	0.889	0.906	0.926	0.948	0.960
	pow	.80	0.749	0.808	0.842	0.866	0.884	0.897	0.908	0.916	0.924	0.930	0.939	0.949	0.960	0.972	0.979
6	nil	.05	0.499	0.632	0.704	0.751	0.785	0.811	0.831	0.847	0.860	0.871	0.889	0.908	0.928	0.950	0.962
	nil	.01	0.696	0.785	0.830	0.859	0.879	0.894	0.906	0.915	0.923	0.929	0.939	0.950	0.961	0.973	0.979
	pow	.50	0.476	0.581	0.647	0.693	0.728	0.755	0.777	0.796	0.811	0.824	0.845	0.869	0.896	0.926	0.942
	pow	.80	0.654	0.734	0.781	0.813	0.836	0.854	0.868	0.880	0.890	0.898	0.911	0.925	0.941	0.959	0.968
	1%	.05	0.514	0.638	0.708	0.754	0.787	0.812	0.832	0.848	0.861	0.872	0.889	0.908	0.928	0.950	0.962
	1%	.01	0.708	0.790	0.833	0.861	0.881	0.895	0.907	0.916	0.923	0.930	0.939	0.950	0.961	0.973	0.979
	pow	.50	0.490	0.590	0.652	0.697	0.731	0.757	0.779	0.797	0.812	0.825	0.847	0.870	0.896	0.926	0.942
	pow	.80	0.664	0.740	0.784	0.815	0.838	0.855	0.869	0.881	0.890	0.898	0.912	0.926	0.941	0.959	0.968
	5%	.05	0.566	0.664	0.724	0.765	0.795	0.818	0.837	0.852	0.864	0.875	0.891	0.910	0.929	0.951	0.962
	5%	.01	0.747	0.807	0.844	0.868	0.886	0.899	0.910	0.918	0.925	0.931	0.941	0.951	0.962	0.973	0.980
	pow	.50	0.542	0.619	0.674	0.713	0.743	0.767	0.787	0.803	0.817	0.830	0.850	0.872	0.898	0.927	0.943
	pow	.80	0.701	0.759	0.798	0.824	0.845	0.861	0.874	0.884	0.893	0.901	0.913	0.927	0.942	0.959	0.968
8	nil	.05	0.399	0.527	0.604	0.657	0.697	0.729	0.754	0.775	0.792	0.807	0.831	0.858	0.887	0.920	0.938
	nil	.01	0.585	0.684	0.740	0.778	0.806	0.827	0.844	0.858	0.869	0.879	0.895	0.912	0.931	0.962	0.962

(continued on next page)

One-Stop *PV* Table (continued)

df_err			1	2	3	4	5	6	7	8	9	10	12	15	20	30	40
	pow	.50	0.382	0.476	0.539	0.585	0.624	0.654	0.679	0.703	0.721	0.737	0.766	0.798	0.836	0.880	0.905
	pow	.80	0.561	0.642	0.692	0.727	0.756	0.777	0.795	0.811	0.824	0.835	0.854	0.875	0.900	0.928	0.943
	1%	.05	0.418	0.537	0.610	0.662	0.701	0.731	0.756	0.776	0.794	0.808	0.832	0.858	0.888	0.920	0.938
	1%	.01	0.603	0.692	0.745	0.781	0.808	0.829	0.845	0.859	0.870	0.880	0.895	0.912	0.931	0.951	0.962
	pow	.50	0.401	0.487	0.547	0.591	0.629	0.657	0.682	0.705	0.723	0.741	0.767	0.799	0.837	0.880	0.905
	pow	.80	0.576	0.650	0.697	0.731	0.759	0.780	0.797	0.813	0.825	0.837	0.855	0.876	0.900	0.928	0.943
	5%	.05	0.482	0.573	0.634	0.679	0.714	0.742	0.764	0.783	0.800	0.813	0.836	0.861	0.889	0.921	0.939
	5%	.01	0.658	0.721	0.764	0.794	0.818	0.836	0.851	0.864	0.874	0.883	0.898	0.914	0.932	0.952	0.963
	pow	.50	0.465	0.528	0.578	0.615	0.646	0.674	0.696	0.717	0.734	0.749	0.775	0.805	0.840	0.882	0.906
	pow	.80	0.625	0.679	0.718	0.747	0.770	0.790	0.806	0.820	0.832	0.842	0.859	0.879	0.902	0.929	0.944
10	nil	.05	0.332	0.451	0.527	0.582	0.624	0.659	0.687	0.711	0.731	0.749	0.778	0.810	0.847	0.890	0.914
	nil	.01	0.501	0.602	0.663	0.706	0.738	0.764	0.784	0.802	0.816	0.829	0.850	0.872	0.898	0.927	0.943
	pow	.50	0.319	0.400	0.459	0.503	0.539	0.570	0.596	0.620	0.640	0.659	0.691	0.731	0.776	0.833	0.866
	pow	.80	0.491	0.568	0.618	0.655	0.684	0.708	0.729	0.746	0.761	0.775	0.798	0.825	0.856	0.893	0.915
	1%	.05	0.353	0.463	0.535	0.588	0.629	0.662	0.690	0.713	0.733	0.750	0.779	0.811	0.848	0.890	0.914
	1%	.01	0.524	0.613	0.670	0.711	0.742	0.767	0.787	0.804	0.818	0.830	0.851	0.873	0.899	0.927	0.944
	pow	.50	0.339	0.416	0.468	0.510	0.545	0.575	0.600	0.623	0.643	0.665	0.696	0.733	0.778	0.833	0.867
	pow	.80	0.509	0.579	0.626	0.661	0.689	0.712	0.732	0.749	0.764	0.778	0.800	0.826	0.856	0.893	0.915
	5%	.05	0.425	0.507	0.566	0.611	0.647	0.677	0.702	0.724	0.742	0.758	0.785	0.815	0.851	0.892	0.915
	5%	.01	0.591	0.652	0.696	0.730	0.756	0.778	0.796	0.812	0.825	0.836	0.855	0.876	0.900	0.928	0.944
	pow	.50	0.410	0.465	0.507	0.542	0.572	0.598	0.621	0.641	0.659	0.676	0.705	0.739	0.784	0.837	0.869
	pow	.80	0.568	0.617	0.653	0.682	0.706	0.727	0.744	0.760	0.773	0.785	0.806	0.830	0.860	0.895	0.916

The column header group is labelled **df_hyp**.

12	nil	.05	0.283	0.393	0.466	0.521	0.564	0.600	0.630	0.655	0.677	0.696	0.729	0.766	0.809	0.860	0.890
	nil	.01	0.437	0.536	0.598	0.643	0.678	0.707	0.730	0.750	0.767	0.782	0.806	0.834	0.865	0.902	0.923
	pow	.50	0.274	0.346	0.396	0.437	0.472	0.502	0.529	0.553	0.575	0.595	0.625	0.667	0.718	0.786	0.826
	pow	.80	0.436	0.509	0.557	0.594	0.623	0.648	0.670	0.689	0.706	0.721	0.744	0.775	0.811	0.858	0.885
	1%	.05	0.307	0.407	0.476	0.528	0.570	0.604	0.634	0.658	0.680	0.699	0.731	0.767	0.810	0.861	0.890
	1%	.01	0.464	0.550	0.607	0.650	0.684	0.711	0.734	0.753	0.769	0.784	0.808	0.835	0.866	0.903	0.924
	pow	.50	0.296	0.360	0.408	0.446	0.479	0.508	0.534	0.558	0.579	0.598	0.627	0.670	0.719	0.787	0.827
	pow	.80	0.457	0.522	0.566	0.601	0.629	0.653	0.674	0.692	0.709	0.723	0.747	0.777	0.812	0.858	0.885
	5%	.05	0.384	0.457	0.512	0.556	0.592	0.623	0.649	0.672	0.692	0.709	0.739	0.773	0.814	0.863	0.891
	5%	.01	0.540	0.597	0.640	0.675	0.703	0.727	0.747	0.764	0.779	0.792	0.814	0.839	0.869	0.904	0.925
	pow	.50	0.371	0.415	0.452	0.483	0.512	0.537	0.560	0.580	0.599	0.617	0.643	0.682	0.728	0.792	0.830
	pow	.80	0.523	0.566	0.600	0.628	0.652	0.673	0.691	0.707	0.722	0.735	0.756	0.784	0.818	0.861	0.887
14	nil	.05	0.247	0.348	0.417	0.471	0.514	0.550	0.580	0.607	0.630	0.650	0.685	0.725	0.773	0.832	0.866
	nil	.01	0.388	0.482	0.544	0.590	0.626	0.656	0.681	0.703	0.721	0.738	0.765	0.797	0.834	0.878	0.903
	pow	.50	0.240	0.304	0.351	0.389	0.416	0.446	0.472	0.496	0.518	0.532	0.569	0.610	0.666	0.738	0.785
	pow	.80	0.393	0.461	0.507	0.543	0.571	0.596	0.618	0.637	0.655	0.669	0.696	0.728	0.769	0.821	0.854
	1%	.05	0.272	0.364	0.429	0.479	0.521	0.555	0.585	0.611	0.633	0.653	0.687	0.727	0.774	0.832	0.867
	1%	.01	0.418	0.499	0.555	0.598	0.633	0.662	0.686	0.706	0.725	0.740	0.767	0.798	0.835	0.878	0.904
	pow	.50	0.264	0.320	0.363	0.399	0.430	0.453	0.478	0.501	0.523	0.543	0.572	0.612	0.668	0.739	0.786
	pow	.80	0.416	0.476	0.518	0.551	0.579	0.602	0.623	0.642	0.659	0.674	0.699	0.730	0.770	0.822	0.854
	5%	.05	0.353	0.418	0.469	0.511	0.547	0.577	0.604	0.627	0.648	0.666	0.697	0.735	0.780	0.835	0.868
	5%	.01	0.499	0.552	0.594	0.628	0.657	0.681	0.702	0.721	0.737	0.751	0.776	0.804	0.838	0.880	0.905
	pow	.50	0.341	0.379	0.411	0.440	0.467	0.485	0.508	0.528	0.547	0.559	0.592	0.628	0.679	0.746	0.791
	pow	.80	0.488	0.526	0.557	0.583	0.607	0.625	0.644	0.660	0.675	0.687	0.711	0.740	0.778	0.826	0.857
16	nil	.05	0.219	0.312	0.378	0.429	0.471	0.507	0.538	0.564	0.588	0.609	0.645	0.688	0.740	0.804	0.843
	nil	.01	0.348	0.438	0.498	0.544	0.581	0.612	0.638	0.660	0.680	0.698	0.727	0.762	0.803	0.853	0.883
	pow	.50	0.213	0.271	0.310	0.345	0.376	0.403	0.422	0.446	0.468	0.489	0.519	0.561	0.615	0.696	0.746

(continued on next page)

One-Stop *PV* Table (continued)

df_err				1	2	3	4	5	6	7	8	9	10	12	15	20	30	40
	pow	.80		0.357	0.421	0.464	0.498	0.527	0.551	0.571	0.591	0.609	0.625	0.652	0.685	0.728	0.786	0.823
	1%	.05		0.245	0.329	0.390	0.439	0.479	0.513	0.543	0.569	0.592	0.613	0.648	0.690	0.741	0.805	0.844
	1%	.01		0.380	0.456	0.511	0.554	0.589	0.618	0.643	0.665	0.684	0.701	0.730	0.764	0.804	0.854	0.883
	pow	.50		0.238	0.289	0.328	0.361	0.385	0.411	0.436	0.452	0.473	0.493	0.523	0.564	0.617	0.697	0.747
	pow	.80		0.382	0.437	0.477	0.509	0.535	0.558	0.579	0.596	0.613	0.629	0.655	0.688	0.730	0.788	0.824
	5%	.05		0.328	0.387	0.434	0.475	0.509	0.539	0.565	0.588	0.609	0.628	0.660	0.699	0.748	0.809	0.846
	5%	.01		0.465	0.514	0.554	0.588	0.617	0.641	0.663	0.682	0.699	0.714	0.740	0.771	0.809	0.857	0.885
	pow	.50		0.318	0.350	0.379	0.406	0.425	0.447	0.469	0.482	0.501	0.519	0.546	0.583	0.632	0.706	0.753
	pow	.80		0.458	0.492	0.521	0.546	0.566	0.586	0.604	0.618	0.633	0.647	0.670	0.700	0.739	0.793	0.827
18	nil	.05		0.197	0.283	0.345	0.394	0.435	0.470	0.500	0.527	0.551	0.573	0.610	0.654	0.709	0.778	0.821
	nil	.01		0.315	0.401	0.459	0.504	0.541	0.572	0.599	0.622	0.643	0.661	0.692	0.729	0.774	0.829	0.863
	pow	.50		0.190	0.242	0.280	0.313	0.342	0.362	0.386	0.409	0.423	0.444	0.474	0.517	0.573	0.654	0.706
	pow	.80		0.327	0.387	0.428	0.461	0.488	0.511	0.532	0.552	0.567	0.584	0.611	0.646	0.691	0.752	0.792
	1%	.05		0.224	0.301	0.358	0.405	0.444	0.477	0.507	0.533	0.556	0.577	0.613	0.657	0.711	0.779	0.822
	1%	.01		0.349	0.421	0.473	0.515	0.550	0.580	0.605	0.627	0.647	0.665	0.695	0.731	0.775	0.830	0.864
	pow	.50		0.218	0.263	0.299	0.324	0.352	0.377	0.394	0.416	0.437	0.449	0.478	0.520	0.575	0.656	0.711
	pow	.80		0.354	0.405	0.443	0.471	0.497	0.521	0.539	0.558	0.575	0.589	0.615	0.649	0.693	0.754	0.794
	5%	.05		0.308	0.361	0.406	0.444	0.477	0.506	0.531	0.554	0.575	0.594	0.627	0.668	0.718	0.784	0.824
	5%	.01		0.437	0.483	0.521	0.553	0.582	0.606	0.628	0.647	0.665	0.680	0.708	0.741	0.782	0.834	0.866
	pow	.50		0.298	0.327	0.353	0.372	0.394	0.416	0.430	0.449	0.467	0.478	0.504	0.542	0.592	0.667	0.715
	pow	.80		0.433	0.463	0.490	0.511	0.532	0.551	0.567	0.583	0.598	0.610	0.633	0.664	0.704	0.761	0.798
20	nil	.05		0.178	0.259	0.317	0.364	0.404	0.438	0.468	0.495	0.518	0.540	0.577	0.623	0.680	0.754	0.799
	nil	.01		0.288	0.369	0.426	0.470	0.506	0.537	0.564	0.588	0.609	0.627	0.660	0.698	0.746	0.806	0.843

df_hyp

N																	
	pow	.50	0.172	0.220	0.256	0.286	0.307	0.332	0.356	0.370	0.391	0.403	0.441	0.475	0.533	0.612	0.669
	pow	.80	0.301	0.358	0.397	0.428	0.453	0.477	0.498	0.515	0.532	0.546	0.576	0.609	0.655	0.719	0.762
	1%	.05	0.206	0.277	0.331	0.376	0.413	0.446	0.475	0.501	0.524	0.545	0.581	0.626	0.682	0.755	0.800
	1%	.01	0.324	0.391	0.441	0.482	0.516	0.545	0.571	0.594	0.614	0.632	0.663	0.701	0.748	0.808	0.844
	pow	.50	0.201	0.242	0.270	0.298	0.324	0.341	0.364	0.385	0.398	0.418	0.446	0.479	0.536	0.614	0.675
	pow	.80	0.330	0.378	0.411	0.440	0.465	0.485	0.505	0.524	0.538	0.554	0.580	0.613	0.658	0.720	0.764
	5%	.05	0.291	0.340	0.381	0.417	0.449	0.477	0.502	0.525	0.545	0.564	0.597	0.639	0.691	0.760	0.804
	5%	.01	0.414	0.456	0.492	0.524	0.551	0.575	0.597	0.616	0.634	0.650	0.678	0.712	0.756	0.812	0.847
	pow	.50	0.285	0.307	0.331	0.348	0.369	0.389	0.402	0.420	0.431	0.448	0.473	0.503	0.555	0.627	0.679
	pow	.80	0.412	0.439	0.463	0.483	0.503	0.521	0.536	0.552	0.564	0.578	0.601	0.630	0.671	0.729	0.769
22	nil	.05	0.163	0.238	0.294	0.339	0.377	0.410	0.439	0.466	0.489	0.511	0.548	0.594	0.653	0.730	0.779
	nil	.01	0.265	0.342	0.396	0.440	0.475	0.506	0.533	0.557	0.578	0.597	0.630	0.670	0.720	0.784	0.824
	pow	.50	0.158	0.202	0.235	0.263	0.283	0.307	0.322	0.343	0.356	0.375	0.404	0.446	0.495	0.578	0.638
	pow	.80	0.280	0.333	0.370	0.400	0.424	0.447	0.465	0.484	0.499	0.515	0.541	0.577	0.622	0.688	0.734
	1%	.05	0.192	0.258	0.308	0.351	0.387	0.419	0.447	0.472	0.495	0.516	0.553	0.598	0.655	0.731	0.780
	1%	.01	0.302	0.365	0.413	0.453	0.486	0.515	0.541	0.563	0.584	0.602	0.634	0.673	0.722	0.786	0.825
	pow	.50	0.187	0.224	0.250	0.276	0.301	0.317	0.338	0.351	0.371	0.382	0.409	0.451	0.499	0.579	0.639
	pow	.80	0.310	0.354	0.386	0.413	0.437	0.456	0.476	0.491	0.508	0.521	0.547	0.581	0.625	0.690	0.735
	5%	.05	0.277	0.322	0.360	0.394	0.425	0.452	0.476	0.498	0.519	0.537	0.571	0.612	0.665	0.737	0.784
	5%	.01	0.393	0.433	0.467	0.497	0.524	0.548	0.569	0.588	0.605	0.622	0.651	0.686	0.731	0.791	0.829
	pow	.50	0.271	0.291	0.312	0.327	0.347	0.359	0.378	0.388	0.406	0.415	0.439	0.476	0.519	0.594	0.649
	pow	.80	0.393	0.418	0.440	0.459	0.478	0.493	0.509	0.522	0.536	0.547	0.570	0.600	0.640	0.700	0.742
24	nil	.05	0.151	0.221	0.273	0.316	0.353	0.385	0.414	0.440	0.463	0.484	0.522	0.568	0.628	0.708	0.759
	nil	.01	0.246	0.319	0.371	0.413	0.448	0.478	0.505	0.528	0.550	0.569	0.603	0.644	0.695	0.763	0.806
	pow	.50	0.146	0.187	0.218	0.244	0.263	0.285	0.299	0.320	0.332	0.351	0.378	0.411	0.460	0.544	0.600
	pow	.80	0.261	0.312	0.347	0.376	0.398	0.420	0.438	0.456	0.471	0.486	0.513	0.545	0.591	0.659	0.705
	1%	.05	0.180	0.241	0.289	0.329	0.364	0.395	0.422	0.447	0.470	0.490	0.527	0.572	0.631	0.709	0.760

(continued on next page)

One-Stop *PV* Table (continued)

df_err			1	2	3	4	5	6	7	8	9	10	12	15	20	30	40
	1%	.01	0.284	0.343	0.389	0.427	0.459	0.488	0.513	0.536	0.556	0.575	0.607	0.647	0.698	0.765	0.807
	pow	.50	0.175	0.210	0.233	0.258	0.274	0.296	0.308	0.328	0.347	0.358	0.384	0.416	0.473	0.546	0.609
	pow	.80	0.292	0.333	0.363	0.389	0.410	0.430	0.447	0.464	0.481	0.493	0.519	0.550	0.597	0.661	0.709
	5%	.05	0.264	0.306	0.342	0.375	0.403	0.430	0.453	0.475	0.495	0.513	0.546	0.588	0.642	0.716	0.765
	5%	.01	0.376	0.413	0.445	0.474	0.500	0.523	0.544	0.563	0.581	0.597	0.626	0.662	0.708	0.770	0.811
	pow	.50	0.259	0.276	0.296	0.310	0.328	0.340	0.357	0.367	0.384	0.392	0.415	0.452	0.495	0.562	0.621
	pow	.80	0.377	0.399	0.420	0.437	0.455	0.469	0.485	0.497	0.511	0.522	0.543	0.574	0.613	0.672	0.717
26	nil	.05	0.140	0.206	0.256	0.297	0.332	0.363	0.391	0.417	0.439	0.460	0.498	0.544	0.605	0.687	0.740
	nil	.01	0.229	0.298	0.349	0.389	0.423	0.453	0.479	0.503	0.524	0.543	0.577	0.619	0.672	0.743	0.788
	pow	.50	0.135	0.174	0.202	0.222	0.245	0.259	0.280	0.291	0.311	0.320	0.347	0.388	0.436	0.512	0.570
	pow	.80	0.245	0.293	0.326	0.352	0.376	0.395	0.414	0.429	0.445	0.458	0.484	0.519	0.564	0.631	0.679
	1%	.05	0.169	0.226	0.271	0.310	0.343	0.373	0.400	0.424	0.446	0.467	0.503	0.549	0.608	0.689	0.741
	1%	.01	0.268	0.323	0.367	0.404	0.436	0.464	0.488	0.511	0.531	0.550	0.582	0.623	0.675	0.744	0.789
	pow	.50	0.165	0.197	0.218	0.241	0.257	0.277	0.289	0.308	0.318	0.336	0.362	0.393	0.440	0.515	0.580
	pow	.80	0.277	0.315	0.343	0.368	0.388	0.407	0.423	0.440	0.453	0.468	0.493	0.524	0.568	0.633	0.683
	5%	.05	0.254	0.293	0.327	0.357	0.385	0.410	0.433	0.454	0.474	0.492	0.524	0.566	0.620	0.696	0.747
	5%	.01	0.360	0.395	0.426	0.453	0.478	0.501	0.522	0.540	0.558	0.574	0.603	0.639	0.686	0.751	0.794
	pow	.50	0.248	0.264	0.282	0.295	0.312	0.322	0.339	0.348	0.364	0.372	0.395	0.421	0.463	0.540	0.593
	pow	.80	0.362	0.383	0.402	0.418	0.435	0.448	0.463	0.475	0.488	0.498	0.520	0.547	0.586	0.648	0.692
28	nil	.05	0.130	0.193	0.240	0.279	0.314	0.344	0.371	0.396	0.418	0.439	0.476	0.522	0.583	0.667	0.722
	nil	.01	0.214	0.280	0.329	0.368	0.401	0.430	0.456	0.480	0.501	0.520	0.554	0.596	0.650	0.723	0.771
	pow	.50	0.126	0.162	0.189	0.208	0.229	0.243	0.263	0.273	0.292	0.301	0.327	0.357	0.405	0.491	0.541

df_hyp

	pow	.80	0.230	0.276	0.308	0.333	0.355	0.373	0.392	0.407	0.422	0.435	0.460	0.492	0.536	0.607	0.653
	1%	.05	0.160	0.213	0.256	4.293	0.325	0.354	0.380	0.404	0.426	0.446	0.481	0.527	0.586	0.669	0.724
	1%	.01	0.254	0.306	0.348	0.383	0.414	0.442	0.466	0.488	0.508	0.527	0.559	0.600	0.653	0.725	0.772
	pow	.50	0.156	0.185	0.206	0.227	0.241	0.261	0.272	0.291	0.300	0.318	0.333	0.373	0.419	0.493	0.551
	pow	.80	0.263	0.299	0.325	0.349	0.368	0.387	0.402	0.418	0.431	0.446	0.467	0.500	0.544	0.609	0.658
	5%	.05	0.245	0.281	0.313	0.342	0.368	0.392	0.415	0.435	0.454	0.472	0.504	0.545	0.600	0.677	0.729
	5%	.01	0.346	0.379	0.409	0.435	0.459	0.481	0.501	0.520	0.537	0.553	0.581	0.618	0.666	0.733	0.777
	pow	.50	0.239	0.253	0.270	0.281	0.298	0.307	0.323	0.331	0.339	0.354	0.376	0.402	0.443	0.511	0.565
	pow	.80	0.349	0.368	0.386	0.401	0.417	0.430	0.444	0.455	0.465	0.478	0.498	0.525	0.563	0.623	0.668
30	nil	.05	0.122	0.181	0.226	0.264	0.297	0.326	0.353	0.377	0.399	0.419	0.455	0.502	0.563	0.648	0.705
	nil	.01	0.201	0.264	0.311	0.349	0.381	0.410	0.435	0.458	0.479	0.498	0.532	0.574	0.629	0.705	0.754
	pow	.50	0.118	0.152	0.178	0.195	0.216	0.228	0.247	0.258	0.276	0.284	0.309	0.339	0.385	0.461	0.522
	pow	.80	0.217	0.261	0.292	0.315	0.337	0.354	0.372	0.386	0.402	0.414	0.438	0.469	0.513	0.581	0.631
	1%	.05	0.152	0.202	0.243	0.278	0.309	0.337	0.362	0.385	0.407	0.426	0.462	0.507	0.566	0.650	0.706
	1%	.01	0.241	0.291	0.331	0.365	0.395	0.422	0.446	0.467	0.487	0.506	0.538	0.579	0.633	0.707	0.755
	pow	.50	0.149	0.176	0.194	0.215	0.228	0.247	0.257	0.275	0.284	0.292	0.316	0.344	0.389	0.464	0.523
	pow	.80	0.251	0.285	0.310	0.332	0.350	0.368	0.383	0.399	0.411	0.422	0.446	0.476	0.518	0.584	0.633
	5%	.05	0.236	0.271	0.300	0.328	0.353	0.377	0.398	0.418	0.437	0.454	0.485	0.526	0.581	0.659	0.713
	5%	.01	0.334	0.365	0.393	0.418	0.442	0.463	0.483	0.501	0.518	0.533	0.562	0.598	0.647	0.715	0.761
	pow	.50	0.231	0.243	0.259	0.269	0.285	0.294	0.309	0.317	0.324	0.339	0.359	0.385	0.425	0.483	0.539
	pow	.80	0.338	0.355	0.372	0.386	0.401	0.413	0.426	0.437	0.447	0.459	0.479	0.505	0.542	0.599	0.645
40	nil	.05	0.092	0.139	0.176	0.207	0.234	0.259	0.282	0.304	0.323	0.342	0.375	0.419	0.479	0.567	0.628
	nil	.01	0.155	0.206	0.244	0.277	0.305	0.331	0.353	0.374	0.394	0.412	0.444	0.486	0.542	0.623	0.679
	pow	.50	0.090	0.116	0.132	0.150	0.160	0.176	0.184	0.200	0.207	0.213	0.234	0.259	0.300	0.362	0.413
	pow	.80	0.170	0.205	0.229	0.249	0.265	0.282	0.295	0.309	0.320	0.330	0.351	0.378	0.418	0.480	0.528
	1%	.05	0.123	0.162	0.194	0.222	0.248	0.272	0.294	0.314	0.333	0.350	0.383	0.425	0.484	0.570	0.631
	1%	.01	0.196	0.234	0.267	0.296	0.321	0.345	0.366	0.386	0.404	0.421	0.452	0.493	0.547	0.626	0.681

(continued on next page)

One-Stop *PV* Table (continued)

df$_{err}$			1	2	3	4	5	6	7	8	9	10	12	15	20	30	40
									df$_{hyp}$								
	pow	.50	0.121	0.140	0.154	0.169	0.180	0.188	0.203	0.210	0.216	0.231	0.251	0.275	0.305	0.365	0.415
	pow	.80	0.206	0.231	0.251	0.268	0.283	0.296	0.310	0.320	0.331	0.343	0.363	0.389	0.425	0.485	0.532
	5%	.05	0.207	0.231	0.255	0.277	0.298	0.317	0.335	0.352	0.369	0.384	0.413	0.450	0.503	0.583	0.640
	5%	.01	0.288	0.312	0.334	0.355	0.375	0.393	0.410	0.426	0.442	0.456	0.483	0.518	0.566	0.639	0.690
	pow	.50	0.200	0.211	0.219	0.231	0.237	0.243	0.256	0.262	0.266	0.279	0.288	0.309	0.344	0.398	0.444
	pow	.80	0.294	0.306	0.317	0.329	0.339	0.348	0.359	0.367	0.375	0.386	0.400	0.421	0.455	0.509	0.551
50	nil	.05	0.075	0.113	0.143	0.170	0.194	0.215	0.235	0.254	0.272	0.288	0.319	0.359	0.416	0.503	0.566
	nil	.01	0.125	0.168	0.201	0.229	0.254	0.277	0.297	0.316	0.334	0.350	0.381	0.420	0.475	0.557	0.616
	pow	.50	0.073	0.094	0.107	0.121	0.130	0.143	0.150	0.156	0.169	0.174	0.192	0.214	0.240	0.296	0.334
	pow	.80	0.140	0.169	0.189	0.206	0.220	0.234	0.244	0.254	0.266	0.275	0.293	0.317	0.350	0.407	0.450
	1%	.05	0.106	0.136	0.163	0.187	0.209	0.229	0.248	0.266	0.282	0.298	0.328	0.367	0.422	0.507	0.569
	1%	.01	0.167	0.198	0.225	0.250	0.272	0.292	0.311	0.329	0.346	0.362	0.390	0.428	0.481	0.561	0.619
	pow	.50	0.103	0.118	0.128	0.136	0.149	0.156	0.168	0.174	0.179	0.192	0.200	0.220	0.245	0.299	0.348
	pow	.80	0.177	0.196	0.212	0.225	0.238	0.249	0.261	0.270	0.278	0.289	0.304	0.326	0.358	0.412	0.457
	5%	.05	0.185	0.206	0.225	0.243	0.261	0.278	0.293	0.308	0.322	0.336	0.361	0.396	0.446	0.523	0.582
	5%	.01	0.257	0.277	0.295	0.313	0.330	0.346	0.361	0.375	0.389	0.402	0.426	0.459	0.505	0.578	0.631
	pow	.50	0.182	0.187	0.197	0.202	0.207	0.211	0.222	0.226	0.229	0.240	0.247	0.264	0.286	0.334	0.378
	pow	.80	0.263	0.272	0.282	0.290	0.298	0.305	0.314	0.321	0.327	0.336	0.347	0.366	0.392	0.440	0.481
60	nil	.05	0.062	0.095	0.121	0.144	0.165	0.184	0.202	0.218	0.234	0.249	0.277	0.314	0.368	0.452	0.515
	nil	.01	0.105	0.142	0.171	0.196	0.218	0.238	0.256	0.273	0.290	0.305	0.333	0.370	0.423	0.503	0.563
	pow	.50	0.061	0.079	0.090	0.102	0.109	0.115	0.126	0.131	0.135	0.147	0.155	0.173	0.205	0.245	0.280
	pow	.80	0.118	0.144	0.161	0.176	0.187	0.198	0.209	0.217	0.225	0.235	0.249	0.270	0.302	0.350	0.390
	1%	.05	0.094	0.119	0.141	0.162	0.181	0.198	0.215	0.231	0.246	0.260	0.287	0.323	0.375	0.456	0.519

Group																	
	1%	.01	0.147	0.173	0.196	0.217	0.237	0.255	0.272	0.288	0.303	0.317	0.344	0.379	0.430	0.508	0.567
	pow	.50	0.091	0.103	0.111	0.117	0.128	0.133	0.138	0.149	0.153	0.157	0.171	0.189	0.211	0.260	0.294
	pow	.80	0.156	0.172	0.185	0.196	0.207	0.216	0.224	0.234	0.241	0.248	0.263	0.283	0.310	0.360	0.399
	5%	.05	0.172	0.188	0.204	0.220	0.235	0.249	0.263	0.276	0.288	0.301	0.324	0.355	0.402	0.476	0.534
	5%	.01	0.235	0.251	0.267	0.282	0.297	0.311	0.324	0.337	0.349	0.361	0.383	0.413	0.458	0.528	0.582
	pow	.50	0.166	0.174	0.178	0.182	0.190	0.194	0.197	0.200	0.210	0.213	0.218	0.233	0.251	0.295	0.326
	pow	.80	0.241	0.249	0.256	0.262	0.270	0.276	0.281	0.287	0.295	0.299	0.309	0.325	0.348	0.391	0.425
70	nil	.05	0.054	0.082	0.105	0.125	0.143	0.160	0.176	0.191	0.206	0.219	0.245	0.279	0.329	0.410	0.472
	nil	.01	0.091	0.123	0.149	0.171	0.190	0.208	0.225	0.241	0.256	0.270	0.296	0.331	0.381	0.459	0.519
	pow	.50	0.053	0.068	0.077	0.088	0.094	0.099	0.109	0.114	0.117	0.128	0.134	0.150	0.170	0.205	0.249
	pow	.80	0.103	0.125	0.140	0.153	0.163	0.172	0.182	0.190	0.197	0.206	0.218	0.236	0.262	0.306	0.346
	1%	.05	0.086	0.106	0.125	0.143	0.160	0.176	0.190	0.205	0.218	0.231	0.255	0.289	0.337	0.415	0.476
	1%	.01	0.132	0.154	0.174	0.193	0.210	0.226	0.242	0.256	0.270	0.283	0.308	0.341	0.389	0.465	0.523
	pow	.50	0.083	0.092	0.099	0.108	0.113	0.117	0.121	0.131	0.134	0.137	0.150	0.166	0.185	0.220	0.251
	pow	.80	0.142	0.154	0.164	0.175	0.183	0.191	0.198	0.207	0.213	0.219	0.232	0.250	0.274	0.316	0.351
	5%	.05	0.160	0.175	0.189	0.202	0.215	0.228	0.240	0.251	0.263	0.274	0.295	0.324	0.367	0.437	0.494
	5%	.01	0.218	0.232	0.246	0.259	0.272	0.285	0.296	0.308	0.319	0.330	0.350	0.378	0.419	0.487	0.540
	pow	.50	0.157	0.160	0.163	0.171	0.174	0.176	0.179	0.187	0.190	0.192	0.203	0.209	0.225	0.255	0.293
	pow	.80	0.224	0.230	0.236	0.242	0.247	0.252	0.257	0.263	0.268	0.272	0.283	0.294	0.314	0.350	0.384
80	nil	.05	0.047	0.072	0.093	0.111	0.127	0.142	0.157	0.170	0.183	0.196	0.219	0.251	0.298	0.375	0.435
	nil	.01	0.080	0.109	0.131	-0.151	0.169	0.185	0.201	0.215	0.229	0.242	0.266	0.299	0.346	0.421	0.480
	pow	.50	0.046	0.060	0.068	0.077	0.083	0.087	0.096	0.100	0.103	0.106	0.118	0.133	0.151	0.183	0.213
	pow	.80	0.091	0.111	0.124	0.136	0.145	0.153	0.162	0.168	0.175	0.180	0.193	0.210	0.233	0.273	0.307
	1%	.05	0.079	0.096	0.113	0.129	0.144	0.158	0.171	0.184	0.196	0.208	0.230	0.261	0.307	0.381	0.440
	1%	.01	0.121	0.140	0.158	0.174	0.190	0.204	0.218	0.231	0.244	0.256	0.278	0.309	0.355	0.428	0.485
	pow	.50	0.078	0.083	0.089	0.097	0.101	0.105	0.108	0.117	0.120	0.122	0.134	0.140	0.165	0.197	0.226
	pow	.80	0.130	0.139	0.149	0.158	0.165	0.172	0.178	0.186	0.191	0.196	0.208	0.221	0.246	0.284	0.316

(continued on next page)

One-Stop *PV* Table (continued)

df_err			1	2	3	4	5	6	7	8	9	10	12	15	20	30	40
	5%	.05	0,152	0.164	0.176	0.189	0.200	0.212	0.222	0.232	0.243	0.253	0.272	0.298	0.338	0.405	0.460
	5%	.01	0.204	0.217	0.229	0.241	0.253	0.264	0.274	0.285	0.295	0.305	0.323	0.349	0.388	0.453	0.505
	pow	.50	0.147	0.153	0.156	0.158	0.161	0.162	0.170	0.172	0.174	0.176	0.186	0.190	0.204	0.231	0.257
	pow	.80	0.211	0.216	0.221	0.225	0.229	0.233	0.239	0.243	0.247	0.250	0.260	0.270	0.287	0.319	0.347
90	nil	.05	0.042	0.064	0.083	0.099	0.114	0.128	0.141	0.154	0.166	0.177	0.199	0.228	0.272	0.345	0.404
	nil	.01	0.071	0.097	0.118	0.136	0.152	0.167	0.181	0.194	0.207	0.219	0.242	0.272	0.317	0.390	0.447
	pow	.50	0.041	0.053	0.060	0.069	0.074	0.078	0.086	0.089	0.092	0.094	0.106	0.119	0.135	0.165	0.193
	pow	.80	0.081	0.099	0.111	0.122	0.130	0.137	0.145	0.151	0.157	0.162	0.174	0.189	0.210	0.246	0.277
	1%	.05	0.072	0.089	0.104	0.118	0.131	0.144	0.156	0.168	0.179	0.190	0.210	0.239	0.281	0.352	0.409
	1%	.01	0.111	0.129	0.144	0.159	0.173	0.186	0.199	0.211	0.223	0.234	0.255	0.284	0.326	0.397	0.453
	pow	.50	0.071	0.077	0.081	0.088	0.092	0.095	0.103	0.106	0.108	0.110	0.121	0.126	0.150	0.179	0.195
	pow	.80	0.119	0.128	0.136	0.144	0.151	0.156	0.164	0.169	0.174	0.178	0.189	0.201	0.223	0.258	0.284
	5%	.05	0.144	0.156	0.167	0.178	0.188	0.198	0.208	0.217	0.227	0.235	0.253	0.277	0.315	0.378	0.431
	5%	.01	0.193	0.205	0.216	0.226	0.237	0.247	0.257	0.266	0.275	0.284	0.301	0.326	0.362	0.424	0.474
	pow	.50	0.142	0.144	0.146	0.148	0.154	0.156	0.158	0.160	0.161	0.169	0.171	0.182	0.195	0.221	0.236
	pow	.80	0.200	0.204	0.208	0.212	0.216	0.220	0.223	0.227	0.230	0.235	0.241	0.253	0.269	0.298	0.320
100	nil	.05	0.038	0.058	0.075	0.090	0.103	0.116	0.128	0.140	0.151	0.161	0.182	0.209	0.251	0.320	0.377
	nil	.01	0.064	0.088	0.107	0.123	0.138	0.152	0.165	0.177	0.189	0.200	0.221	0.250	0.292	0.362	0.418
	pow	.50	0.037	0.048	0.055	0.062	0.067	0.070	0.077	0.081	0.083	0.085	0.096	0.108	0.123	0.150	0.166
	pow	.80	0.074	0.090	0.101	0.110	0.118	0.124	0.132	0.137	0.142	0.147	0.158	0.172	0.191	0.225	0.250
	1%	.05	0.067	0.082	0.096	0.108	0.121	0.132	0.143	0.154	0.164	0.174	0.193	0.220	0.260	0.327	0.383
	1%	.01	0.104	0.119	0.133	0.147	0.160	0.172	0.183	0.194	0.205	0.215	0.235	0.262	0.303	0.370	0.424
	pow	.50	0.066	0.071	0.075	0.081	0.085	0.087	0.094	0.097	0.099	0.101	0.111	0.115	0.128	0.154	0.179

	pow	.80	0.111	0.119	0.126	0.133	0.139	0.144	0.150	0.155	0.159	0.163	0.173	0.184	0.202	0.233	0.260
	5%	.05	0.139	0.150	0.158	0.168	0.178	0.187	0.196	0.204	0.213	0.221	0.237	0.260	0.295	0.355	0.406
	5%	.01	0.184	0.195	0.205	0.214	0.224	0.233	0.242	0.250	0.259	0.267	0.283	0.306	0.340	0.399	0.448
	pow	.50	0.135	0.137	0.142	0.144	0.145	0.147	0.148	0.155	0.156	0.157	0.160	0.169	0.181	0.204	0.218
	pow	.80	0.190	0.194	0.198	0.201	0.204	0.208	0.211	0.215	0.218	0.221	0.226	0.236	0.250	0.277	0.297
120	nil	.05	0.032	0.049	0.063	0.075	0.087	0.098	0.108	0.118	0.128	0.137	0.155	0.179	0.216	0.279	0.332
	nil	.01	0.054	0.074	0.090	0.104	0.117	0.129	0.140	0.151	0.161	0.171	0.189	0.215	0.253	0.317	0.370
	pow	.50	0.031	0.040	0.046	0.049	0.056	0.059	0.061	0.068	0.070	0.072	0.080	0.084	0.096	0.119	0.142
	pow	.80	0.062	0.076	0.085	0.092	0.099	0.105	0.110	0.116	0.120	0.124	0.133	0.143	0.159	0.188	0.212
	1%	.05	0.061	0.073	0.084	0.095	0.105	0.115	0.124	0.133	0.142	0.151	0.167	0.191	0.226	0.287	0.339
	1%	.01	0.092	0.105	0.117	0.128	0.139	0.149	0.159	0.169	0.178	0.187	0.204	0.228	0.264	0.326	0.377
	pow	.50	0.059	0.063	0.068	0.071	0.073	0.075	0.081	0.083	0.085	0.086	0.095	0.098	0.109	0.132	0.154
	pow	.80	0.098	0.105	0.111	0.116	0.121	0.125	0.130	0.134	0.137	0.141	0.149	0.158	0.173	0.199	0.223
	5%	.05	0.130	0.138	0.147	0.154	0.162	0.170	0.178	0.185	0.192	0.199	0.213	0.233	0.264	0.318	0.365
	5%	.01	0.170	0.179	0.187	0.195	0.203	0.211	0.219	0.226	0.233	0.241	0.254	0.274	0.305	0.358	0.404
	pow	.50	0.126	0.128	0.129	0.134	0.135	0.136	0.137	0.138	0.144	0.145	0.147	0.155	0.159	0.178	0.198
	pow	.80	0.175	0.178	0.181	0.184	0.187	0.189	0.192	0.194	0.198	0.200	0.204	0.213	0.222	0.244	0.265
150	nil	.05	0.025	0.039	0.051	0.061	0.070	0.079	0.088	0.096	0.104	0.112	0.127	0.148	0.179	0.235	0.282
	nil	.01	0.043	0.060	0.073	0.084	0.095	0.105	0.114	0.123	0.132	0.140	0.156	0.178	0.211	0.268	0.315
	pow	.50	0.025	0.032	0.037	0.040	0.045	0.047	0.049	0.054	0.056	0.058	0.065	0.068	0.078	0.097	0.108
	pow	.80	0.050	0.061	0.069	0.075	0.080	0.085	0.089	0.094	0.097	0.101	0.108	0.116	0.129	0.153	0.170
	1%	.05	0.054	0.063	0.072	0.080	0.089	0.096	0.104	0.112	0.119	0.126	0.140	0.160	0.190	0.243	0.289
	1%	.01	0.080	0.090	0.099	0.108	0.117	0.126	0.134	0.142	0.149	0.157	0.171	0.192	0.223	0.277	0.323
	pow	.50	0.052	0.056	0.058	0.060	0.062	0.066	0.068	0.069	0.071	0.071	0.078	0.081	0.090	0.108	0.119
	pow	.80	0.086	0.090	0.094	0.098	0.102	0.106	0.109	0.112	0.115	0.117	0.124	0.131	0.143	0.165	0.181
	5%	.05	0.120	0.126	0.132	0.139	0.146	0.152	0.158	0.165	0.170	0.176	0.187	0.204	0.230	0.277	0.319
	5%	.01	0.155	0.162	0.168	0.175	0.181	0.188	0.194	0.200	0.206	0.212	0.224	0.240	0.267	0.313	0.354

(continued on next page)

One-Stop *PV* Table (continued)

df_err				1	2	3	4	5	6	7	8	9	10	12	15	20	30	40
		pow	.50	0.116	0.120	0.121	0.122	0.123	0.123	0.124	0.125	0.130	0.130	0.132	0.139	0.141	0.157	0.167
		pow	.80	0.160	0.163	0.164	0.166	0.168	0.169	0.171	0.173	0.176	0.178	0.181	0.188	0.194	0.212	0.226
200		nil	.05	0.019	0.030	0.038	0.046	0.053	0.060	0.067	0.073	0.080	0.086	0.097	0.114	0.139	0.185	0.225
		nil	.01	0.033	0.045	0.055	0.064	0.072	0.080	0.087	0.094	0.101	0.108	0.120	0.138	0.165	0.212	0.253
		pow	.50	0.019	0.024	0.028	0.030	0.034	0.036	0.037	0.041	0.042	0.043	0.045	0.051	0.059	0.068	0.083
		pow	.80	0.038	0.046	0.052	0.057	0.061	0.064	0.068	0.071	0.074	0.076	0.081	0.088	0.098	0.114	0.130
		1%	.05	0.046	0.053	0.060	0.065	0.072	0.078	0.084	0.089	0.095	0.100	0.111	0.127	0.151	0.195	0.234
		1%	.01	0.067	0.074	0.081	0.088	0.095	0.101	0.107	0.113	0.119	0.125	0.136	0.153	0.178	0.223	0.262
		pow	.50	0.045	0.047	0.048	0.051	0.052	0.053	0.054	0.055	0.059	0.060	0.062	0.067	0.070	0.084	0.092
		pow	.80	0.071	0.075	0.078	0.081	0.083	0.085	0.088	0.090	0.093	0.095	0.098	0.105	0.112	0.128	0.141
		5%	.05	0.109	0.114	0.118	0.123	0.128	0.133	0.138	0.142	0.147	0.151	0.160	0.173	0.194	0.232	0.267
		5%	.01	0.138	0.143	0.148	0.153	0.158	0.163	0.168	0.172	0.177	0.182	0.191	0.204	0.225	0.263	0.298
		pow	.50	0.106	0.106	0.109	0.110	0.110	0.111	0.111	0.112	0.112	0.112	0.117	0.118	0.124	0.132	0.139
		pow	.80	0.142	0.143	0.145	0.146	0.148	0.149	0.150	0.151	0.152	0.153	0.157	0.160	0.167	0.177	0.187
300		nil	.05	0.013	0.020	0.026	0.031	0.036	0.041	0.045	0.050	0.054	0.058	0.067	0.078	0.097	0.130	0.160
		nil	.01	0.022	0.030	0.037	0.043	0.049	0.054	0.059	0.064	0.069	0.073	0.082	0.095	0.114	0.150	0.181
		pow	.50	0.013	0.016	0.018	0.020	0.023	0.024	0.025	0.025	0.028	0.029	0.030	0.035	0.040	0.046	0.052
		pow	.80	0.025	0.031	0.035	0.038	0.041	0.044	0.046	0.047	0.050	0.052	0.055	0.060	0.066	0.077	0.086
		1%	.05	0.037	0.042	0.046	0.050	0.054	0.05B	0.062	0.066	0.070	0.074	0.081	0.092	0.109	0.141	0.170
		1%	.01	0.053	0.058	0.062	0.067	0.071	0.075	0.079	0.084	0.088	0.092	0.100	0.111	0.129	0.162	0.192
		pow	.50	0.036	0.037	0.038	0.040	0.041	0.042	0.042	0.043	0.043	0.046	0.047	0.048	0.053	0.058	0.064
		pow	.80	0.056	0.0SB	0.060	0.062	0.063	0.064	0.066	0.067	0.068	0.070	0.073	0.076	0.081	0.091	0.099
		5%	.05	0.097	0.100	0.103	0.107	0.109	0.112	0.115	0.119	0.122	0.125	0.131	0.140	0.154	0.182	0.208

	5%	.01	0.119	0.122	0.126	0.129	0.132	0.136	0.139	0.142	0.145	0.149	0.155	0.164	0.179	0.207	0.233
	pow	.50	0.094	0.095	0.095	0.095	0.098	0.098	0.098	0.098	0.099	0.099	0.099	0.103	0.104	0.108	0.113
	pow	.80	0.122	0.123	0.123	0.124	0.126	0.126	0.127	0.127	0.128	0.129	0.130	0.133	0.136	0.142	0.149
400	nil	.05	0.010	0.015	0.019	0.023	0.027	0.031	0.034	0.038	0.041	0.044	0.051	0.060	0.074	0.100	0.124
	nil	.01	0.016	0.023	0.028	0.033	0.037	0.041	0.045	0.049	0.052	0.056	0.063	0.072	0.088	0.116	0.141
	pow	.50	0.009	0.012	0.014	0.015	0.017	0.018	0.019	0.019	0.021	0.022	0.023	0.026	0.030	0.035	0.039
	pow	.80	0.019	0.024	0.026	0.029	0.031	0.033	0.034	0.036	0.038	0.039	0.041	0.045	0.050	0.058	0.065
	1%	.05	0.033	0.036	0.039	0.042	0.045	0.048	0.051	0.054	0.057	0.060	0.065	0.073	0.087	0.112	0.135
	1%	.01	0.045	0.049	0.052	0.055	0.059	0.062	0.065	0.068	0.071	0.074	0.080	0.089	0.103	0.129	0.153
	pow	.50	0.032	0.033	0.033	0.034	0.034	0.036	0.036	0.036	0.037	0.037	0.040	0.040	0.044	0.049	0.053
	pow	.80	0.048	0.049	0.050	0.051	0.052	0.054	0.054	0.055	0.056	0.057	0.059	0.061	0.066	0.073	0.079
	5%	.05	0.089	0.092	0.094	0.097	0.099	0.101	0.104	0.106	0.109	0.111	0.115	0.122	0.133	0.155	0.175
	5%	.01	0.108	0.111	0.113	0.116	0.118	0.121	0.123	0.126	0.128	0.130	0.135	0.142	0.154	0.175	0.196
	pow	.50	0.088	0.088	0.089	0.089	0.089	0.089	0.089	0.089	0.089	0.092	0.092	0.092	0.093	0.096	0.100
	pow	.80	0.111	0.111	0.112	0.112	0.113	0.113	0.113	0.114	0.114	0.116	0.116	0.118	0.119	0.124	0.128
500	nil	.05	0.008	0.012	0.015	0.014	0.022	0.025	0.028	0.030	0.033	0.036	0.041	0.048	0.060	0.081	0.102
	nil	.01	0.013	0.018	0.022	0.026	0.030	0.033	0.036	0.039	0.042	0.045	0.051	0.059	0.071	0.094	0.115
	pow	.50	0.008	0.010	0.011	0.012	0.014	0.014	0.015	0.015	0.017	0.018	0.018	0.021	0.022	0.028	0.032
	pow	.80	0.015	0.019	0.021	0.023	0.025	0.026	0.028	0.029	0.030	0.031	0.033	0.036	0.039	0.047	0.052
	1%	.05	0.030	0.032	0.035	0.037	0.040	0.042	0.044	0.046	0.049	0.051	0.056	0.062	0.073	0.093	0.113
	1%	.01	0.040	0.043	0.046	0.048	0.051	0.053	0.056	0.058	0.061	0.063	0.068	0.075	0.086	0.108	0.128
	pow	.50	0.029	0.030	0.030	0.030	0.031	0.031	0.032	0.033	0.033	0.033	0.033	0.036	0.037	0.040	0.043
	pow	.80	0.043	0.044	0.044	0.045	0.046	0.046	0.048	0.048	0.049	0.049	0.051	0.053	0.055	0.061	0.065
	5%	.05	0.085	0.087	0.089	0.091	0.092	0.094	0.096	0.098	0.100	0.102	0.105	0.111	0.120	0.137	0.154
	5%	.01	0.101	0.103	0.105	0.107	0.109	0.111	0.113	0.115	0.117	0.119	0.123	0.128	0.138	0.155	0.173
	pow	.50	0.083	0.083	0.083	0.083	0.083	0.083	0.085	0.085	0.085	0.085	0.086	0.086	0.088	0.089	0.092
	pow	.80	0.103	0.103	0.104	0.104	0.104	0.104	0.106	0.106	0.106	0.106	0.107	0.108	0.110	0.112	0.116

(continued on next page)

One-Stop *PV* Table (continued)

			df_{hyp}														
df_{err}			1	2	3	4	5	6	7	8	9	10	12	15	20	30	40
600	nil	.05	0.006	0.010	0.013	0.016	0.018	0.021	0.023	0.025	0.028	0.030	0.034	0.040	0.050	0.069	0.086
	nil	.01	0.011	0.01S	0.019	0.022	0.025	0.028	0.030	0.033	0.035	0.038	0.042	0.049	0.060	0.080	0.098
	pow	.50	0.006	0.008	0.009	0.010	0.011	0.012	0.012	0.013	0.014	0.015	0.015	0.017	0.018	0.023	0.026
	pow	.80	0.013	0.016	0.018	0.019	0.021	0.022	0.023	0.024	0.025	0.026	0.028	0.030	0.033	0.039	0.043
	1%	.05	0.027	0.029	0.032	0.034	0.036	0.038	0.040	0.041	0.043	0.045	0.049	0.055	0.063	0.081	0.097
	1%	.01	0.037	0.039	0.041	0.044	0.046	0.048	0.050	0.052	0.054	0.056	0.060	0.066	0.075	0.093	0.110
	pow	.50	0.026	0.027	0.028	0.028	0.028	0.028	0.029	0.030	0.030	0.030	0.031	0.031	0.033	0.036	0.039
	pow	.80	0.039	0.040	0.040	0.041	0.041	0.042	0.042	0.043	0.044	0.044	0.045	0.046	0.049	0.053	0.057
	5%	.05	0.081	0.083	0.084	0.086	0.087	0.089	0.091	0.092	0.094	0.096	0.099	0.103	0.111	0.125	0.140
	5%	.01	0.096	0.098	0.100	0.101	0.103	0.104	0.106	0.108	0.109	0.111	0.114	0.119	0.127	0.142	0.156
	pow	.50	0.080	0.081	0.081	0.081	0.081	0.081	0.081	0.081	0.081	0.081	0.081	0.083	0.083	0.096	0.086
	pow	.80	0.098	0.098	0.099	0.099	0.099	0.099	0.099	0.100	0.100	0.100	0.100	0.102	0.103	0.106	0.107
1,000	nil	.05	0.004	0.006	0.008	0.009	0.011	0.012	0.014	0.015	0.017	0.018	0.021	0.024	0.031	0.042	0.053
	nil	.01	0.007	0.009	0.011	0.013	0.015	0.017	0.018	0.020	0.021	0.023	0.026	0.030	0.037	0.049	0.061
	pow	.50	0.004	0.005	0.006	0.006	0.007	0.007	0.007	0.008	0.009	0.009	0.009	0.010	0.011	0.014	0.016
	pow	.80	0.008	0.010	0.011	0.012	0.013	0.013	0.014	0.014	0.015	0.016	0.017	0.018	0.020	0.023	0.026
	1%	.05	0.023	0.024	0.025	0.026	0.028	0.029	0.030	0.031	0.032	0.033	0.035	0.039	0.044	0.055	0.065
	1%	.01	0.030	0.031	0.032	0.033	0.034	0.036	0.037	0.038	0.039	0.040	0.043	0.046	0.052	0.063	0.074
	pow	.50	0.022	0.023	0.023	0.023	0.023	0.023	0.023	0.024	0.024	0.024	0.024	0.024	0.026	0.028	0.028
	pow	.80	0.031	0.031	0.031	0.032	0.032	0.032	0.032	0.033	0.033	0.033	0.034	0.034	0.036	0.038	0.040
	5%	.05	0.073	0.074	0.075	0.076	0.077	0.078	0.079	0.080	0.081	0.082	0.084	0.087	0.091	0.100	0.109
	5%	.01	0.085	0.086	0.087	0.087	0.088	0.089	0.090	0.091	0.092	0.093	0.095	0.098	0.103	0.112	0.121

10,000	pow	.50	0.073	0.073	0.073	0.073	0.073	0.073	0.073	0.073	0.073	0.073	0.073	0.074	0.074	0.074	0.075	0.076
	pow	.80	0.086	0.086	0.086	0.086	0.086	0.086	0.086	0.086	0.087	0.087	0.087	0.088	0.088	0.088	0.089	0.090
	nil	.05	0.000	0.001	0.001	0.001	0.001	0.001	0.001	0.002	0.002	0.002	0.002	0.002	0.002	0.003	0.004	0.006
	nil	.01	0.001	0.001	0.001	0.001	0.001	0.002	0.002	0.002	0.002	0.002	0.003	0.003	0.003	0.004	0.005	0.006
	pow	.50	0.000	0.000	0.001	0.001	0.001	0.001	0.001	0.001	0.001	0.001	0.001	0.001	0.001	0.001	0.001	0.001
	pow	.80	0.001	0.001	0.001	0.001	0.001	0.002	0.001	0.002	0.002	0.002	0.002	0.002	0.002	0.002	0.002	0.003
	1%	.05	0.013	0.014	0.014	0.014	0.014	0.014	0.014	0.014	0.014	0.014	0.015	0.015	0.015	0.015	0.016	0.011
	1%	.01	0.015	0.015	0.015	0.015	0.015	0.016	0.016	0.016	0.016	0.016	0.017	0.017	0.017	0.017	0.018	0.019
	pow	.50	0.013	0.013	0.013	0.013	0.013	0.013	0.013	0.013	0.013	0.013	0.013	0.013	0.013	0.013	0.013	0.013
	pow	.80	0.015	0.015	0.015	0.015	0.015	0.015	0.015	0.015	0.015	0.015	0.015	0.015	0.015	0.015	0.015	0.015
	5%	.05	0.057	0.057	0.057	0.057	0.057	0.057	0.057	0.057	0.057	0.058	0.058	0.058	0.059	0.059	0.059	0.060
	5%	.01	0.060	0.060	0.060	0.060	0.060	0.060	0.061	0.061	0.061	0.061	0.061	0.061	0.062	0.062	0.063	0.064
	pow	.50	0.057	0.057	0.057	0.057	0.057	0.057	0.057	0.057	0.057	0.057	0.057	0.057	0.057	0.057	0.057	0.057
	pow	.80	0.060	0.060	0.060	0.060	0.060	0.060	0.060	0.060	0.060	0.060	0.060	0.060	0.060	0.060	0.060	0.060

Appendix D

The df_{err} Needed for Power = .80 (α = .05) in Tests of Traditional Null Hypothesis

										df_{hyp}								
PV	d	1	2	3	4	5	6	7	8	9	10	12	15	20	30	40	60	120
.01	0.20	775	952	1072	1165	1260	1331	1394	1451	1504	1580	1670	1825	1992	2302	2565	3027	4016
.02	0.29	385	473	533	579	627	662	694	722	762	787	832	909	993	1176	1313	1413	2010
.03	0.35	255	313	353	384	416	439	460	479	505	522	552	603	660	782	874	1008	1341
.04	0.41	190	233	263	286	310	328	343	358	377	390	413	451	494	585	654	774	1031
.05	0.46	151	186	209	228	247	261	273	285	300	310	329	359	402	466	522	618	825
.06	0.51	125	154	173	189	204	216	227	236	249	257	273	298	333	388	434	514	687
.07	0.55	106	131	148	161	174	184	193	204	212	220	233	255	285	331	371	440	601
.08	0.59	92	114	128	140	152	160	168	178	185	191	203	222	248	289	324	384	525
.09	0.60	81	100	113	124	134	142	149	157	164	169	179	196	220	256	287	341	466
.10	0.67	73	90	101	110	120	127	133	141	146	152	161	176	197	230	258	312	419
.11	0.70	66	81	91	101	108	115	120	127	132	137	148	159	178	208	238	283	388
.12	0.74	60	74	83	92	99	104	110	116	121	125	135	145	163	190	218	259	355
.13	0.77	55	68	76	84	90	96	101	106	111	115	124	133	150	178	200	238	327
.14	0.81	50	62	70	78	83	88	94	98	102	106	114	123	138	165	185	220	302
.15	0.84	47	58	65	72	77	82	87	91	95	98	106	115	129	153	172	205	286
.16	0.87	43	54	61	67	72	76	81	85	88	92	99	107	120	143	161	192	268
.17	0.91	40	50	57	63	68	72	76	80	83	86	93	101	112	134	151	183	251

.18	0.94	38	47	53	59	63	67	71	75	78	81	87	96	106	126	142	172	236
.19	0.97	36	44	50	55	59	63	67	70	73	77	82	90	101	119	136	163	227
.20	1.00	34	42	47	52	56	60	64	67	69	73	77	85	96	112	129	154	214
.22	1.06	30	37	42	47	51	54	57	60	62	65	70	76	86	102	116	139	194
.24	1.12	27	34	39	42	46	49	52	54	57	59	63	69	78	93	105	128	178
.26	1.19	25	31	35	38	42	44	47	49	52	54	58	63	71	85	96	117	163
.28	1.25	22	28	32	35	38	41	43	45	48	49	53	58	65	78	90	107	152
.30	1.31	21	26	30	32	35	37	40	42	44	45	49	53	61	72	83	100	142
.32	1.37	19	24	27	30	33	35	37	39	40	42	45	50	56	68	76	93	131
.34	1.44	18	22	25	28	30	32	34	36	38	39	42	46	52	63	72	87	123
.36	1.50	16	20	23	26	28	30	32	33	35	37	39	43	49	59	67	81	115
.38	1.57	15	19	22	24	26	28	30	31	33	34	37	40	45	55	62	76	108
.40	1.63	14	18	20	23	24	26	28	29	31	32	35	38	43	52	59	72	101
.42	1.70	13	17	19	20	23	24	26	27	29	30	32	36	40	48	55	67	96
.44	1.77	12	15	18	20	21	23	24	26	27	28	30	33	38	45	52	64	91
.46	1.85	12	14	17	19	20	22	23	24	25	26	29	31	35	43	49	60	85
.48	1.92	11	14	16	18	19	20	22	23	24	25	27	30	34	40	46	57	81
.50	2.00	10	13	15	16	18	19	21	21	22	24	25	28	32	38	44	54	76
.60	2.45	8	10	11	12	13	14	15	16	17	18	19	21	24	29	33	41	58
.70	3.06	6	7	8	9	10	11	11	12	13	13	15	16	18	22	25	30	44

Appendix E

The df$_{err}$ Needed for Power = .80 (α = .05) in Tests of the Hypothesis That Treatments Account for 1% or Less in the Variance of Outcomes

									df$_{hyp}$									
PV	d	1	2	3	4	5	6	7	8	9	10	12	15	20	30	40	60	120
.02	.29	3225	3242	3301	3266	3334	3349	3364	3429	3442	3454	3479	3570	3621	3900	4042	4379	5260
.03	.35	1058	1086	1104	1122	1139	1176	1185	1199	1212	1254	1271	1303	1377	1518	1615	1833	2299
.04	.41	573	590	607	623	650	658	670	683	694	716	736	779	836	920	993	1151	1458
.05	.46	373	389	405	422	444	445	457	472	483	492	509	541	586	652	728	843	1075
.06	.51	269	285	299	313	323	334	343	357	365	373	387	414	450	506	568	654	854
.07	.55	208	223	245	246	255	267	275	283	290	297	315	338	362	419	460	533	718
.08	.59	166	180	192	202	211	219	226	236	243	249	265	279	307	357	393	457	606
.09	.63	139	151	161	170	180	187	193	199	208	214	224	241	266	303	343	400	532
.10	.67	117	130	139	147	154	162	168	174	179	187	196	212	234	268	297	355	473
.11	.70	101	113	122	129	136	143	149	154	159	166	174	189	205	240	266	318	426
.12	.74	89	99	108	115	121	127	133	138	142	147	157	170	185	217	241	289	388
.13	.77	80	89	97	104	109	114	121	125	129	133	142	152	168	197	220	264	355
.14	.81	72	80	87	94	99	104	110	114	118	121	130	139	154	181	202	243	327
.15	.84	65	73	80	86	91	95	101	105	108	112	120	128	142	168	187	225	303
.16	.87	59	67	73	79	84	88	93	97	100	103	111	119	132	156	174	209	283
.17	.91	54	61	68	73	77	81	85	90	93	96	103	110	123	145	162	195	269

.18	.94	49	57	63	68	72	76	79	83	86	89	96	103	115	136	152	183	252
.19	.97	45	53	58	63	67	71	74	78	81	84	90	97	108	127	144	172	238
.20	1.00	42	49	55	59	63	67	69	73	76	79	84	91	101	120	137	162	234
.22	1.06	37	43	48	52	56	59	62	65	68	70	75	81	91	107	123	146	204
.24	1.12	32	38	43	47	50	53	56	59	61	63	68	74	83	97	111	134	185
.26	1.19	29	34	38	42	45	48	51	53	55	57	61	67	75	90	101	122	169
.28	1.25	26	31	35	38	41	43	46	48	50	53	56	61	69	82	92	111	156
.30	1.31	24	28	32	35	37	40	42	44	46	48	51	56	63	75	86	103	144
.32	1.37	21	26	29	32	34	37	39	40	42	44	47	52	58	69	79	96	135
.34	1.44	20	24	27	30	32	34	36	37	39	41	44	48	54	64	73	89	125
.36	1.50	18	22	25	27	29	32	33	35	36	38	41	44	50	60	68	83	117
.38	1.57	17	20	23	25	27	29	31	32	34	35	38	41	47	56	64	78	110
.40	1.63	15	19	21	23	25	27	29	30	32	33	35	39	44	53	60	73	103
.42	1.70	14	18	20	22	24	25	27	28	30	31	33	36	41	49	56	69	98
.44	1.77	13	16	19	20	22	24	25	27	28	29	31	34	39	47	53	65	92
.46	1.85	12	15	17	19	21	22	24	25	26	27	29	32	37	44	50	61	87
.48	1.92	12	14	16	18	19	21	22	23	25	26	28	30	34	41	47	58	82
.50	2.00	11	13	15	17	18	20	21	22	23	24	26	29	32	39	45	54	77
.60	2.45	8	10	11	13	14	14	16	16	17	18	19	21	24	29	34	41	59
.70	3.06	6	7	8	9	10	11	12	12	13	13	14	16	18	22	25	31	44

Author Index

Subject Index